Pancho Villa and John Reed

Pancho Villa and John Reed

Two Faces of Romantic Revolution

JIM TUCK

The University of Arizona Press
TUCSON, ARIZONA

About the Author

JIM TUCK has long maintained active careers in writing, editing, and lecturing. His area of concentration has been mainly, though not exclusively, in the travel and historical fields. For the best reports on Mexico in the foreign press, he won the Francisco Zarco Prize in 1968. A continuing interest in Mexico led to the publication in 1982 of his book, *The Holy War in Los Altos: A Regional Analysis of Mexico's Cristero Rebellion.*

For Maricruz

THE UNIVERSITY OF ARIZONA PRESS

Copyright © 1984
The Arizona Board of Regents
All Rights Reserved

This book was set in 11/13 Linotron Electra.
Manufactured in the U.S.A.

Library of Congress Cataloging in Publication Data

Tuck, Jim.
  Pancho Villa and John Reed.

  Bibliography: p.
  Includes index.
  1. Villa, Pancho, 1878–1923. 2. Reed, John, 1887–
1920. 3. Mexico—History—Revolution, 1910–1920.
4. Revolutionists—Mexico—Biography. 5. Revolutionists
—United States—Biography.   I. Title.
F1234.V63T83   1984   972.08'1'0922   84-8770

ISBN 0–8165–0867–4

Contents

Illustrations

Preface

FRANCISCO VILLA AND JOHN REED were two exciting and controversial men who achieved fame in the first quarter of this century. Superficially they were polar opposites. One sprang from Mexico's rural proletariat, lived a childhood of brutish poverty, and was driven to banditry by the inequities of a social system in which his opportunities for advancement were nonexistent. The other was born into an influential family, attended private schools, and graduated from Harvard.

Yet these dissimilar figures—whose paths crossed for a brief period—became symbols of the romantic tradition in revolution. Here the qualifier is important. Reed and Villa were representatives of revolution in its springtime phase, the exhilarating era before a "new class" of bureaucrats—Orwell's "little beetlelike men"—arose to do its dulling and dehumanizing work.

One of the most interesting aspects of Reed's short life is that he was such a pivotal figure. Armed with boundless enthusiasm, a high sense of adventure, and good contacts, he went everywhere and knew everybody. His circle of acquaintances, as eclectic as it was wide, included presidents like Theodore Roosevelt and Woodrow Wilson, established intellectuals like Lincoln Steffens and Charles Townsend Copeland, rising ones like Walter Lippmann, rich dilettantes playing with power like William C. Bullitt and Mabel Dodge, serious power players like Lenin and Trotsky, and libertarian radicals like Emma Goldman. A special case is that of Eugene O'Neill, who combined the roles of protégé-playwright and romantic rival. Given these antecedents, it is hardly surprising that Reed should have come into contact with Villa. In early 1914—before World War I stole the headlines—revolution-torn Mexico was the center of world attention. Reed went where the action was, and, in those turbulent days, it bubbled and flowed around the flamboyant figure of Francisco Villa.

Neither Villa nor Reed was a self-generated phenomenon. Both were motivated by mentors they revered and loved. These men, interestingly, bore the first names of Abraham and Lincoln. The roles of Governor Abraham González and Lincoln Steffens in molding their protégés' thinking will be fully evaluated, as will the factors that propelled Villa and Reed into revolution.

In the portion of this study devoted to Reed's actual stay in Mexico, two areas will receive particular scrutiny. One involves Villa's "foreign legion," the band of reporters and combatants that included Reed, the doomed Ambrose Bierce, range and radio idol Tom Mix, Giuseppe Garibaldi's grandson-namesake, and two dissimilar San Franciscans, an ex–bank robber picturesquely known as the "Dynamite Devil" and a dentist named Bernard Freyberg who later became Field Marshal Lord Freyberg, commander of New Zealand's troops in the Second World War. The other area relates to Reed's vibrant book, *Insurgent Mexico*, a work in which art at times proved to be larger than life. In this chapter the pageantry of *Insurgent Mexico* will be measured dispassionately against the reality of insurgent Mexico.

Both Villa and Reed were controversial figures, men who attracted the warmest friendship and the most vindictive enmity. Among the friends, there were two who served them as indispensable helpmates—though in vastly differing contexts. Felipe Angeles was a gifted artillery commander who masterminded Villa's greatest victories. The catastrophic defeats took place when he failed to heed Angeles's advice. Louise Bryant, completely apart from the romantic relationship, was the same sort of irreplaceable companion. She buoyed Reed, their careers complemented each other, and she was constantly at his side during the tensest days of the October Revolution.

The enemies tended to be organization men. Chapter 8 will focus on Villa's travails with Carranza and Obregón and Chapter 9 on Reed's with those master intriguers, Grigori Zinoviev and Karl Radek.

Both Villa and Reed died in ambush; the only difference was one of method. Whereas Villa was gunned down in the streets of Parral, Reed's destruction was engineered more subtly but no less effectively. Maneuvered by the Zinoviev-Radek clique into a long, wasting trip to Baku as a test of Party loyalty, he returned a sick, exhausted, and embittered man. A month later he was dead.

The final chapter will assess Villa and Reed as revolutionaries. First a paradigmatic standard will be defined, one embodying the qualities of an ideal revolutionary. By that standard, each protagonist will be measured.

Acknowledgments

Preparing a work that involves leading figures of differing nationality, language, and social background normally adds to an author's work. My task was made gratifyingly easier through the cooperation of both trained specialists and informed and dedicated laypersons.

Because of the mystery that shrouds part of his life, Francisco Villa can be an elusive subject. For their assistance in unearthing data beyond the usual scope of popular histories and romanticized biographies, I wish to thank *doctora* Carmen Castañeda of the *Universidad de Guadalajara*'s library staff, and Lic. Alfonso Rivas Salmón, Research Director of the *Universidad Autónoma de Guadalajara*. An American Guadalajara resident to whom I am indebted is the late Theodore Cohen. Much of the information on Zinoviev and Radek, Reed's organization enemies, derives from my free and frequent access to his extensive library. In Mexico City an expression of gratitude goes to Emil K. Michner, an Austrian-born realtor and diligent amateur historian. Mr. Michner was kind enough to photocopy an extensive body of material from his archives relating to Villa's "foreign legion." For prompt and courteous clarifying statements on the role of their fathers during the *villista* period, I wish to thank Lord Freyberg of Surrey, England, and Mayor Manfred Rommel of Stuttgart, German Federal Republic.

In Cambridge I derived both great profit and pleasure from my examination of the John Reed papers at Harvard's Houghton Library. My work was facilitated by the aid of the library's curator, Mr. Thomas Noonan, and his efficient staff.

My research odyssey next took me to New York. There I enjoyed equally competent staff assistance at the Butler Library of Columbia University, where the Lincoln Steffens papers are stored. Finally, in the area of supplementary general research, I benefited, as always, from the magnificent facilities of the New York Public Library.

— I —

The Mentors:
Abraham and Lincoln

THERE ARE THREE VERSIONS OF THE DEATH of Abraham González, revolutionary governor of Chihuahua and mentor of Pancho Villa. According to one account, he was forced at gunpoint to dismount from a Mexico-City–bound train and then shot by an Army major named Benjamín Camarena.[1] This would have been a classic application of the *ley fuga*, where a prisoner is killed while "trying to escape."

The second and third versions are grimmer than the first. One states that he was shot and that his lifeless body was then placed on a railroad track and run over by a train. In this manner the bullet holes would not be apparent. The final, and most grisly, account alleges that González was not shot but handcuffed and pushed into the path of a moving train.[2] The date of González's murder was 7 March 1913, and the location was Bachimba Canyon, about 40 miles south of Chihuahua City.

However it was accomplished, González's killing was ordered by General Victoriano Huerta, hard-drinking military usurper who had overthrown President Francisco Madero the month before. As one of Madero's most influential followers, González was a marked man. His death took place just thirteen days after that of his chief.

The event was followed by an official statement, issued by Huerta's secretary of *gobernación* (Interior Ministry), that González had been killed by cross fire when a band of pro-Madero partisans tried to rescue him from the train.[3] This story had a familiar ring—an identical explanation had been issued following the killing of Madero and his vice-president, José María Pino Suarez.

González's assassination, and the cynical whitewash that followed it, were greeted with horror and contempt. Nobody believed *gobernación's* self-serving story, and the American consul in Chihuahua, Marion Letcher, commented that "civilization has been mocked in this act of stark, cold-blooded, and vengeful murder."[4]

González was a born victim, a gentle man caught up in a violent epoch that he had little chance of surviving. And he knew it. *"Yo muero en la raya"* ("I will die on the firing line") was a phrase he used frequently.[5]

A year before his death he was given a chilling preview of what lay in store. He and his nemesis, Huerta, had been uneasy allies in a campaign against Pascual Orozco, the first major revolutionary to break with Madero. When Orozco declared himself in rebellion, González was forced to flee the governor's palace. He hid for a few days in the house of a working-class family and then slipped into the countryside in an attempt to join Villa. But Villa, who was coordinating his movements with those of the federal troops, had to move south into Durango. Feeling the need to remain in Chihuahua, González lived for a time as a fugitive in the wilderness, ever in danger from marauding bands of *orozquistas*. Though not an athletic man, he bore the ordeal with the utmost stoicism, a fact attested to even by unfriendly chroniclers.[6] Later, in the Ojinaga region, he joined a band of *maderista* irregulars led by José de la Cruz Sánchez.[7]

In Mexico City, Madero prepared to put down the rebellion. Commanding the punitive expedition was General Jesús González Salas, Minister of War and Madero's relative by marriage. Orozco defeated González Salas so badly that the latter committed suicide.

The disaster sent shock waves through the capital. Would the Madero revolution, product of Mexico's brightest and best, be derailed by the rude Orozco, an ex–mule driver and part-American to boot?[8] Reluctantly turning to Huerta who, drunk or sober, was a first-rate soldier, Madero sent him north with a new army.

Huerta's campaign against Orozco was a *veni, vidi, vici* affair. On 12 May he defeated the *orozquistas* at Conejos, Durango, and on 22–23 May at Rellano, across the Chihuahua line. (This was the scene of González Salas's defeat.) Orozco suffered a third loss on

16 June at La Cruz, near Ciudad Camargo. It was here that the irregulars that Abraham González had joined made contact with the Federals.[9] Orozco's fourth successive defeat came, ironically, at Bachimba Canyon, where González would die the following year. This engagement, fought over 3–4 July, marked the end of the *orozquistas* as a regular force capable of fighting set-piece battles. Three days later Huerta marched into Chihuahua City and reinstalled González as governor. Though Orozco continued to direct a sporadic hit-and-run campaign, his movement no longer posed a threat to Madero's authority.

But González's troubles were far from over. True, the *orozquista* menace had been defused. Nevertheless, the restored governor soon began to suspect that he was proceeding from the frying pan into the fire. Huerta had little use for *maderista* politicians—Francisco Madero included. His heart belonged to the old dictator, Porfirio Díaz, whom he had bidden a tearful farewell after commanding the guard train that carried him into exile. In fighting anti-Madero rebels he was not so much defending the president as knocking off future rivals in his own grab for power. Huerta was a master of intimidation, and now, as he faced the large, soft man in the governor's palace, he spoke in the tones of courtly menace for which he was famous. "May God protect you, *señor* governor," he said, leaving little doubt from whom González would need protection.[10] Within a year both Madero and González would be dead and Huerta master of Mexico.

The life so sordidly snuffed out at Huerta's order began on 7 June 1864. The future governor's birthplace, a ranching community called Ciudad Guerrero, is slightly over 100 miles west of Chihuahua City. His family belonged to the old creole aristocracy, with branches in Mexico and the United States. On both sides of the border the family attained prominence. González's paternal uncle was governor of Chihuahua while an American cousin became governor of New Mexico. Following early education in Chihuahua and Mexico City, he went to the United States and received his university training at a small, then little-known Catholic college in Indiana called Notre Dame. With his heritage and education, González spoke fluent English.[11]

Physically he was tall and corpulent but neither strong nor athletic. His shoulders were narrow and lacking in musculature, and his body inclined to stoutness. In this respect—and in his distaste for personal violence—he resembled the radical journalist and political leader Ricardo Flores Magón, to whose doctrines he was drawn early in his career. Compensating for these unprepossessing physical characteristics were a kindly expression, amiable manner, and easy smile—qualities that added up to a low-key charisma. People instinctively liked the man—then listened to what he had to say. Edward S. ("Tex") O'Reilly, an American soldier of fortune who served González as a bodyguard, describes him as "one of the finest men I have known in Mexico."[12]

González never married. *"Mi novia es la revolución"* ("my sweetheart is the revolution") was another of his favorite sayings, along with the prediction about the manner of his death.[13]

That death was honored in the most ceremonial manner by a man who normally detested ceremony. When Francisco Villa heard of his mentor's slaying, he wept tears of grief and rage. Those tears were repeated at Bachimba Canyon, where Villa had gone to retrieve the remains of his beloved friend. González's body was returned to Chihuahua City and "that night there was a *velada* (candlelight service) in the Theater of the Heroes, an immense auditorium packed with emotional peons and their women." The *velada* consisted of speeches, followed by renditions of Tosti's "Goodbye" and Handel's "Largo." Then Villa "leaped up to the stage, knelt and took up the coffin in his arms." He took it across the square to the Governor's palace, where he arranged for each of four generals to stand a two-hour death watch. In anticipation of this ceremony, "a dense mass of silent, breathing people packed the doorway. Villa unbuckled his sword and threw it clattering into a corner. Then he took his rifle from the table and stood the first watch."[14]

As noted, González had been an early follower of Ricardo Flores Magón. But disillusionment set in. Basically a moderate, he viewed the journalist's accelerating progress to the Left with distaste. Also, a new star had appeared on the political horizon. In a dramatic shift of allegiance, González abandoned *magonismo* and forged the alliance—that would end only in death—with a bearded little man from the neighboring state of Coahuila.

Personally as well as geographically, Abraham González had far more in common with Francisco Madero than with Ricardo Flores

Magón. Where Flores Magón was a Oaxacan of almost pure Indian ancestry, Madero, like González, belonged to the creole elite of the arid north. The Maderos, believed to be of part-Jewish origin, were among the richest families in Mexico. Their economic interests were diverse, distributed in such areas as ranching, cotton planting, banking, mining, and distilling. Madero's grandfather, *don* Evaristo, was reputedly worth fifteen million dollars at the time of his death.

Madero, like González, had an early association with Flores Magón. He joined the Liberal Party and in 1905 was issued membership credential No. 4.[15] But he later broke with Flores Magón, denouncing the *magonistas'* emphasis on violent overthrow of the Díaz system.

The single most influential factor in winning González over to the *maderista* cause was Madero's new famous book, *La sucesión presidencial en 1910* ("The Presidential Succession in 1910"). Though its principal concept—*sufragio efectivo y no reelección* (effective suffrage and no reelection)—is today holy writ, it would be mistaken to view it as some sort of flaming manifesto. Compared to other revolutionary documents, *la sucesión* is remarkable for its blandness. Rejecting revolution, Madero proposed nothing more subversive than creation of an "anti-reelectionist party," and he even hedged on that. Reelection would be acceptable, he added, if the election were honest and if anti-reelectionists were given a fair share of government posts.

As gradualist in his outlook as Madero, González was immensely attracted to the latter's policies of sweet reason. But moderation did not blunt his unshakable antagonism to *díazpotismo*. As *magonista* or as *maderista*, Abraham González saw no hope for Mexico except through extensive political reform.

By early 1909 González had made the transition from literary-intellectual gadfly to political conspirator. Sitting on a Chihuahua park bench, he held court to a band of kindred spirits. These included a disgruntled officer named Colonel Lomelín, an unrelated lawyer named Aureliano González, a Dr. Perea, and an aging *bon vivant* named Manuel de la O, a man few suspected of political activism. Though all these men were from Chihuahua, González's entourage also included two out-of-staters. One was Luis Moya, a fiery Zacatecas rebel who would die fomenting a rising in his home state. The other, a young Coahuila schoolteacher named Braulio Hernández, had such an air of messianic zeal about him that friends humorously compared him with a hellfire Protestant preacher.[16] Yet—following Madero's victory—Hernández was one of the first to go into counterrevolution.

It was in the wake of these park-bench conclaves that González founded the Anti-Reelection Party in Chihuahua and accepted its presidency. This decision took courage. Though Díaz always tried to maintain a façade of legality, dissidents could count on receiving short shrift. The previous year three "subversive" youths, Juan Sarabia, César Canales, and Timoteo Cuellar, had received long prison terms following a drumhead trial before a judge especially imported from Mexico City. Of the three, Cuellar was described as being too young to shave.[17]

Such acts made González feel that political reform might have to be backed by a little military muscle. By late spring of 1909 he was in the sierra, recruiting ranchers to what might be the coming revolution. Though he had not given up on the idea of a peaceful solution, he wanted to be ready in case stronger means were required to break Díaz's grip on Mexico. It was during this journey that he recruited Pascual Orozco, as well as members of the Caraveo, Casavantes, Frias, Dosal, and Estrada families.[18]

Constant travel in such wild country cannot have been easy for a sedentary man like González. Yet he performed brilliantly, turning rural Chihuahua into a hive of *maderismo*.

Though González was not rugged physically he possessed, according to a contemporary, "uncommon energy and . . . a repeatedly proven serenity of mind."[19] These qualities must have come into play when González won over his most famous recruit.

Chroniclers differ as to who first introduced him to Francisco Villa. According to Martín Luis Guzmán, who prepared the autobiographical *Memorias de Pancho Villa*, the intermediary was Victoriano Ávila, one of Villa's many *compadres*.[20] Another source states that it was Colonel Lomelín, González's park-bench co-conspirator.[21]

A full year passed between González's trip to the sierra and his recruitment of Pancho Villa. During that period a series of events convinced him that *díazpotismo* could be toppled only by force.

In April of 1910 González was in Mexico City as a delegate to the Anti-Reelectionist Party convention. The delegates numbered

120 and included such figures as José María Pino Suárez, Madero's future vice-president, Aquiles Serdán, the Puebla martyr, and Emilio Vázquez Gómez, who later turned against Madero.[22]

Madero, who did not attend the convention, was nominated for president on 15 April. The next day he was granted an interview by Porfirio Díaz.

Though no witnesses were at the meeting, indirect reports have seeped out about what was discussed. The octogenarian dictator at times seemed senile and fuzzy. Then he would suddenly regain his mastery of lacerating invective. Unkindly, he compared Madero to *don* Nicolás Zuñiga y Miranda, a stock political figure of fun. Zuñiga, once a comer, had degenerated into a perennial candidate and a perennial loser. Díaz ended the interview with the cynical observation that "a man must be more than honest to govern Mexico."[23]

On 6 June Madero was arrested on charges of fomenting rebellion and disrespect to the person of the president. Fifteen days later, in a flagrantly rigged election, Díaz and Ramón Corral, his handpicked running mate, were declared winners by an overwhelming majority. Thanks to the intervention of his influential family, Madero was released on 19 July. He had been confined to the San Luis Potosí penitentiary and released on condition that he remain in the city. He waited till 4 October, when the Díaz-Corral "victory" was officially certified by the Chamber of Deputies, and then boarded a northbound train. Hiding in the baggage car, he safely crossed the border. On 25 October, in San Antonio, he proclaimed the 2,500-word Plan de San Luis Potosí. Díaz was disavowed as president, the "election" held null and void, and Madero was proclaimed provisional president until free elections could be held. The manifesto concluded with a call to arms.

In the meantime, González had returned to Chihuahua. Moved inexorably by the march of events—the contemptuous Díaz-Madero interview, the fraudulent election, Madero's imprisonment and flight, the Plan de San Luis Potosí—he had entered the third and final phase of his opposition to Díaz: from intellectual gadfly to political conspirator to full-fledged revolutionist. For the violent work ahead he needed violent men, men whose past could be overlooked if they served effectively—men like Francisco Villa.

In the spring of 1910, when the association between these dissimilar individuals began, Villa was living in Chihuahua City. He occupied a three-room adobe house at 500 Calle 10, ostensibly trading horses and operating a butcher shop. At 32 he had a legendary reputation as a bandit, having ridden with sierra brigands since he was 16. Despite his currently respectable exterior, Villa still kept his hand in. It was his practice to pick up information about cattle drives in the stockyards, which he would then relay to outlaw accomplices in the hinterland.[24]

González knew all this when he began to cultivate Villa. But past misdeeds were far outweighed by this rough man's ability to ride and fight, by his intimate knowledge of the sierra he had so recently roamed as a bandit, and by the circle of followers he dominated.

González must also have sensed something else: that Villa's attachment to the *maderista* cause was unquestionably genuine. Had he been simply interested in booty he could have become, as Pascual Orozco did, a hired *pistolero* for the great robber-baron clans, the Creel and Terrazas families.

Violent men can be notoriously sentimental, and Villa was deeply moved by his association with González. Years later, after his mentor's death, he recalled their meetings in Chihuahua. "That house," he said of his modest adobe residence on Calle 10, "I wouldn't trade for the most elegant of palaces. There I had my first meetings with *don* Abraham González, now a martyr of democracy. There I heard his voice inviting me to the Revolution that we must make for the rights of the people. . . ."[25]

Villa entered that revolution a few days before its official beginning. Though 20 November is honored legally as the day Madero launched the armed struggle against Díaz, it is in fact the celebration of an almost comic fiasco. Having crossed the Río Grande the night of the 19th, Madero expected to be met by his uncle, Catarino Benavides, at the head of five hundred men. Only four showed up, with the discouraging news that federal troops were in hot pursuit. A crestfallen Madero slipped back across the border.

Between the launching of the Revolution, in November 1910, and the fall of Díaz, in May 1911, González spent most of his time in the United States. There he used all his hard-headed energy to advance Madero's fortunes. Basing himself in El Paso, he concentrated on keeping the pot boiling in his native Chihuahua. In late October or early November (the exact date is unknown) he sent

Braulio Hernández to seek financial aid from Madero and received 5,000 pesos.[26] In November Madero appointed him provisional governor of Chihuahua. By the second week of December, following the 20 November disaster, González was making plans to have Madero enter Mexico by way of Chihuahua. (The November attempt had been through Eagle Pass into Coahuila.) The key man in this new effort was Pascual Orozco. In December he had captured Ciudad Guerrero (González's birthplace) and won his first major victory of the revolution. The plan was for Orozco to capture Juárez by 5 February so that Madero could make his entry on Mexico's Constitution Day. Though the attack failed, González showed great resourcefulness in spiriting defeated *orozquistas* into the United States and beyond the reach of federal vengeance.[27]

During this period González figured in two incidents in which he demonstrated both humanity and courage. Roque Estrada, a Madero aide, had wanted to accompany the fighting forces into Chihuahua. Since González was provisional governor, protocol dictated that Estrada seek his permission. González at first agreed but almost immediately changed his mind. Estrada, like himself, was a sedentary civilian. Not wishing to expose him to needless danger, González pointed out to Estrada that he could do more important work in the United States. To soften the blow, he told Estrada that he himself merely held the horses during combat actions.[28]

The second episode took place during Madero's first major confrontation with the prickly Pascual Orozco. It was May 1911, and Orozco, aided by Villa, had just captured Ciudad Juárez. The saturnine ex–mule driver had hoped to be named Minister of War in Madero's cabinet, but the appointment went to his enemy, Venustiano Carranza. Sensing Orozco's discontent, representatives of the old order started playing on his vanity, telling him he was the real hero of the revolution. These "devil's advocates" included two Díaz negotiators at Madero's headquarters, Oscar Braniff and Toribio Esquivel Obregón.

Things came to a head on 13 May, following the fall of Ciudad Juárez. Among the captives was General Navarro, the federal commander. Because he had bayoneted prisoners, Orozco wanted to kill him. But the humane Madero refused to hand him over. Tempers flared and Orozco, pulling his pistol, tried to arrest Madero.

Witnessing the confrontation was González. With complete disregard for personal safety he flung himself on the younger, stronger man (he was 46 to Orozco's 29) and pinioned his arms. Aiding him in restraining Orozco was Madero's brother, Gustavo. During the scuffle Madero was able to step out onto a balcony and successfully appeal to Orozco's troops. The incident ended with Madero and Orozco reconciled—for the time being. Villa, who had supported Orozco, emotionally made his way to Madero's side and begged to be punished. Madero smilingly refused, saying he would never execute a brave man. With this victory, Madero successfully weathered the first serious challenge to his authority. Navarro, who precipitated the controversy, was quietly shipped across the border.[29]

Díaz went into exile at the end of May and Madero marched into Mexico City on 7 June. In November, in what is considered to be Mexico's most honest election, he was chosen president with an astounding 99 percent of the vote. After Madero's victory González was given a cabinet post, that of secretary of *gobernación*, the powerful Interior Ministry. Taking advantage of González's absence, political enemies at home staged risings in Dolores and Ciudad Juárez. They also mounted an attack on the Chihuahua City penitentiary, freeing two anti-Madero activists. With trouble mounting, González resigned his federal post on 13 February and returned to Chihuahua to reassume the governorship.[30] The following month Orozco rose, and González had to go into hiding. Restored to office by Huerta, he served until February 1913, the month that Madero was overthrown. Madero's downfall unleashed a chain of events that spelled calamity for González. On 19 February he joined Venustiano Carranza in refusing to recognize Huerta. Three days later he was arrested by a squad led by Major José Alessio Robles. The arrest was ordered by Colonel Antonio Rábago, the pro-Huerta military commander in Chihuahua. There is a tragic parallel between the fall of Madero and the fall of González. Just as the naive Madero failed to get rid of Huerta, so had González allowed Rábago to remain at his post. This was a mistake. Rábago was rewarded for his treachery by being named *huertista* governor of Chihuahua.[31]

On 25 February, under duress, González resigned as governor of Chihuahua. Two days later Pascual Orozco announced his allegiance to Huerta. His marauding bands were incorporated into the *rurales* and given the assignment of securing northern Chihuahua for the usurping regime.[32] On 4 March a military court convicted González of buying weapons from the government, allegedly for the purpose of arming his followers. Though the offense was a misdemeanor, it gave González's enemies a pretext for holding him in captivity.[33] The wait was, at least, mercifully brief. In the evening of 6 March a three-man military detail came to González's cell. It was headed by Major Camarena, the man who reportedly killed him, and two other officers, Captain Hernando Limón and Lieutenant Federico Revilla. González was taken to the station and the party boarded a special Pullman car. The journey that ended for González at Bachimba Canyon began at 11:30. To avoid attracting attention, the train traveled without lights and whistles.[34]

Just before his arrest González received a message from Pancho Villa in El Paso. "*Don* Abraham," it began, "I am safe and sound in El Paso. Here I am at your orders. I am the same Pancho Villa you have known in times past, suffering from misfortune but with no bad thoughts." Villa went on to say that he feared an impending coup against Madero (this was on the eve of his overthrow) and offered to take charge of pro-Madero volunteer forces in Chihuahua.[35] In advising Villa to stay put, González compounded the error he had made in failing to remove Rábago. A cadre of loyal *villistas* might have prevented his arrest on 22 February.

Two days after González's fall, Venustiano Carranza sent off an angry telegram to President Taft, denouncing what he believed to be American recognition of Huerta. (Carranza erred in this assumption.) On the 27th, at the end of an armed band, he set up revolutionary headquarters at the hacienda of Guadalupe. There he issued his *Plan* calling for the usurper's overthrow.[36] The Constitutionalist movement had begun.

González, and not Carranza, would certainly have been First Chief of this movement had he not been put under arrest. Those two fatal mistakes—trusting Rábago and keeping Villa at bay—probably kept him from being president of Mexico. He was closer to Madero than was Carranza, he had held an important cabinet post (*gobernación*), and he was governor of Mexico's largest state. But it was not to be. A more savage destiny awaited this trusting and amiable man.

"WHEN JOHN REED CAME, BIG AND GROWING, handsome outside and beautiful inside, when that boy came from Cambridge to New York, it seemed to me I had never seen anything so near to pure joy. No ray of sunshine, no drop of foam, no young animal, bird or fish, and no star, was as happy as that boy was."[37] The writer of these lines was Lincoln Steffens and the passage is taken from Steffens's final tribute to his protégé, John Reed.

The two mentor-pupil relationships—González-Villa and Steffens-Reed—are as interesting for their differences as for their similarities. Villa outlived his teacher by ten years, while Reed predeceased Steffens by sixteen. The González-Villa relationship lasted less than three years, while Steffens-Reed bumped along for eleven. The latter association was strained several times through disillusionment on the part of the pupil. Villa, on the other hand, was consistently reverent toward González.

Reed came to Steffens as an acolyte to a high priest; with González and Villa it was the union of a senior and junior partner. When they first met, Reed, at 21, was a Harvard junior while the 42-year-old Steffens, author of *The Shame of the Cities*, was one of America's most talked about men. González, though two years older than Steffens, was an unknown provincial agitator when he met Villa, while his 32-year-old pupil was a bandit turned butcher and horse trader. Where Reed was a bright Harvard student coming under the wing of a national celebrity, González and Villa were obscure plotters with no inkling that fame was less than a year away.

Reed met Steffens through his father, Charles Jerome (C. J.) Reed, a successful businessman turned political reformer. The elder Reed and Steffens had become friends when Reed was serving as United States Marshal in Oregon under Theodore Roosevelt. C. J. aided in the prosecution of a land-fraud ring, and Steffens covered the event as a highly partisan reporter.[38]

Of the brilliant Harvard class of 1910—members included T. S. Eliot, Conrad Aiken, H. V. Kaltenborn, Heywood Broun, Alan Seeger, Walter Lippmann, and John Reed—the two most attracted to Steffens were Lippmann and Reed. Steffens was in Boston at the time, having accepted a $10,000-a-year offer from that city's Good Government Association to study municipal corruption. Prime mover behind the offer was merchant prince Edward A. Filene, a private entrepreneur with a highly developed public conscience.[39]

Of the two students, Lippmann was a far more serious political activist than Reed. He was president of the Socialist Club while Reed, though in sympathy with the club's aims, was not even a member. Writing diverted Reed from political activity, as did "football games, beer halls, weekend jaunts to Nantucket (and) dances. . . ."[40] Possibly sensing a tendency toward dilettantism, Steffens soberly told Reed that "there is not enough intellectual curiosity in your college."[41]

Yet Steffens sensed another quality in the brash young Westerner: his magnificent potential as a reporter. Reed was a frequent contributor to the *Monthly*, Harvard's literary magazine. (He also wrote humor for the *Lampoon*.) Steffens had been invited by Reed to meet with the *Monthly*'s staff, and the meetings resulted in some frank talk. It was a common error, said Steffens, for editors to try and "make" a magazine, to decide what would be a good story and then assign it to the most likely writer. Citing from his own experience as managing editor of *McClure's*, he insisted that "what I wanted was what (the writer) cared most to say." Steffens concluded by appealing to each editor "to regard himself as the whole world: whatever will interest him involuntarily (not as an editor, but as a human being) will interest the rest of us as human beings."[42]

How deeply Reed embraced this *engagé* philosophy became apparent when he began his own journalistic career. Following a postgraduation trip to Europe, he was back in New York in March 1911, living temporarily at the Harvard Club and looking for work. Owing to a change in his father's fortunes, Reed needed any job he could get. C. J., fired from his Marshal's job during the Taft administration, was trying to sell insurance in a community where he was regarded as a class renegade. Regretfully, he informed his son that further financial assistance was impossible.

Yet C. J. was able to draw on another line of credit to aid Jack: his friendship with Steffens. Using his influence, he got Reed an assistant editor's position on the *American*. His salary, modest even for those days, was $12.50 a week.[43] The *American*, once a muckraking journal, had degenerated into blandness and was now soliciting works of name authors and sentimental poets of proven commercial appeal.

To supplement his meager salary, Reed began deluging editors with contributions ranging from straight reporting to satirical sketches.

But Reed was an unknown, and rejection slips came thick and fast. When he did sell his first piece he had to share by-line credit— even though he was the sole author. The story, a fine vignette, involved a Harvard classmate named Waldo Peirce. Peirce, of moneyed background and indolent temperament, had rashly agreed to accompany Reed on a cattle boat to Europe. But he was so horrified by the vessel's primitive accommodations that he dived overboard and swam till he was picked up by a fishing boat. No crew member had witnessed the dive, and Peirce had left his wallet on Reed's bunk. Reed made the crossing under suspicion of murder and was not cleared until the boat reached England. The man who exonerated him was none other than Peirce, who had crossed on a fast liner. Reed sold the story's rights to the popular magazine writer Julian Street and was listed in the *Saturday Evening Post* as co-author.

Trying to direct Reed into more serious endeavor, Steffens suggested that he do an exposé on incompetence and political meddling in the New York Fire Department. Though Reed worked hard and came up with a lengthy study, he was unable to sell the story. Interest in muckraking had declined since Theodore Roosevelt's day.

Steffens was a more successful mentor when it came to Reed's private life. While in Europe Jack had become engaged to a French girl named Madeleine Filon. Now, back in New York, he was having doubts. There were many attractive women closer at hand, and his dramatic proposal, made on bended knee in the Roman arena of Fréjus, was beginning to look more like an exercise in high camp than a serious emotional commitment. But in 1910 there was a rigid standard about engagements. "The pact is sacred," was the cant of the day. It was the sophisticated Steffens who brought Reed's emotional travail to an end. Calmly, he persuaded the younger man that it would be a fatal error to marry a girl he no longer loved. In June 1911, Reed wrote Madeleine and broke the engagement.[44]

In September of that year Steffens, recently widowed, moved into the second floor of a run-down brick building at 43 Washington Square South. Occupying the apartment above were four boisterous Harvard graduates; one of them was John Reed. Reed had persuaded Steffens to move into the building after the latter's reversion to bachelor status.

There the relationship took its first turn. At Harvard—and during those early days in New York—Steffens had been very much the guru and Reed the adoring disciple. Though their association was friendly, even warm, Steffens never lost that aura of mystery that Charles de Gaulle later defined as the essence of prestige.

All that changed in the free and easy atmosphere of Washington Square. There "Jack" and "Steff" shared meals, drank together, and had interminable bull sessions on topics ranging from political philosophy to the most intimate concerns of private life. Reed borrowed money from Steffens to finance his evenings on the town and made him the leading confidant of his love life. On these occasions Steffens frequently banked down his protégé's youthful ardor. "You're not in love," he said, "or you'd never put it that way: 'Damn it, I'm afraid I'm falling in love again!' . . . Wait for the real thing. It's worth waiting for. . . ."[45] But growing familiarity had not yet bred contempt. Steffens may have been displaced from the pedestal, but he was still an admired counselor.

The first strain between them came at the time of the McNamara case, a sensational trial which produced almost as much fratricidal struggle on the Left as it did between Left and Right. The McNamara brothers, John and James, were union officials convicted in December 1911 of a bombing that destroyed part of the *Los Angeles Times* Building. The brothers had originally pleaded innocent but later, on the advice of Steffens, changed their pleas to guilty. Steffens took this step because he believed he had made a deal with the court whereby the McNamaras would receive only moderate prison terms in return for their guilty plea. Steffens viewed these efforts as an application of the Golden Rule to labor-management disputes.[46]

The Golden Rule, unfortunately, did not figure in the value system of a devious judge named Walter Bordwell. Denying the existence of any arrangement, he sentenced James McNamara to life imprisonment and John to fifteen years at hard labor.

Stunned and betrayed, Steffens worked for the rest of his life to obtain a pardon for the McNamaras. Equally unpleasant was the fact that he found himself an object of scorn among persons who had once admired him. Ridiculed as "Golden Rule" Steffens, he had to suffer Walter Lippmann's caustic observation that the Rule works best among equals and Max Eastman's denunciation of him as an "old-maidish fuss budget."[47]

The Brutus thrust was dealt by Reed. He wrote a poem, titled "Sangar," about a Christian chieftain who goes to war against the Huns. In the midst of battle he breaks his sword, calls for peace in Christ's name, and offers to mediate between the two armies.

This act enrages his son. He immediately slays Sangar, crying:

> *Father no more of mine!*
> *Shameful old man—abhorred*
> *First traitor of all our line.*[48]

Though the symbolism here is obvious, there is a curious aside to the episode. Reed read the poem to Steffens while his guest at a Christmas Eve dinner. His intention, he insisted, was to praise Steffens, and the poem does in fact end with Sangar receiving a hero's welcome in heaven.

But the shaft went deeply home. Years later, in the *Autobiography*, Steffens wrote that "Jack Reed, my own boy, wrote a fierce poem, 'Sangar,' denouncing me."[49]

Both Reed and Steffens covered the Mexican Revolution. Their approach to it was a reflection of both ideology and life-style. Reed—youthful, reckless, romantic—was immediately drawn to Pancho Villa, serving with him as well as with his bandit *compadre*, Tomás Urbina. Intensely partisan and totally committed, Reed faced *federales* and *colorados* on the battlefield, attended village fiestas, shared tacos and tequila with the men of *la tropa*, and slept with *soldaderas*, the camp following (and fighting) women who shared the lot of the *villistas*.

Steffens, on the other hand, was a pampered junketeer. He rallied to the stodgy Carranza—giving substance to charges that he had become a comfortable establishment liberal—and covered the Revolution from the First Chief's luxurious railroad car. To do Steffens justice, the 21-year age gap between the two men should be explanation enough of his less adventurous stance.

During the Mexican period Steffens and Reed feuded only by proxy, each casting aspersions on the other's hero. Steffens denounced Villa as an "illiterate, unscrupulous, unrevolutionary bandit."[50] Reed, while crediting Carranza with idealism, poked fun at the First Chief's portliness and the "medieval" manner in which he "led them (his peons) to war like any feudal overlord."[51]

With the coming of World War I, Reed and Steffens patched up their ideological differences. Both strongly opposed American participation in the conflict and then deplored the anti-German hysteria and erosion of civil liberties that accompanied American entry into the war. Wilson, to promote martial sentiment, had appointed an able publicist named George Creel to head the so-called Committee on Public Information. Creel quickly succeeded in recruiting a number of reform-minded luminaries to his group. These included not only eminent muckrakers—Ida Tarbell, Ray Stannard Baker, Samuel Hopkins Adams—but also several old-line socialists. Sounded out about aiding the Committee, Steffens refused. Hysteria and repression were mounting, and Steffens, heartsick, witnessed such acts as disruption of public meetings, banning of radical publications, and the jailing of Eugene Debs. He fully shared Reed's view, uttered in September 1917, that "the month just passed has been the blackest month for free men our generation has known. With . . . hideous apathy the country has acquiesced in a regime of judicial tyranny, bureaucratic suppression, and industrial barbarism. . . ."[52] In late summer of 1917, shortly before his departure for Russia, Reed lauded Steffens in extravagant terms. "More than any one man," he wrote, "Lincoln Steffens has influenced my mind. . . . Being with Steffens is like flashes of clear light; it is as if I see him, and myself, and the world with new eyes. . . . He does not judge or advise . . . he simply makes everything clear."[53]

Then came the Bolshevik Revolution—an event that provoked the next, and last, turn in relations between Steffens and Reed. It would be more correct to speak of a Final Rift than a Final Break: the association was never completely severed.

In significant ways, Russia was a replay of Mexico. Both men supported the Revolution but in different ways, for different reasons, and with differing degrees of intensity. Reed had gone to Russia in 1917, witnessed the Bolshevik Revolution at first hand, and returned to America in April of 1918. With him was the manuscript—confiscated on his arrival in New York—of *Ten Days that Shook the World*. He was by now a dedicated Communist and party organizer. As a zealot and fanatic, he had little use for trimmers, compromisers, and half-hearted fellow travelers.

It was in this category that Reed placed Steffens. In early 1918 Steffens was on the lecture circuit, questioning Allied policy and "interpreting" (rather than propagandizing) the Bolshevik Revolution for the American people. But he ran into so much harassment from local police and federal agents that by the end of April he had been forced to cancel the tour. One newspaper attack denounced him for "glorifying the bolsheviki and deriding the war aims of the United States and her allies."[54]

Yet this "dangerous subversive" maintained a hot line to the highest levels of the administration whose policies he was attacking. His contact was Colonel Edward House, Wilson's closest adviser. Wilson had announced his Fourteen Points in January 1918, and Steffens, for all his opposition to the superpatriots, believed in the president's sincerity and desire for world peace. In February 1918, Steffens told House that a serious obstacle to world peace was "the failure of Trotsky and the Russians to believe in the sincerity of President Wilson."[55] (The Bolsheviks had issued a statement denouncing the Fourteen Points and stigmatizing Wilson as the "prophet of American imperialism."[56])

At the time, Reed was in Christiana, Norway, his return visa to the United States having been held up by the State Department. Steffens, thinking that Reed would be the ideal person to mediate between the Wilson administration and the Bolsheviks, sent him an open telegram:

TROTSKY MAKING EPOCHAL BLUNDER DOUBTING WILSON LITERAL SINCERITY. I AM CERTAIN PRESIDENT WILSON WILL DO WHATEVER HE ASKS OTHER NATIONS TO DO. IF YOU CAN AND WILL CHANGE TROTSKY'S AND LENIN'S ATTITUDES YOU CAN RENDER HISTORICAL INTERNATIONAL SERVICE.
STEFFENS[57]

Reed thought the idea preposterous; still, he routinely transmitted Steffens's cable to Russia through local Bolshevik contacts.[58]

Though Reed never felt any personal antagonism toward Steffens, he increasingly began to see him as a man who was no longer pulling his weight. Gone was the ambivalence he displayed when he wrote "Sangar," trying to sugar-coat repudiation with triumphal entry into heaven. His criticisms of Steffens were now open and unequivocal. On 17 June 1918, Steffens wrote Reed suggesting that he tone down his activities and ride out the current wave of war hysteria: "Jack you do wrong to buck this thing. . . . it is wrong to try and tell the truth now. We must wait. I know it's hard. . . . Only feelings exist, and the feelings are bewildered. I think it is undemocratic to try and do much now. Write, but don't publish."[59] Reed's response, written on 29 June, was almost truculent. Rejecting Steffens's view that it is "undemocratic to buck this thing," he pointedly reminded the old muckraker that "all movements have had somebody to start them and, if necessary, go under for them." He also assailed Steffens's quietist counsels, taxing his old mentor with being "wrong to think this business (the war hysteria) is unanimous. There are many . . . who crowd to my meetings—thousands; and they are with us. And it's growing, growing fast. . . . My people weep with joy that there is something like dreams-come-true in Russia."[60] This last, particularly the reference to "my people," is a clear implication that Steffens was a man time had passed by, a man frightened into silence because he had lost touch with the mainstream of American radicalism.

Yet personal friendship never slackened. In what amounted to almost a reversal of their original relationship, Reed invited Steffens to share his house in Croton-on-Hudson. There, presumably, Steffens could be revitalized by his old pupil's ardor.

Reed was even negative when Steffens made *his* pilgrimage to Russia and uttered—on many occasions and to many people—the line for which he is most famous: "I have been over into the future and it works." (Usually incorrectly rendered as "I have seen the future and it works.") This was actually Steffens's second trip; he had been over in the spring of 1917 to observe the bourgeois-democratic revolution that overthrew the Czar.

Steffens made the trip in March 1919, as a member of the unofficial mission headed by a 28-year-old career diplomat named William C. Bullitt. Bullitt, from a wealthy Philadelphia family, was a strange compendium of charm, chutzpah, dilettantism, and savage vindictiveness. Then a fervent pro-Bolshevik, he would later take that familiar journey to the Neanderthal caverns of America's far Right—a journey marked by vicious personal attacks on such enemies as Woodrow Wilson (whom he believed to have aborted his mission) and Sumner Welles. With typical audacity (and, in this

case, intelligence) Bullitt insisted on inclusion of the "subversive"
Steffens in his group. Steffens, the only man the Bolsheviks trusted,
was the Bullitt party's passport. Steffens interviewed Lenin and quite
mistakenly saw him as a moderate, a sort of Russian Carranza. Bullitt, echoing Steffens's views, placed Lenin "well to the right in the
existing political life of Russia. . . ."[61] Though Bullitt and Steffens
found the hard-pressed Bolsheviks in a mood to make concessions,
the group's report was brushed off by Wilson, who broke an appointment with Bullitt. Also contributing to the mission's failure
was a stunning about-face by its original sponsor. This was Lord
Northcliffe, editor of the London Daily Mail. Abandoning previous counsels of conciliation, a Daily Mail editorial rejected any
idea of treating with the Bolsheviks. Undoubtedly contributing to
the attitude of Wilson and Northcliffe was the fact that a White
army led by Admiral Kolchak was then reported nearing Moscow.
Reed's reaction to the Bullitt-Steffens mission was one of ridicule.
"Did you see," he wrote Louise Bryant, "that President Wilson has
sent Lincoln Steffens, Bill Bullitt, and two or three of that sort on
a destroyer to investigate the Soviets?"[62]

Then came their dramatic final meeting. Steffens was back from
Russia, and Reed had not yet left on what would turn out to be a
one-way trip. They met in New York one night, under a street lamp,
and Steffens's affectionate greeting was brushed aside by an embittered Reed. Reed was now working full-time as a Communist Party
organizer, and his associates—unlike those of earlier days—were
no longer persons of relatively privileged background. These new
comrades had as frequently come to Communism from poverty as
from idealism.

The self-imposed transformation from exuberant idealist to Party
drudge had done little to improve Reed's disposition. "Why don't
you join us?" he angrily asked Steffens. "We are trying to do what
you used to talk and write about."[63] Steffens confirmed the meeting. "He met me on the street," he wrote, "and gave me hell for not
getting into it and doing something."[64] Steffens and Reed never saw
each other again.

After Reed's death Steffens wrote a final tribute that appeared in
the 3 November 1920 issue of The Freeman. Titled "John Reed:
Under the Kremlin," it is interesting both as confession and endorsement. As we see from this excerpt, Steffens had a motive in

dampening Reed's revolutionary ardor: "Convictions were what I was afraid of. I tried to steer him away from convictions, that he might play; that he might play with life; and see it all, live it all; tell it all; that he might be it all; but all, not any one thing. And why not? A poet is more revolutionary than any radical."

Yet Steffens, unlike others, did not see Reed's death in the typhus ward as a waste rather than a sacrifice. Though he tried to divert his protégé from political activism to poetry, he still felt his death had meaning. This feeling rose from the faith they both shared in the future of

> Soviet Russia, where there are lice and hunger and discipline and death; where it is hell now . . . [but where] . . . The future is coming . . . really and truly coming, and soon. And it is good. . . . So, to a poet, to a spirit like Jack Reed, the communist, death in Moscow must have been the most wonderful thing in the world: a vision of the resurrection and the life of Man.

2

1910: The End
of the Beginning

FOR BOTH FRANCISCO VILLA AND JOHN REED, 1910 was a threshold year. It was a year of metamorphosis—as dramatic as a caterpillar turning into a butterfly or the fictional horror depicted by Kafka. (Only with Villa and Reed it was more a case of the cockroach turning into Gregor Samsa.) It was in 1910 that Villa and Reed abandoned identities that could never have brought them fame: Reed as the campus dilettante insufficiently motivated to join the Socialist Club; Villa as the sierra marauder more interested in cattle than causes.

Neither man changed overnight into a revolutionary. The process was halting, uncertain, a thing of fits and starts. Youthful lifestyles are not easily discarded and—in that evolution to revolution—the bandit and the dilettante died hard. But die they did, with 1910 witnessing the passing of the early Villa and the early Reed.

Since Villa was almost a decade older than Reed, his transformation was more complex. At 32, his personality was more mature and tempered than Reed's. That 1910 marked the beginning of his change into a revolutionary is beyond question. But change from *what?*

A bandit—and nothing more—is too simplistic an explanation. Villa was a bandit, to be sure, but he was also a sharecropper, a butcher, a horse trader, a keeper of accounts, and, according to one source, an unwilling military conscript. All these identities must be considered when evaluating the personality of the 32-year-old man who came under the spell of Abraham González. Therefore, a fuller understanding of the earlier Francisco Villa is indispensable to an understanding of Francisco Villa in that crossroads year of 1910.

The forty-five years of Villa's life can be divided into three stages—the first two lasting sixteen years apiece and the third thirteen years. These time spans could be roughly labeled "Boy," "Bandit," and "International Celebrity." The events of phase III are known in detail, those of phase I are partly known, and those of phase II are obscured in a fog of contradictory claims, press agentry, half-truths, and outright lies. In the analysis that follows, covering phases I and II, provable facts will be used as a foundation and conflicting pieces of information will be assessed on the basis of source, probability, and personal prejudice, with biased accounts more open to question than objective ones.

It is a matter of record that Francisco Villa was born with the baptismal name of Doroteo Arango on 5 June 1878. His birthplace was the village of Río Grande in a rural Durango municipality called San Juan del Río. Doroteo was the eldest of five legitimate children born to Agustín Arango and Micaela Arámbula.

Immediately, we are faced with our first mystery. How did he come to be saddled with the unlikely name of Doroteo, a male version of Dorotea (Dorothy)? In Latin countries, the phenomenon of transsexual names almost always has a religious basis. Boys unlucky enough to be born on the feast days of female saints will be given a masculinized version of the saint's name, e.g., Tereso for Teresa, Margarito for Margarita. But this was not true in Villa's case. The 5th of June is the feast day of San Fernando; besides, Santa Dorotea (St. Dorothy) does not even rate a listing in the Mexican religious calendar. The most logical hypothesis is that the boy was named after a relative or family friend.

The father died (or disappeared) early and Doroteo became head of the family when he was still a boy. His siblings were two brothers, Antonio and Hipolito, and two sisters, Martina and Mariana.

From the beginning young Doroteo demonstrated signs of extraordinary intelligence and industry. He cut wood, farmed, and functioned as general factotum to a local merchant named Pablo Valenzuela.[1] By this time the family had moved from Río Grande to Rancho Gogojito in the municipality of Canatlán, about 35 miles north of Durango City. The ranch belonged to the wealthy López Negrete family, and the Arangos worked as sharecroppers on a *medieros* basis, meaning they kept half of what they farmed.[2]

In September of 1894, when he was 16, Doroteo took to the sierra and became a bandit. What impelled him to this decision is still being debated today.

The most popular explanation (and the one most firmly ensconced in *villista* mythology) involves an alleged affront to the honor of his sister. On 22 September, as he tells it, Doroteo was returning from work in the fields. When he arrived at the house, he witnessed a disturbing scene. At the door was the landowner, *don* Augustín López Negrete. Apparently a man of pedophilic tendencies, he was attracted to 12-year-old Martina and had come to take her away. Shielding Martina in her arms, a tearful Señora Arango was attempting to dissuade him.[3]

When he saw what was happening, Doroteo ran to the house of his cousin, Romualdo Franco, and took a pistol down from the wall. Returning to the scene of the attempted abduction, he fired three shots at López Negrete before being seized by the landlord's retainers. The wounded López Negrete ordered that the boy be taken to a nearby hacienda, there, presumably, to await his pleasure. (He had specifically forbidden his men to kill Doroteo on the spot.) But surveillance at the hacienda was lax. The boy slipped out, found his horse, and galloped off into the sierra.[4]

This version, deriving from the *Memorias*, differs significantly from the account of an American biographer. Here the dishonored victim is Mariana, the older sister, and the culprit Leonardo, López Negrete's son. López Negrete himself is called "Arturo" rather than "Augustín," and Doroteo's revenge is depicted as the killing of Leonardo rather than the wounding of Agustín (or Arturo). But both narratives end with Arango's flight into the sierra.[5]

The day after his escape Arango visited a friend's house and was informed that López Negrete had sent armed men from Canatlán to track him down. Apart from concerns for his own safety, Doroteo feared that his family might become targets of the wounded landlord's revenge. So he told his friend, Antonio Lares, to warn his mother that she should leave the area immediately and go to the original family home in Río Grande.[6]

Arango then returned to the mountains. Since a dead-or-alive warrant had been put out on him, he never dared show his face in any village. Instead, he roamed from the Sierra de la Silla to the Sierra de Gamón, feeding himself as best he could and leading the life of a hunted criminal.

On one occasion he was captured. Though Arango would later become one of history's most elusive guerrillas, at 16 he was still inexperienced enough to let himself be taken by three bounty hunters. They took him to San Juan del Río, about 65 miles north of Durango City, and locked him up in the city jail. As noted, he was under sentence of death for assaulting the influential López Negrete.[7]

But this unenviable status did not exempt Arango from work details. One morning he was taken outside the prison to grind a barrel of corn into paste. Seeing a chance to escape, he seized a grinding slab roller and threw it at one of the guards with such force that the man was instantly killed. Taking advantage of the confusion, Doroteo bolted into the nearby Cerro de los Remedios. Arriving at a stream, he found a wild colt that had been separated from its herd. He mounted the animal and rode him upriver until he reached a point about 6 miles from San Juan del Río. Seeing the colt was tired, Arango released him and made it on foot to a cousin's house. There he obtained a horse, saddle, and food to last him several days. He then returned to his previous haunts in the sierras of Gamón and de la Silla.[8]

How much of this is true? As a reliable source points out, no researcher or student of Villa's career has ever been able to locate a copy of the decree that allegedly sentenced him to death.[9] Another source, frenziedly hostile to Villa, states that he told Abraham González that he left for the sierra at age 17 (not 16) for the sole purpose of banditry, with no mention of any "dishonored sister."[10] This information derives, however, from a writer so antagonistic to Villa that she will seemingly go to any lengths to discredit him. There are, for example, charges against Villa of repeated battlefield cowardice—with no explanation of how the hard-fighting *Division del Norte* would continue to accept the authority of a "cowardly" commander.

So what is the explanation? Did external factors impel young Doroteo Arango in his flight to the sierra—or was he simply a born bandit following natural instincts?

I believe the latter theory can be ruled out. Bandits of Villa's era conformed to a macho stereotype that prevailed in rural Mexico at the turn and early years of this century. They were prodigious drinkers and womanizers, passionately addicted to violence and adventure, they scorned humdrum people who pursued "square" occupations, and they were anti-intellectual to the point of regarding not only education but even literacy as somehow sissified. (An archetype of this genre was Tomás Urbina, Villa's *compadre* and later his victim.)

Villa partly adhered to the stereotype—yet differed from it in interesting and significant ways. In his lust for adventure—and women—he fitted it in every respect. At the same time he was a diligent worker at a number of "square" jobs, a teetotaler and non-smoker, and his affinity for education amounted to obsession. ("Let's put a school here," was his most frequent directive when he was civil governor of Chihuahua.[11]) Mindless machismo (the type Villa rejected) found its ideal spokesman in a later war on another continent. This spokesman was General Millán Astray, commander of Franco's Foreign Legion, whose slogan was "Down with intelligence! Long live death!"[12] Such a sentiment would have horrified Villa.

It is, therefore, doubtful that the flight into banditry of a sober, intelligent, upwardly mobile youth like Doroteo Arango was a case of "natural instincts" asserting themselves. There had to be a stimulus somewhere. That one of his sisters was sexually harassed is a distinct probability. In the rough, semi-feudal, male-dominated world of Porfirian Mexico, daughters and sisters of peons were as fair game as black slave girls in the antebellum South. A logical hypothesis is that the assailant was one of López Negrete's ranch hands, and his chastisement a beating from Doroteo. In later years, Villa's flair for public relations led to the incident being magnified. The ranch hand became a landowner and the beating a shooting. A peon who beat up a rich man's employee would have been well advised to take to the hills. At the same time, the offense would not have been serious enough to justify a death warrant. Hence the absence of such a document.

Villa also demonstrated image-building skill in public statements about his literacy. He told John Reed that he was illiterate till the age of 34, when he taught himself to read and write in prison.[13]

This is simply untrue. During his confinement he wrote letters which were corrected and recopied by the court clerk, Carlos Jáuregui, who later helped him escape.[14] There are also evidences of his writing in 1910, the year he joined the Revolution.[15] Though Reed and other foreign admirers were enchanted by the spectacle of an *analfabeto* ex-bandit learning to read and write during a 6-month prison term, it is likely that Villa was at least marginally literate as far back as his teens. (We recall that he kept ledgers and accounts for his employer Pablo Valenzuela.)

We now move in for a closer look at those sixteen "lost" years— the period when Villa rode in and out of the sierra, alternately practicing banditry and more respectable professions. This is a frustrating task. There are sharp contradictions between Villa's own narrative, as unfolded in the *Memorias*, and accounts of other writers. Luis Garfías, military historian and general in the Mexican Army, writes that Villa rode with three bands during this period. Since Garfías has access to army intelligence files (an entrée denied other reporters), his information must be weighed seriously. He identifies the leaders of these gangs as Ignacio Parra, José Beltrán, and "the real Francisco Villa . . . (whose name) Doroteo Arango adopted."[16] The prototpye Villa, described as "a troublemaker originating in Zacatecas," was killed in a shoot-out, and Doroteo Arango took his name either because "he was implicated in the attack on . . . López Negrete or . . . because he had demonstrated his authority over the rest of the group, and the best way of insuring it was by using the name of the former leader."[17]

There is no mention of an earlier Francisco Villa in the *Memorias*. To explain his change of name, Villa states that his father, Agustín Arango, was the natural son of one Jesús Villa. It was presumably to wipe out the stain of his father's illegitimacy that Doroteo Arango took his grandfather's name.[18] Yet, according to an American writer, Durango state records list the paternal grandfather's name as Arango and not Villa.[19]

Does this revive the theory of a bandit predecessor from whom he took his name? Though absolute proof is lacking, the existence of an earlier Francisco Villa cannot be ruled out. Throughout the *Memorias*, Villa consistently played down the bandit part of his career. He pictured himself as the victim of an unjust social system, driven to brigandage by the malevolence of its representatives and persistently thwarted when he tried to find honest work. So it would be logical for him to omit mention of his service with the bands of Francisco Villa and José Beltrán.

When Villa does admit to banditry, it is always from the loftiest of motives, with the Durango sierra at times appearing as an extension of Sherwood Forest. Chided by his mother for becoming an outlaw, he replies (somewhat pompously) that he "prefers to be the first bandit in the world who went into banditry for the honor of his family."[20] Following the robbery of a rich mine owner, Villa showers his portion of the loot on family and friends. One of these beneficiaries is the nearly blind Antonio Retana, set up by Villa in a tailor shop and furnished with an assistant.[21] Villa quits the Ignacio Parra gang in disgust when José Solís, a fellow member of the band, kills an old man who won't sell him bread.[22]

Along with this chronicle of Robin Hood-ism, the *Memorias* also reflect Villa's personal prejudices. Gleefully he reports how he stole a magnificent horse from a man named Ramón Amparán. He was able to do so, he scornfully recounts, because Amparán was getting drunk in a cantina.[23] Villa's distaste for alcoholic excess was well known.

Villa was to become the scourge of the federal army, with his tactics compared by an admiring John Reed to those of Napoleon. Was he briefly a federal soldier himself? In Porfirian Mexico it was common practice for press gangs to arbitrarily round up men who did not look prosperous and force them into military service. It is recorded that Villa was caught up in one of these sweeps. Imprisoned for an infraction, he broke out of the Durango pentientiary and made his accustomed bolt for the sierra.[24]

Through the haze of legend, contradiction, and unconfirmed reports, there emerges a discernible behavior pattern. It is one of Villa seeking the path of honest work but, for one reason or another, repeatedly having to revert to banditry. In Tejame he starts a tanning business but has to flee from pursuing police.[25] In San Juan del Río he makes a promising start as a butcher, selling twenty-five head of cattle to his old employer Pablo Valenzuela.[26] Then, riding through the field of a local landowner, he is ordered off the property and savagely threatened by one of the rancher's hands. The dispute leads to drawn pistols and Villa has to flee after killing his assailant.[27] In Parral he performs so competently as a mason that his employer,

Señor Santos Vega, sets him up in his own business. But police come around and start asking Santos Vega questions. The master mason tips off Villa and—again!—that familiar trip to the sierra.[28] He goes to work in a Santa Eulalia mine, but the work is so hard and low-paid that he again rides off into the bush.[29]

It is by now obvious that what we have here is an agonizingly split personality. One part is the bandit and killer, the sierra marauder, the prodigious sexual macho, the man of passion and violence. The other side is the sober, intelligent, and ambitious do-gooder, the fighter for social justice and builder of schools.

The miracle of 1910 is that this split was healed. The two Francisco Villas, up to now locked in mutually destructive struggle, suddenly made peace and began working as a team. It was Abraham González who effected this fusion. He legitimized the fury of the violent Villa and directed it toward the goal of revolution. Never again would Villa feel shame over shooting and marauding; these activities were now channeled into service of a noble cause. Later, when he functioned as a civil administrator, he was able to give free rein to his intelligence, ambition, and yearning for progress. Before 1910—and the influence of Abraham González—"bandit" Villa and "do-gooder" Villa waged a Manichean struggle for the soul of this able but confused man. Then they joined forces and collaborated in the forging of a mighty revolutionary.

LIKE FRANCISCO VILLA, JOHN REED ALSO SUFFERED from an identity crisis. This conflict had strong parental roots. C. J., Reed's father, had left a well-paid job with an insurance company to accept a position as United States Marshal under Theodore Roosevelt. The year was 1905 and C. J.'s predecessor, Jack Mathews, had been removed from office for attempting to block investigation of a land-fraud ring. On 13 July 1910, with Taft in the White House and Roosevelt out of sympathy with his policies, the pro-T. R. Reed was fired from his Marshal's post. He went back to selling insurance but did poorly, being regarded by former friends and associates as a class traitor. In August 1910, C. J. sought the Republican congressional nomination and was badly defeated. Troubles continued to mount, and on 1 July 1911 C. J. died at 56 of a heart attack. On his death, the liabilities of this once prosperous businessman far outnumbered his assets.

Though Jack idolized his quixotic, dragon-slaying father, he also had something of his mother in him. Margeret Green Reed was an entirely different proposition from her husband. Her father, Henry Green, was a successful self-made man, a living testimonial to the American Dream. Born in upstate New York, he rounded the Horn in a sailing ship, settled on the Oregon frontier, prospered in utilities, married a fellow New York émigré, fathered four children, and built an estate, Cedar Hill, considered the most magnificent in Portland.

Among Green's children, the sexes were equally represented. Neither of the boys showed any respect for convention. But they defied it in different ways. Henry ("Hal") was the family tragedy: a drunkard, wastrel, woman-chaser, and suicide at 25. Horatio ("Ray") was a far more interesting figure. A picaresque adventurer and soldier of fortune, he sailed the South Seas, fomented Central American revolutions, and served with the Second Oregon during the Spanish-American War.

None of this adventurous spirit carried over to Green's daughters. Katherine dutifully married an Army officer, and Margaret was as turned off by her husband's Bull Moose sympathies as she would later be by her son's Marxism. For years she badgered Jack with entreaties to give up his coarse radical friends and associate with people of "the better sort."[30]

Perhaps Margaret succeeded in this design better than she realized. At Harvard, Reed was by no means immune to the temptations of social advancement. And he could be quite cold-blooded about it. Between his freshman and sophomore years, Reed had made plans to room with a Jewish youth from New York named Carl Binger. Harvard was at the time a citadel of WASP elitism, and Jews suffered from snobbery and discrimination. Feeling that too close an association with Binger might damage his social prospects, Reed abruptly informed him that he had found another roommate. Later, Reed had the grace to admit that his behavior had been reprehensible and friendship with Binger was resumed. He also began to perceive that those privileged scions of Eastern wealth were by no means as godlike as he had once supposed. "The more I met," he wrote, "the more their cold cruel stupidity repelled me. I began to pity them for their lack of imagination and the narrowness of their glittering lives. . . ."[31] Also contributing to the decline of Reed's social ambitions was his increasing radicalism and, of course, the influence of Steffens.

But they had not died completely. In December 1909, an election was held to choose officers who would preside over the graduation-week ceremonies. This election, an annual affair, was normally won by members of the social elite. These privileged students lived in private apartments on Mount Auburn Street, while other undergraduates occupied dormitories in Harvard Yard. The Mount Auburn faction's previous record of unbroken victory was due to its slate never having been contested by students from the Yard. But this year it was different. The Yard put up its own ticket, and the numerically inferior Mount Auburnites faced certain defeat. Seeking to broaden their base by inclusion of a well-known campus radical, they offered Reed a place on their slate.

Unwisely, he accepted. Reed's presence on the snobs' ticket failed to effect the outcome and the Mount Auburnites were swamped by plebians from the Yard.

It was a double defeat for Reed. He had let himself be used by the elitists and seriously damaged his credibility as an anti-establishment activist. With a petulance unworthy of him, he turned on the Yard faction in a bitter parody of Tennyson which he called "The Charge of the Political Brigade." Accusing the Yard men of organizing a "Fools' Brigade," he stigmatized them as "traitors to 1910." He also heaped scorn on their objective—"Let the Street [Mount Auburn] go to hell, we'll do the job as well"—and ended with a denunciation of the *yardistes* as "scoundrels and ignorant."[32] As in the case of Carl Binger, Reed would later suffer pangs of conscience and describe the Yard's victory as a "democratic revolution."[33]

This was Reed's final spasm of social climbing. In early 1910— that threshold year—he wrote some lyrics for the Hasty Pudding Club's musical show, *Diana's Debut*. In these lines he mercilessly mocked the Brahmins. Here he was completely his father's son, rejecting the snobs' "cold, cruel stupidity" as well as Margaret's wistful yearning for intimacy with people of "the better sort."

The most dramatic changes took place in 1910. On 24 June he graduated from Harvard and prepared to leave for Europe. Postgraduation jaunts to the continent were common among collegians of Reed's day, but most of them (particularly Ivy Leaguers) traveled in luxury or at least in comfort.

Reed would have none of this. The snob was behind him, the dilettante was fading, but the adventurer was very much alive and his adventures would pave the way for the revolutionist. On 9 June he shipped out of New York as a crew member on the S.S. *Bostonian*, a British cattle boat carrying 648 steers. With him was Waldo Peirce, whose defection and subsequent reappearance were described in Chapter 1. It was Reed's intention to rough it not only on the cattle boat but all over Europe, sleeping in barns and haylofts and rubbing elbows on a day-to-day basis with farm hands, workers, sailors, Paris toughs, and prostitutes.

There was another reason why Reed did not travel in the style of the Waldo Peirces. C. J., foreseeing that he would be eased out of his marshal's job under the Taft administration, saw rough times ahead financially. Though as generous and supportive as ever, the most he could give Jack on graduation was a hundred dollars and a letter of credit. Encouraged by his literary success at Harvard, Reed expected to earn his own way by selling travel articles to magazines and newspaper syndicates.

The boat trip was a good indoctrination for the roughing it that lay ahead. That Reed was crossing as a suspected murderer helped as much as hindered him. His "criminal" reputation won him the crew's grudging respect. Three tough Irishmen, Dunn, McNally, and Mahoney, had been in the habit of stealing Reed's food. "Now all that changed. No one touched my plate . . . I think they all thought I had drowned Peters (pseudonym for Peirce). . . ."[34] Reed must have been almost disappointed when Peirce materialized in Liverpool and stripped him of his desperado's credentials.

Reed's time in England was something of a rustic "roots" trip. With his English heritage, excellent grounding in English literature and history, and romantic attachment to England's past, Reed found himself wonderfully in tune with his environment. He strode down country lanes, visited castles and Roman ruins, and—in a perhaps unconscious imitation of Mark Twain's *Connecticut Yankee*—saw himself as "an example of American pluck, democracy, and independence."[35]

In London he rejoined Peirce, who had comfortably made the trip by train. Apprehensively, he found himself being drawn into his sybaritic classmate's life-style. As the two ate at expensive restaurants and savored London nightlife, Reed was forced to draw on his father's credit. He was almost relieved when Peirce went on a golfing trip, and he was able to start doing London on the cheap. He became an indefatigable sightseer, conscientiously visiting such landmarks as the British Museum, Westminster Abbey, the Tower of London, and Parliament.

By late August he was in Dover, poised for an invasion of the continent. Peirce was again with him and—on a minor scale and with variations—the drama of the *Bostonian* was reenacted. Reed inveigled Peirce into stowing away on a Calais-bound packet. They remained undiscovered until within sight of the French mainland. Apprehended by crew members, they would have been turned over to the police had they not produced money for the fare.

Though Reed regarded the incident as a lark, being manhandled by sailors was anything but funny to a self-indulgent young man like Peirce. He angrily blamed Reed for his difficulties, and they parted company at Calais.

Reed went to Paris where he ran into two other Harvard friends, Carl Chadwick and Joe Adams. After a few days in the capital— which included a pub crawl in Montmartre—the three drove to the Normandy coast in Chadwick's car.

There, in St. Pierre, they were exposed to an enchanting Proustian scenario of *"jeunes filles en fleur"* and, predictably, the romance-prone Reed found his Albertine. She was Madeleine Filon, one of three sisters who were vacationing at St. Pierre. Slender, dark, and petite, she lighted fires in Reed that would culminate in that theatrical bended-knee proposal in the Fréjus arena.

But these fires did not flame immediately. Jack was partly diverted by a letter from home announcing C. J.'s entry into the congressional race. (Reed's offer to come back and campaign for his father can be taken more as dutiful-son rhetoric than as a serious declaration of intent.) Another distraction was a long-planned trip to Spain, a country that had captured his imagination from early boyhood. Accompanying him were Chadwick, Adams, and Peirce. Easy-going Waldo, no man to bear a grudge, had gotten over the pique that parted them at Calais.

The quartet broke up in San Sebastian. Adams and Chadwick (who shared Peirce's aversion to budget travel) decided, with Peirce, to return to France after a disastrous night at the gaming tables. Unable to see Spain in style, they would not see it at all.

To be freed of these *jeunesse dorée* companions was the best thing that could have happened to Reed. Spain, by European standards, was a primitive country, and traveling it on foot and by third-class rail was an excellent education for a future revolutionary. Spain was also a valuable primer for a later journey to another Hispanic country—the assignment in Mexico that would make Reed world famous.

Though not as well-heeled as his departed friends, Reed was still able to interrupt his self-imposed regimen of austere living with periodic retreats into the world of the first-class traveler. Spain was something of a bargain paradise in those days, and foreign visitors of relatively modest means had no difficulty enjoying the best restaurants and hotels. Though Reed had accompanied Peirce, Chadwick, and Adams that disastrous night at the casino, his own losses had been slight. With his bankroll intact, he could have traveled all that September in comfort had he wished to.

Instead, Reed charted a desert-and-oasis course—a norm of picturesque poverty interrupted by lapses of splurging. In Valladolid he shared not only a room but a bed with a sailor. The next morning he uncovered a plot on the part of the sailor and the landlady to stick him with the full price of the grimy room. To add, in this case, injury to insult, Reed carried away a souvenir of the unpleasant experience in the form of *papillons d'amour* ("butterflies of love")—that marvelous French euphemism for crab lice.[36] At the Medina del Campo railroad station an ill-clad Reed was seized by military police and put under guard. The King's train was due and Spanish security forces were on the lookout for foreign anarchists.[37]

In the "oasis" phase of his trip, Reed derived great amusement from walking into an elegant Madrid hotel looking like a tramp. The manager's frigid demeanor instantly melted when Reed produced his bankroll. In a smart café, the haunt of elegant *madrileños*, he found himself the target of disapproving stares as he drank chocolate and wrote letters to friends.[38]

These rags and riches antics did not prevent Reed from immersing himself in Spain's rich culture and strange, and sometimes horrifying, folkways. In Burgos he stood at the foot of a hill called El

Castillo, where the Cid was born, and imagined a "splendid caval-
cade of knights . . . off to drive the Moor from Toledo."[39] In Salamanca he lamented over the decline of the university, once a world
center of learning, but marveled that he was treading paving stones
that had been walked on by Cervantes and Calderón. Toledo jolted
him with its disturbing mixture of wretched present and glorious
past. On the one hand, El Greco paintings in the San Tomé Church
and that magnificent view of the city from the Alcantará bridge; on
the other, abject hovels and narrow, vermin-infested *callejones* that
passed for streets. Though Reed found Toledo "more regal than
Madrid, more gloriously disdainful than Burgos," he was distressed
by its decline into "that pathetic thing, a city living for its ruins."[40]

In Madrid, it was modernity rather than antiquity that offended
Reed. "Joseph Bonaparte tried to make a Paris of Madrid which
would be like making New York of London."[41] Reed noted how
wide boulevards made an incongruous spectacle against a background of filth and poverty. He concluded—unkindest cut of all—
that Spain's capital was "the Newark New Jersey of Europe."[42]

Reed's glimpses of Spain's seamy side played their part in his cautious progress, still more a drift than a march, toward revolution.
In Burgos he saw a sight that increased his distaste for cruelty and
superstition. ". . . an old dame hobbling along on a cane was pursued by a crowd of men and children, who yelled insults, sang
derisive songs, and even threw rocks."[43] The woman was suspected
of witchcraft.

Accompanying Reed's hatred of superstition was intensified identification with the masses he would one day be exhorting to revolution. In Salamanca he took pride in the fact that he was the only
foreigner never accosted by beggars. Presumably discouraged by his
proletarian appearance, the mendicants gave him a wide berth. What
a contrast with the Reed of nine months ago, pathetically grateful
for his place on the Mount Auburn political slate!

Though his contacts with humbler Spaniards were generally
friendly, Reed did have an unpleasant experience on a third-class
train to Madrid. An old peasant woman with "a wrinkled face like
a squally lake" had offered him her market basket as a pillow. But
her demeanor abruptly changed when she learned he was an American. ". . . that squally lake became a raging sea of tears . . . she

kicked me, she clawed at my face . . . she cursed and wept." Other Spaniards in the compartment, who found the incident hilarious, explained that the old woman had lost a son in the Spanish-American war.[44]

By the end of September Reed was back in Paris. Propped up financially by another letter of credit, he took a room at a Left Bank hotel (the Jacob) and prepared to enjoy Paris to the hilt.

Here Jack renewed his association with Madeleine Filon, back from St. Pierre and primed to enjoy the fall-winter season. Though attraction was mounting, Madeleine had not yet established a dominant claim on him. The insouciant Waldo Peirce, nominally an art student, had settled down to a life of café lounger and stud-about-town. He invited Reed to his merry company, and Reed eagerly accepted the invitation. Jack fully shared Waldo's admiration for *parisiennes*—as well as its wide range. Daughters of wealth, shopgirls, sleek *cocottes* from the Champs Élysées, their coarser sisters from the Place Pigalle—all enjoyed the attentions of Reed and Peirce. Though fanatical in his aversion to "the strenuous life," Peirce was no stuffed shirt. Freewheeling bohemianism was fine as long as it didn't entail physical discomfort.

But there was one aspect of the American presence in Paris that disturbed Reed. Some Harvard respectables had ensconced themselves in the capital and, far from adapting culturally, were behaving like bearers of the white man's burden in darkest Africa. Most of them were Mount Auburn men. Reed's irritation was not caused by any snubs from the elitists. On the contrary, they considered him an old Paris hand and assiduously cultivated him. Though he attended some of their meetings (placing bets on the Yale game with transplanted Elis), the snobs soon palled on him. Having crossed on a cattle boat as a suspected murderer, tramped over half of England, and endured lice and hostile gendarmes in Spain, the cocktail chitchat of privileged émigrés seemed puerile and insipid.

Reed was also turned off by his encounters with Professor W. H. Schofield, a Harvard exchange scholar at the Sorbonne. Schofield, a man of towering pomposity, was given to entertaining the Harvard Paris contingent at a series of punitively formal dinners. Having got wind of Reed's adventures in less respectable sections of town, Schofield undertook to upbraid him for his waywardness. After that, Reed stopped attending Schofield's starchy soirées.

Family vicissitudes also contributed to the making of the "new" Reed. C. J., defeated in the Republican primary, faced the last year of his life with grim prospects and a mountain of debt. As November yielded to a bleak, cheerless December, it was stocktaking time for Reed *fils* as well as Reed *père*. Though he had dreamed of sustaining himself in Europe as a writer, to date he had produced nothing of note. Lacking the financial resources of Peirce and others, a life of leisure in Paris cafés was closed to him.

In 1910 Jack Reed got his values straight. Twelve months earlier he had happily accepted a meaningless gesture of tokenism from people of "the better sort." Now, having rejected the rejecters, he was determinedly charting his course in a chill Paris hotel room.

But determination had not dampened Reed's innate *joie de vivre*. Deciding on a final fling, he began with a holiday bash at Grez with Chadwick and his family.[45] In January he fled Paris's inhospitable climate and headed for the south of France. Meeting Peirce in Toulon, he joined a group for a walking tour of the Riviera. In the group was Madeleine Filon. The trip included that picture-book proposal at Fréjus and ended with Madeleine as his fiancée. Though the engagement was later broken, belief that he would soon be supporting a wife added to Reed's resolve and sense of responsibility. It was this resolve, and reordering of values, that unleashed the flood of euphoric happiness that possessed Reed when he came to New York in the spring of 1911. Lincoln Steffens immediately noticed it. It was almost in awe that he recalled never having seen "anything so near to pure joy."

3

Villa's Road
to Revolution

FRANCISCO VILLA'S ROAD TO REVOLUTION began with two political assassinations. Previously his killings had been either for booty or in self-defense. But now he participated in two slayings that deviated from the previous norm—one far more than the other. The first killing was both a political execution and an act of vengeance; the second was as impersonal as a high-altitude bombing. The victims, both from Chihuahua, were Claro Reza and Pedro Domínguez.

Claro Reza had been a close friend of Villa, one of his many *compadres*. In late summer of 1910, when Villa was still being indoctrinated by Abraham González, Reza was in the Chihuahua jail on a charge of stealing burros. Tiring of confinement, he got out a message to Juan Creel, a member of the baronial clan whose holdings were exceeded only by those of the Terrazas family. If *don* Juan would arrange Reza's release and an appointment to the *rurales*, he would deliver Pancho Villa. Creel, who had a double reason to hate Villa, immediately accepted Reza's offer. As a bandit, Villa had rustled many of Creel's cattle. Now, as a protégé of the dangerous Abraham González, he also posed a political threat to the power structure Creel represented. (Reza was intimately acquainted with the location of Villa's adobe house and must have told Creel of the subversive meetings going on there.)

A few nights later Reza led a raiding party of *rurales* against his former friend's house. But Villa was ready for him. He had been tipped off to Reza's treachery by a friend in the rurales named José— "whose last name I do not remember."[1] To meet the expected attack, Villa had garrisoned the house with a picked group of followers. A nocturnal gun battle raged till 0400, when the attackers gave up the siege. Though several *rurales* lay dead, Reza got away.

Villa was almost maniacal in his rage against Reza and his thirst for revenge. Not only had Reza betrayed him personally—thus violating the bond of *compadrazgo*—but had also voluntarily offered his services to a hated oppressor. The now politically conscious Villa saw Reza as a class traitor as well as a personal enemy.

With his closest confidant, Eleuterio Soto, Villa discussed plans for Reza's elimination. Soto, who had also befriended Reza, was as aggrieved as Villa by his treachery. "That's the way this traitor pays us after all we've done for him," he said bitterly. Soto suggested that they track Reza down and kill him.[2]

Villa fully endorsed Soto's proposal but added a condition: the killing had to be public. "Even in front of Government Palace," he insisted, "do you agree, *compadre*?"[3]

This was another reflection of Villa's growing political consciousness. Reza was more than a personal enemy. He belonged to the rural police, one of the Díaz regime's most hated organs of repression. The public killing of a *rural* had ideological as well as practical value.

After spending the night by the nearby Chuvícazar Dam, Villa and Soto rode into Chihuahua in the early morning. Having heard it was an area Reza frequented, they ranged the length of Avenida Zarco. Then they saw him—he was at an *expendio*, a meat stall, across the street from a cantina called "Las 15 Letras." Drawing their pistols, they emptied them into the unsuspecting Reza. He died instantly.

By now a crowd was beginning to pour into the street. Reza was a much disliked man, and the bystanders wanted to make sure he was dead. Though nobody intended to impede the killers' escape, the crowd's density had exactly that effect. And now hoofbeats were heard—a party of soldiers was on the way.

With threats and drawn pistols, Villa and Soto secured an escape route through the crowd. As they thundered back toward the Sierra

Azul, Villa got the impression that the soldiers were not following with great enthusiasm. "They were all praying to God for the pursuit to fail," he noted ironically.[4]

Back at La Estacada, their hideout in the sierra, Villa and Soto continued recruiting men for the revolution. One of these recruits, Feliciano Domínguez, took Villa aside one day about a matter that was causing him concern. Domínguez told Villa that his uncle, Pedro Domínguez, had just returned from Chihuahua with the credentials of *juez de acordada*, a sort of rural judge. The uncle, a staunch Díaz supporter, had personally vowed to track down and kill every member of the Villa band. This put Feliciano in a difficult position. Though he detested his uncle's political role, he liked and admired him personally. "I'm very sorry, chief," he told Villa, "because he's my uncle and a good man and very brave. But I believe for the good of our cause we have to kill him."[5] Domínguez added that his uncle lived at a nearby ranch called Del Encino. "You're right," Villa is recorded as saying. "We have to finish off these men who don't listen to the voice of the people or their consciences and who uphold tyranny and cause suffering to the poor."[6] Though his real words were undoubtedly more earthy, the meaning was the same. Villa selected eight men, and they rode off to the judge's ranch.

Feliciano Domínguez had not exaggerated his uncle's valor. When he saw the band approaching, he positioned himself behind a fence and brought down two riders. The attackers dismounted, trying to encircle the ranch, and Domínguez dropped a third man as he was approaching the kitchen. Villa and Soto made a rush for the fence, firing at will and wounding Domínguez. A bullet narrowly missed Soto, passing through his sombrero. The wounded judge tried to escape but was hit twice more while making for a second fence and a fourth time while trying to climb it. This time he fell to the ground. Villa rushed to the scene and tried to grab the fallen man's rifle but Domínguez, still full of fight, reached up and sank his teeth into Villa's hand. It was Soto who delivered the *coup de grace*, a bullet through the head.

Though definite dates are not given, the Reza killing probably took place in late summer and the Domínguez execution toward the end of September. We know this because on 4 October Villa brought his entire band (now fifteen in number) to the adobe house at 500 Calle 10.[7] He did so in response to a request by Abraham González. Villa had gone to Chihuahua alone to confer with his mentor right after the Domínguez killing. He found González jittery, his nerves worn from constant police surveillance. Fearing arbitrary arrest—with all that that entailed—he needed the protection of men who could fight and shoot. Villa agreed, detaching two of the band to serve as bodyguards. In event of capture, the others would act as a rescue team.

Though the Mexican Revolution was officially launched on 20 November, the Pancho Villa Revolution began three days earlier. On 17 November Abraham González arrived at the adobe house for what would be their last meeting. Accompanying him was Cástulo Herrera, one of his chief lieutenants. After a hearty *comida*, González made the announcement they had all been waiting for. "I'm going to the north, to Ojinaga, and you, Pancho, go south. All must recognize Cástulo Herrera as your chief."[8]

If Villa felt chagrin over Herrera's appointment, he concealed it with good grace. "It didn't surprise me much," he records in the *Memorias*, "that I wasn't named chief of the men gathered here and those who would join us." Then he addressed González: "Señor, be sure you will be obeyed," he began. "Since we are uneducated, we need men who know more to lead us. We will always obey the orders of Cástulo Herrera."[9] Villa would later think differently about the more educated Herrera, a man with few military skills.

González exchanged an emotional *abrazo* with each man present, and that night the band rode into the sierra. These were the Original Fifteen—the first men with whom Villa rode as a revolutionary and not as a bandit. The group included Tomás Urbina, that paragon of mindless *machismo*; Feliciano Domínguez, who had so cold-bloodedly engineered the death of his "beloved" uncle; and Eleuterio Soto, Villa's closest friend, soon to die. Not wanting to attract attention, the fifteen maintained silence until they were beyond the city limits. Then pent-up emotion burst forth and a chorus of ¡vivas! split the night air—to Abraham González, to Francisco Madero, to the rights of the poor. Villa records that he had not been so close to tears since the death of his mother.[10]

In the first five days Villa succeeded in recruiting 375 men. On orders from Cástulo Herrera they swarmed down from the sierra and attacked the town of San Andrés, about 27 miles west of Chihuahua City. Because a garrison of *rurales* had fled, the action was bloodless. Though it was not much of a victory, these inexperienced men celebrated as if they'd just marched into Mexico City. They whooped, shouted, and rode through the streets firing their pistols. Enraged at this waste of ammunition, Villa immediately ordered them to stop. He also noted that Cástulo Herrera, his nominal superior, had stood by placidly while this wasteful display was taking place.[11] The rebels also appointed new civil officials for the newly captured town.

The next attack was at Estación San Andrés, a rail spur near the town they had just liberated. In this action Villa used only his most experienced men, the original fifteen.[12] A passenger train from Chihuahua was carrying a troop contingent and the rebels wanted to seize it. Though they failed to capture the train, they managed to kill the troop commander and three soldiers.[13]

Returning to action, the rebels scored another bloodless victory as they seized Santa Isabel. Again, new civil officials were appointed and local recruiting proved so successful that Villa was able to beef his force up to 500 men.[14]

On 27 November, following the fall of Santa Isabel, Villa ordered a march on Chihuahua City. For the first time, he gave an order on his own without consulting Herrera. Fed up with Herrera's do-nothing leadership, Villa commented that "Cástulo Herrera, who passed for our leader, commanded so little that it was I who was leading the Revolution's campaign."[15]

About a mile and a half from Chihuahua, the *villistas* (as they were now) engaged the Army's 20th Battalion near a hill called El Tecolote. The inexperienced rebels were almost surrounded, and it was with difficulty that they managed to break out to the north. Three of the Original Fifteen were killed in the engagement, among them Eleuterio Soto. Villa himself was wounded in the leg.[16]

Shortly after this engagement Villa received a telegram from Pascual Orozco, requesting that he bring as much ammunition as he could to Ciudad Guerrero. There, on 10 December, a high-level meeting took place that included Villa, Orozco, and possibly Cástulo Herrera. Uncertainty stems from the fact that one source has Herrera conferring with Madero in the United States on that date.[17]

But the point is academic. Villa and Orozco were now in charge of the Revolution in Chihuahua and what remained of Herrera's authority was rapidly evaporating. The Ciudad Guerrero meeting produced a decision to make a frontal assault on a strong federal force that was approaching from Chihuahua under General Navarro. The attack, to be launched the following day, was the boldest operation the rebels had planned to date.

Thus began a bloody, seesaw battle that lasted three and one-half hours. First the *villistas*, in a screening action, seized an elevation called Cerro Prieto. Since the hill blocked Navarro's advance, the Federals launched a furious attack to dislodge Villa's men. The assault gained ground and Villa admitted that at one point he was almost *"abatido"* (defeated).[18] Then Orozco's cavalry, in strategic reserve, came thundering onto the scene and eased the pressure on the beleaguered *villistas*. But Navarro had a hole card of his own: artillery. He wheeled up his guns and superior firepower left the Army in possession of the field. The *orozquistas* escaped over the Sierra de Picachos, while Villa's men melted into the safety of a closer range. Night had fallen and many wounded were saved by lanterns of friendly *campesinos* lighting the way to safety.[19]

Though Villa was learning fast, he still made mistakes. After the Cerro Prieto defeat, he and Orozco intercepted a letter concerning delivery of ammunition to the Federal-held town of Santa Isabel. (Villa states unequivocally that he read the letter—"because at that time I knew how to read"—debunking later claims that he was illiterate until his Mexico City incarceration.[20]) To prepare an attack on Santa Isabel, Villa quartered his men and stabled his horses in nearby San Andrés. Told by the widow of a fallen *villista* that Federals were near, he mistakenly assumed she was referring to the Santa Isabel garrison. But this was another force—even now crossing a mountain that overlooked San Andrés. Led by an unpopular native son, a *porfirista* tax collector, they were following the course of a stream that flowed down the mountain and into the town.

Their attack took Villa so completely by surprise that he lost all his horses. Without time to get their mounts out of the stables, the *villistas* had to flee on foot.[21] That winter in the sierra was Villa's Valley Forge. Cold, hungry, lacking horses, his people survived mainly through the aid, some of it involuntary, of local ranchers. Particularly "generous" was a well-to-do family named Cuilty, whom the *villistas* relieved of four hundred horses. More were obtained when Villa attacked a fifty-man detachment of *rurales* at Satevó, about 50 miles south of Chihuahua City. Some of the *rurales* were killed and others joined the rebels.

But not all aid was extracted by force. Small ranchers in Santa Gertrudis and Ojo de Obispo enthusiastically furnished food, supplies, and what money they could spare. At La Boquilla, Villa routed a twenty-five–man garrison guarding a dam being built by a private company. Seizing the payroll, he offered the manager a *pagaré* (I.O.U.). The man refused, on grounds that it was company money and not his own.[22]

On 7 February 1911, the re-equipped *villistas* attacked Camargo, one of the largest cities in the state. A strong federal relief force appeared and Villa had to break off the attack. The *villistas* retired in good order and their casualties were minimal.[23] Camargo demonstrated that Villa was learning. Though he would retreat before *force majeure*, there was no repetition of his amateurish errors at El Tecolote and San Adnrés.

Villa next undertook a personal espionage mission to Parral, the town where he was to die. Leaving his men at an unidentified location ("100 kilometers from Rancho Tarais"), he told them to wait there until he returned. He slipped into Parral and spotted the location of four federal detachments—three inside the city and one guarding a hill outside. All belonged to the 7th Regiment of Dragoons.[24] On the way out of town Villa had the misfortune to run into a personal enemy named Jesús Bailón. Apparently fearing a confrontation, Bailón pretended not to recognize Villa. Then he made his way straight to military headquarters and reported the encounter. The force sent to track down Villa surrounded him at Rancho Tarais. With him was one of his captains, Albino Frías. Though their pursuers numbered 150, both Villa and Frías managed to escape. But they were separated in the melee, and Villa made it back to his camp alone. On the way he stopped for food at the house of Santos Vega, the master mason who had befriended him in pre-Revolutionary days.

Villa received an unpleasant surprise when he arrived at his base camp: the troops had completely disappeared. Weary and disgusted, he hitched his horse, spread his blanket, and went to sleep on the ground.

The next morning he proceeded to the nearby village of San José. There he saw one of his captains, Natividad García, and four men. Angrily he asked García why the troops had not obeyed his orders to stay put. García replied that Frías, following his escape from Rancho Tarais, had come to the camp and reported that Villa was dead. (After their separation, Frías was positive that Villa had been overwhelmed by the Federals.) So the troop had moved on; with Villa dead there was no further sense in waiting.

Aided by García, Villa rounded up his scattered men and moved north to Satevó, where he set up headquarters on 8 March.[25] His force now numbered seven hundred, including five captains.[26] One of these officers was that model of family solidarity, Feliciano Domínguez.

Shortly after setting up his new base camp, Villa defeated a federal force at Terrero, between Satevó and Chihuahua City. His losses in the engagement were a modest twenty-three dead and fourteen wounded.[27]

After the Terrero victory, Villa's men moved into San Andrés, the town from which he had been so ignominiously expelled in December. It was now mid-March, exactly a month since Francisco Madero had crossed into Mexico to take charge of the rebellion. Though he and Villa had never met, Madero had heard great things about this bandit-turned-guerrilla from their mutual friend Abraham González. He sent a message to Villa in San Andrés, summoning him to his headquarters at Hacienda Bustillos.

This first meeting was little more than an exchange of amenities. Madero, radiating enthusiasm, greeted Villa with his most charming smile. "Pancho Villa, *hombre*, what a boy you are! And here I was thinking you were an old man." The less articulate Villa's response was an aw-shucks mumble of self-deprecation. But he expresses himself with complete clarity in the *Memorias*. "This is a rich man who fights for the good of the poor. . . . If all the rich and powerful in Mexico were like him, there would be no struggle and no suffering, for all of us would be doing our duty."[28]

There were two more meetings, an official reception with marching bands at San Andrés and a second one at Bustillos where more substantive matters were considered. There Pascual Orozco joined Villa and Madero, and the three men discussed strategy. The idea of a frontal attack on Chihuahua was rejected in favor of intensified guerrilla activity. In addition, the rebels were to make greater use of trains. They would be needed to increase mobility and to accommodate the heavy guns and supplies Madero was expecting.

Then Madero addressed himself to another problem: internal dissension. Shortly after the second Bustillos meeting, he ordered Villa to meet him at a rail junction called Estación Guzmán. There he told him of difficulties he was having with three *cabecillas* (leaders of semi-autonomous bands) named Salazar, García, and Alaniz. They had sent Madero insolent letters and were attempting to repudiate him. And—forerunner of things to come—the situation was further complicated by the attitude of Pascual Orozco. Madero had asked him to disarm the rebellious trio, but Orozco refused, protesting that such a step could not be taken without bloodshed. Faced with three (four, if we count Orozco) leaders who were openly defying his authority, Madero turned in desperation to Villa.[29]

Villa instantly agreed to disarm the refractory *cabecillas*. Making the most of surprise, his men swooped down on the Salazar, García, and Alaniz bands in a daring night raid. So fast and surely did the *villistas* move that the operation was accomplished completely without bloodshed.[30]

That Madero entrusted Villa with such a challenging assignment was a mark of his growing confidence in the former bandit. He had commissioned him a colonel at Bustillos, followed by a blanket pardon for all the crimes of which he had been accused. Shortly afterward (in an apparent move to justify himself before world opinion) Madero wrote a letter to the *El Paso Times*. It was unfair, he argued, to call Villa a bandit because he had been prevented by an unjust political system from earning an honest living. His victims had always been the exploiting rich, and he had only killed in self-defense. (It isn't difficult to deduce from whom this Robin-Hood image derived.)[31]

Free from the threat of internal revolt, Madero could now get on with the business of revolution. Until then the fighting had centered around Chihuahua City, over 200 miles south of the U.S. border. Now the rebellion dramatically moved north. Madero's next attack took place on 16 April. The target was Estación Bauche, only 10 miles south of Ciudad Juárez. Spearheading the assault was a 150-man detachment under José Orozco. But the rebels made little headway against stiff federal resistance. The attack was on the point of failing when Madero despatched a relief column under Villa. These *villista* reinforcements turned the tide and the Federals were sent reeling back to Juárez. Texans once read about the Mexican Revolution in newspapers: now it was at their back door.[32]

This proximity caused complications. Both Mexican factions feared and abhorred the specter of American intervention. With a major battle raging across the river from El Paso, there was a strong probability that stray rounds might fall on the American side. Then what? Colonel Edgar Z. Steever, commander of the 4th Cavalry at Fort Bliss, served notice on both Madero and the garrison chief at Juárez that misplaced bullets and shells might cause U.S. units to cross the border.[33]

In issuing this warning, Steever probably exceeded his authority. Though Juárez would be bloodily contested by Federals and *maderistas*, at no time did American troops intervene. Steever's admonition, delivered on 7 May, could well have been a bluff designed to shield El Paso civilians from accidental exposure to a foreign civil war raging on their doorstep.

But Madero had no way of knowing this. Since 19 April, three days after Villa's victory at Estación Bauche, his revolutionary army had been at the gates of Juárez. The 80-year-old federal commander, General Juan Navarro, had rejected a message from Madero demanding his surrender. But he did agree to a 10-day armistice; two unofficial negotiators had arrived in El Paso from Mexico City to explore the possibility of a peaceful settlement. These intermediaries were Oscar Braniff and Toribio Esquivel Obregón, the same men who would later play a role in seducing Pascual Orozco from revolution.

Confused negotiations continued for over two weeks. Contributing to the confusion was Madero's unending vacillation. First he wanted the resignation of Díaz and Corral; then he declared himself satisfied with such concessions as the appointment of *maderista* governors, withdrawal of federal troops from northern Mexico, and recognition of the no-reelection principle.

On 3 May an official Díaz negotiator arrived, a supreme court justice named Francisco Carbajal. Carbajal was no more successful than his predecessors in pinning Madero down. One day he came away with the impression that Madero was not pressing for the resignation of Díaz and Corral; the next he was informed by *maderista* negotiators that the old dictator and his handpicked vice-president would have to step down. (Corral, gravely ill with cancer, was already on leave of absence in Paris.)

Then came Steever's warning. It had such an effect on Madero that he told his troops that the attack on Juárez was being abandoned in favor of a march on Mexico City.[34]

Madero's hesitation waltz was observed with mounting anger by two hard men: Pascual Orozco and Francisco Villa. Though the ex–mule driver and the ex-bandit would soon become bitter enemies, today they were united in contempt for their indecisive chief's game of diplomatic patty cake.

Moreover, the military situation definitely favored the rebels. Madero new had 2,500 effectives while federal strength consisted of 908 officers and men plus a governor's militia of 130 auxiliaries. But, of this total, 186 were sick or wounded.[35] So the *maderistas* had an amost 3–1 numerical advantage.

There was another—and more personal—factor that militated toward a showdown in Juárez. The garrison's second-in-command, Colonel Manuel Tamborel, had given a series of boastful interviews to an *El Paso Times* reporter named Tim Turner. He scorned the rebels as chicken thieves and despoilers of defenseless ranchers, adding that they were not men enough to take Juárez.[36]

These taunts were a red flag to such machos as Orozco and Villa. Stung by Tamborel's jibes and hampered by Madero's indecision, they decided to take matters into their own hands. On the morning of 8 May a band of Orozco followers, led by a Captain Reyes Robinson, approached a federal outpost called El Molino and began shouting insults at the defenders. The Federals responded in kind, and it wasn't long before billingsgate escalated to bullets. Orozco and Villa, in a show of innocence, had taken care to be in El Paso when the El Molino incident took place. Now they hurried back across the border, and Villa disingenuously asked Madero what had happened. Madero tried to arrange a cease-fire but Villa and Orozco, openly disobeying him, ordered more men into the rapidly spreading conflict. Having stoked the flames till the fire was out of control, Orozco and Villa "sorrowfully" informed Madero that fighting could no longer be contained. Madero, befuddled as ever, ordered two more cease-fires and countermanded both directives when it appeared that his forces were gaining the upper hand.

In the two-day action Villa attacked from the south and Orozco from the west. Colonel Tamborel, who lost his life in the action, had organized an ingenious system of fortifications. Though these took their toll, the *maderistas* were too numerous and motivated to be denied. The final blow came when the Federals' water and electricity were cut off. Faced with a hopeless situation, General Navarro surrendered.

In victory, Villa amply demonstrated his half-adoring, half-patronizing attitude toward "little *señor* Madero." Explaining his disobedience, he said he had decided "to launch our attack by military logic, circumventing Sr. Madero, who was no military man."[37]

This victory was followed by the incident related in Chapter 1, when Madero saved General Navarro from the vengeance of Villa and Orozco. In prevailing against Orozco's bluster—and eliciting that emotion-charged apology from Villa—Madero recaptured much of the prestige he had lost during the attack on Juárez.

The fall of Ciudad Juárez was soon followed by the fall of Porfirio Díaz. Demoralized, in agony from an abscessed jaw, the old dictator signed an act of resignation on 25 May. Six days later he boarded the *Ypiranga*, a German steamer that took him into exile. *Don Porfirio* settled in Paris, living quietly and avoiding ostentation. A treasured urn of Oaxaca earth was the only Mexican soil he would ever see again. He died in July 1915 in the first year of the First World War.

Before boarding the *Ypiranga*, Díaz made a prophetic remark. "Madero has unleashed a tiger," he said to a companion, "let us see if he can control him."[38] Despite his astounding electoral victory in November, the "tiger"—or "tigers," to be more exact—were not long in turning on Madero. Zapata repudiated him even before his election. Feeling that Madero was dragging his feet on land reform, Zapata denounced the Plan de San Luis in favor of his more radical Plan de Ayala. The Vázquez Gómez brothers, Emilio and Francisco, declared themselves in revolt against Madero three days after his inauguration. (Francisco, Madero's running mate in the old Anti-Reelectionist Party, had been dumped in favor of José María Pino Suarez in the 1911 election.) General Bernardo Reyes, an old soldier and ex-political boss, led a farcical rebellion in December and voluntarily surrendered when it failed. A second abortive rising was headed by Felix Díaz, the dictator's nephew. Instead of being shot, Reyes and Díaz were imprisoned by the soft-hearted Madero. Another potential troublemaker was Victoriano Huerta. Having obstructed Madero's efforts to negotiate with Zapata, he was angrily chafing in enforced retirement.

But the worst betrayal came from the north. If the Mexican Revolution produced a Benedict Arnold, he appeared in the person of Pascual Orozco. True, others had turned against Madero but their motives were far cleaner than Orozco's. Zapata and the Vázquez Gómez brothers opposed him from the Left; all three considered the new president insufficiently revolutionary. As for Reyes, Díaz, and Huerta, personal ambition was mingled with genuine attachment to the old order.

No such ideological considerations animated Orozco. His motive was greed and—interesting similarity!—the same wounded vanity that caused Arnold to turn traitor. Both were enraged at being cheated of the recognition they felt they deserved. Just as Arnold had been seduced by Tory sympathizers, so did Orozco become the creature of the Creel-Terrazas clan. Disappointed ambition made him easy prey to the cattle barons' blandishments. He had hoped for a 50,000-peso donative for his part in the Revolution but received only 5,000. He had expected to be named Minister of War but was made commander of rural irregulars in Chihuahua. He had aspired to be state governor but saw the post go to the popular Abraham González.[39]

Orozco's wealthy backers were not limited to Chihuahua or even to Mexico. Among them was the press mogul, William Randolph Hearst, who had extensive Mexican holdings. In a report to Vienna, the Austrian Minister charged that "Mr. Hearst's newspapers, which are hoping to benefit from Madero's overthrow . . . are therefore supporting Orozco's people with money, arms, and good advice in El Paso, San Antonio, and Douglas, Arizona."[40]

The Orozco rising had the effect of reactivating Francisco Villa. With 10,000 pesos received from Madero, he had returned to the butchering business. In December 1911, Madero sent him another 500 pesos and a request that he come to Mexico City. Though Madero was naive and trusting, his trust did not extend to the resentful Orozco. He told Villa that he had heard adverse reports about the ambitious ex–mule driver. Villa replied that Orozco was spending a great deal of time with Juan Creel and Alberto Terrazas, "and you know what those people are."[41] Madero did indeed. He told Villa to return to Chihuahua and keep a close eye on Orozco. Should rebellion break out, Villa should be ready to help suppress it. Villa accepted Madero's commission and prepared to return north.

In February Villa reported that he had been visited by Orozco's father, Pascual Orozco, Sr. Purpose of the visit was to offer Villa a 300,000-peso bribe to go to the United States and "not meddle in the affairs of my son."[42] Villa, by his account, spurned the offer but told the elder Orozco that he would take no action against him— "even though you are in my hands." The day being unusually cold, he even gave the old man a blanket when he left.[43]

When Orozco rose, Villa formed a band of irregulars and was promoted from colonel to brigadier-general. It was during the Orozco campaign that Villa and Huerta first met. The meeting was a classic dog-cat confrontation—the educated, hard-drinking, Indian regular officer and the rough-mannered, teetotaling, light mestizo ex-bandit. Huerta detested Villa for the role he played in the overthrow of his idol, Díaz; Villa loathed Huerta both for his dubious allegiance to Madero and fanatical one to Hennessy and Martel, Huerta's favorite brandies. Huerta sardonically referred to Villa as "the honorary general," while Villa, with equal venom, called Huerta "the little drunkard." (Yet Villa was fair-minded enough to admire Huerta's military gifts.)

Following the Rellano victory, Huerta saw an opportunity to permanently rid himself of Villa. The latter had refused to return a fine mare seized from a local rancher, and Huerta, in a savagely disproportionate punishment, sentenced him to be shot. Villa came so close to death that he was actually against the wall and facing the firing squad. Fortunately, he had made a friend of Colonel Rubio Navarrete, an artilleryman on Huerta's staff. Rubio got word to Colonel Raul Madero, the President's brother, who telegraphed Mexico City. A return wire halted the execution. According to one source, the officer in charge of the firing squad had already given the "¡Preparan armas!" ("Ready arms!") order when the reprieve came.[44]

Villa was placed on a train and sent to Mexico City. There he spent a little over six months in detention, four in the penitentiary and two in the military prison of Santiago Tlatelolco.

As noted earlier, the version that Villa was illiterate until this confinement was pure fabrication. That doesn't mean that he didn't benefit intellectually from his imprisonment. In the penitentiary he was lodged in a special section for *presos distinguidos* (distinguished prisoners).[45] There he made friends with Gildardo Magaña, one of the radical intellectuals who surrounded Zapata. Though Villa sympathized with Zapata's land reform program, he could not condone his repudiation of Madero.

In Tlatelolco Villa was wooed by the Right. Old guard elements were plotting against Madero; a key figure in the conspiracy was the imprisoned General Bernardo Reyes. Antonio Tamayo, a lawyer representing Reyes, visited Villa in his cell and tried to enlist him for the coming *cuartelazo* (military coup).

This ill-advised overture only increased Villa's determination to escape and aid his beloved "little *señor* Madero." With the aid of Carlos Jáuregui, his literary collaborator, he procured a disguise and slipped out on Christmas Eve of 1912. Jáuregui, who feared his part in the escape would be found out, decided to accompany Villa. Following a circuitous route, they made their way to the United States by car, rail, and sea. By February Villa was in El Paso.

It was from there that Villa wrote to Abraham González, warning him of the impending coup and offering to take control of *maderista* forces in Chihuahua. González's unwise refusal was followed—in rapid succession—by Huerta's treachery against Madero, Madero's arrest and death, Rabago's treachery against González, González's arrest and death.

For Villa, it was a case of starting all over again. On 17 November 1910, he had ridden into the Sierra Azul with fifteen men. Now, on 9 March 1913, he crossed the border with eight.

What followed was a military success story almost without parallel in history. His first act was to send an insolent telegram to Rábago, whom Huerta had installed as governor of Chihuahua:

KNOWING THAT THE GOVERNMENT YOU REPRESENT WAS PREPARING TO EXTRADITE ME I DECIDED TO COME HERE AND SAVE YOU THE TROUBLE. HERE I AM IN MEXICO RESOLVED TO MAKE WAR ON THE TYRANNY WHICH YOU DEFEND. FRANCISCO VILLA.[46]

Fifteen and a half months passed between 9 March 1913, when Villa's tiny party crossed the Río Grande, and 23 June 1914, when bloody defeat at Zacatecas sent Huerta on the road to exile. These fifteen and a half months saw Villa rise to his apogee as a revolutionary leader, both in the military and civil fields. When he crossed the river, he was an escaped convict and proscribed follower of a defeated cause; when his forces triumphed at Zacatecas, he was a world celebrity.

Once he crossed his Rubicon, success came to Villa with dazzling speed. *Maderista* sympathy was strong in Chihuahua and Villa's band did not remain small for long. Recruiting went so well that within a month he was able to defeat a federal force of 500 at Bustillos, where he had first met Madero. Of the enemy, 300 were line soldiers and 200 followers of his former ally, Pascual Orozco.[47] Ever the opportunist, Orozco had made his peace with Huerta and received a combat command. It is ironic that Orozco's men were known as *colorados* (the Americans called them "Red Flaggers") because of their distinctive insignia. Far from being "red," they rode gun for the cattle barons and imposed a cruel white terror on the Chihuahua countryside.

The Bustillos victory was followed by another *villista* triumph. At Casas Grandes, about 200 miles southwest of Juárez, Villa had the satisfaction of routing an all-*colorado* force of 400. Of sixty prisoners taken, all were shot. Villa's rule of warfare mandated the killing of federal officers and *colorados*. Federal enlisted men were usually spared (though not when they fell into the hands of such brutish Villa subordinates as Tomás Urbina and Rodolfo Fierro) on the ground that many were unwilling conscripts.[48]

June and July were devoted to consolidation, with Villa setting up headquarters at Ascención in northwestern Chihuahua. Aiding him was Julián Medina, a former federal cavalry lieutenant who had been commissioned a *villista* colonel.

On 26 August Villa scored another satisfying victory over a force of *colorados*—doubly satisfying because its commander was "General" Felix Terrazas, a pampered aristocrat on active duty with the hooligans financed by his family fortune. The *villistas*, who now numbered 1,028 effectives, captured two pieces of artillery (their first), 20,000 rounds, and 249 prisoners. Of these, 237 were shot. In sparing twelve men, Villa was not motivated by sentiment. They were artillerists who would be needed to operate the captured field pieces.[49]

All this time the *División del Norte* (as Villa's growing force was now known) had been confining operations to Chihuahua. But now Villa had his eye on Torreón, an important rail center in southwestern Coahuila. Seizure of this key point would prevent *huertista* reinforcements from entering Chihuahua. The assault began on 29 September and by dawn of 2 October the city was in *villista* hands. It was Villa's greatest triumph to date. It also marked the *villistas'* transition from a hit-and-run band to a modern army, one complete with machine guns, heavy artillery, and troop trains. The booty taken from the Federals included 13 cannons (including a 3-inch railroad gun), 600 grenades, 1,000 rifles, 6 machine guns, and 500,000 cartridges.[50]

Leaving a garrison in Torreón, Villa turned back to secure Chihuahua. Torreón is 288 miles southeast of Chihuahua City, and by 27 October the *División del Norte* had defeated the Federals at Ciudad Camargo, less than 100 miles from the state capital. Villa continued to roll north, and by 5 November he had reached the outskirts of Chihuahua.

It was here that he suffered the only setback of that brilliant fifteen-and-a-half-month campaign. The assault on Chihuahua City began on 5 November and lasted two days. But the *huertistas* were too well entrenched and their artillery worked with murderous precision. On 7 November, with night falling, Villa broke off the attack.

Villa reacted to this reverse with all the resilience and quick intelligence for which he was famous. Instead of retreating south, as the Federals had expected him to do, he wheeled north, bypassed Chihuahua City, and seized a coal train heading south from Juárez. The *villistas* unloaded the coal from the cars, substituted themselves, and rode the train into Juárez on 15 November. Surprise was so complete that Villa took only an hour to secure the city.[51]

Juárez proved a bonanza. With a base on the border Villa was able to appropriate the gambling money from the casinos and buy vast stores of arms and supplies from willing American sellers.

Seeing how badly they had been tricked, the Federals of the Chihuahua garrison made a pell-mell rush north to do battle with Villa. Perhaps previous success had made them overconfident. The battle was joined on 23 November at Tierra Blanca, about 20 miles south of Juárez. This time it was a different story. The *villistas* were fresh and re-equipped and the *huertistas* no longer enjoyed the entrenched positions that had served them so well at Chihuahua. By 25 November the Federals were shattered. A remnant made its way back, not to Chihuahua but to the more distant border town of Ojinaga, 125 miles southeast of Juárez. This force was annihilated by Villa on 9 January in an engagement that lasted sixty-five minutes. Among the enemy survivors who crossed the border was Pascual Orozco. Prior to the encounter Orozco had threatened to kill a 26-year-old American journalist if he crossed into Mexico. The reporter was John Reed.[52]

By mid-March of 1914 the *División del Norte* was ready for the final offensive against Huerta. In barely a year the jailbreaker who slipped furtively across the Río Grande had become chief of the most famous military formation in Mexican history. With nine brigades, including one of artillery, the *División del Norte* now numbered 9,000 men.[53]

Adding to the *División's* efficiency was the fact that it had recently been joined by one of Mexico's most brilliant soldiers. General Felipe Angeles, a loyal *maderista*, had been exiled to Europe by Huerta in the guise of a "study mission." Making his way back to Mexico, he had first joined Carranza and Obregón. But relations had been acrimonious and a transfer was arranged to the *División del Norte*. Villa's respect for Angeles approached hero worship, and Angeles fully justified the Centaur's confidence in him. It was only when he stopped taking Angeles's advice that Villa began losing battles.

The two engagements that broke Huerta were Torreón (which had been evacuated by the *villistas* while they secured Chihuahua) and Zacatecas.

Between 21 and 27 March the *División* battled for the approaches to Torreón. Fighting for every town, falling back in good order, the *huertistas* contested Tlahualilo, Peronal, Bermejillo, San Pedro de las Colonias, Gómez Palacio, and Lerdo. Particularly bloody was the attack on Cerro de la Pila, a hill overlooking Torreón. Though the assault was made at night, Villa recalls that "darkness (never reigned) on the hill, since at every moment it was illuminated. . . .by powder flashes. . . ."[54] The attack on Torreón began on 28 March. Though the city fell on 3 April, *huertista* resistance in the Laguna cotton-growing area (which comprised Lerdo, Gómez Palacio, and San Pedro de las Colonias as well as Torreón) continued for another ten days. Then the beaten Federals moved eastward to regroup at Saltillo.

This led to a brief—and, for Villa, unwelcome—diversion before the showdown at Zacatecas. Carranza, Villa's nominal chief in the revolutionary movement, wanted the *División del Norte* to capture Saltillo, whereas Villa and Angeles preferred to move south against the main *huertista* stronghold of Zacatecas. (As ex-governor of Coahuila, Carranza had a personal reason for wanting to liberate the capital of his home state.) Reluctantly, Villa and Angeles agreed to what they thought was an unnecessary detour. Saltillo proved to be easy pickings. The defenders were a dispirited remnant of the federal force shattered at Torreón, and by 20 May Saltillo was in rebel hands. The stage was now set for the attack on Zacatecas.

The mounting tension between Villa and Carranza that preceded this operation will be discussed in another chapter. Suffice it now to say that the Villa-Angeles attack on Zacatecas was in the mold of the Villa-Orozco attack on Juárez: a successful assault undertaken without official sanction. (The only difference was that Villa had none of the affection for Carranza that he had had for Madero.)

The attack began on 23 June at 1000. Thanks to Angeles's expertise (he was an artillery specialist), Villa's thirty-nine guns were mounted in emplacements preselected by Angeles himself. These field pieces created a "hecatomb" for the defenders. The cover they provided made the assault infinitely easier for Villa's infantry and cavalry.[55] By early afternoon the *villistas* had captured El Grillo, a strategic hill to the west; by nightfall the city was theirs. General José Medina Barrón, the *huertista* commander, was wounded in the leg but escaped. Federal losses came to between 5,000 and 8,000, while Constitutionalist casualties were about 4,000 dead and wounded.[56]

Zacatecas finished Huerta. He resigned on 15 July and two days later boarded a German cruiser bound for Spain. Zacatecas was also a turning point for Villa. His career as a revolutionist began with the killings of Claro Reza and Pedro Domínguez and peaked, if not ended, with the victory at Zacatecas. It peaked because Zacatecas—and Huerta's subsequent flight—eliminated the system against which Villa was rebelling.

This raises an important question: was Villa a true revolutionary or, like Pascual Orozco, a man who served revolution because it suited his convenience? Was Lincoln Steffens right in his appraisal of Villa as an "unscrupulous, unrevolutionary bandit"?

There can be no doubt that Villa's commitment to revolution was genuine. In four glory years between the killing of Claro Reza and the fall of Zacatecas, Villa battled not one but three anti-revolutionary movements: the old order of Díaz, the landlord-backed rising of Orozco, and the usurpation of Huerta. His constancy was unwavering. He spurned Tamayo's invitation to join in the *cuartelazo*, he rejected the bribe offer from Orozco's father, he remained loyal to Madero even while being imprisoned by him. Villa's rage against Orozco was fueled by the fact that he saw him as a magnified Claro Reza: both had been his friends and both betrayed him and went over to Creel and Terrazas.

A further confirmation of Villa's sincerity and effectiveness was his role as civil administrator—one that will be analyzed in a later chapter. Here we will also place Villa in correct historical perspective and determine exactly what *kind* of revolutionary he was.

If Francisco Villa declined as a revolutionary after Zacatecas, it was not due to any flagging of zeal. He was a man who saw the world in black-and-white terms and now black and white were being replaced by confusing shades of gray. Díaz, the senile tyrant; Orozco, the traitor; Huerta, the usurper—these were highly visible enemies. Zacatecas changed all that. Some of his future adversaries had revolutionary credentials as impeccable as his own. The targets were no longer clearly defined; for the rest of his life, Francisco Villa would be fighting in the dark.

4

Reed's Road
to Revolution

JOHN REED'S PROGRESS TOWARD REVOLUTION was a good deal more gradual than Francisco Villa's. Villa's debut was literally accomplished with a bang—the revenge killing of Claro Reza in the streets of Chihuahua. Reed's began in that euphoric spring of 1911 when he came to seek fame and fortune in New York. He was then no enemy of the capitalist system. Though he had rejected the values of the Harvard snobs, his commitment was to reform, not revolution. A Bull Mooser like his father, he believed that capitalism could be cured of its failings and saw nothing wrong with the idea of prospering under it. As he left Europe, his two announced goals were "to make a million dollars and get married."[1]

His journey to the Left began under the auspices of Lincoln Steffens. This is ironic because it had never been Steffens's intention to radicalize Reed. "Don't let him get a conviction right away, or a business or a career. . . . Let him play." This instruction was given Steffens by his old friend, C. J. Reed. Agreeing with the counsels of "that wise father," Steffens got Reed his job on *American Magazine*, "on condition that he use it as a springboard from which to dive into life."[2] As noted in the first chapter, Steffens tried to steer Reed away from conviction, in line with his view that "a poet is more revolutionary than any radical."

As part of this consciousness-enhancing program, Steffens introduced Reed to Socialists, anarchists, and single taxers, recommended radical books at Frank Shay's bookstore, and made him look at poverty. "During my rambles about the city," wrote Reed, "I couldn't help but observe the ugliness of poverty (and) the cruel inequality between rich people who had too many motor cars and poor people who didn't have enough to eat. It didn't come to me from books that workers produced all the wealth of the world."[3] "That," records Granville Hicks, "was what Socrates Steffens wanted."[4]

In the end, Steffens proved more Pandora than Socrates. He opened a world of radical thought to Reed in hopes that this would enlarge his capacity as a writer and poet. Instead, he initiated the process which, within a decade, transformed a warmly idealistic young liberal into a grim zealot who sat on the Executive Committee of the Communist International.

Reed had already turned his back on Harvard's elitists. As he moved Left, his scorn for them intensified. In late 1911 he wrote a satiric short story titled "Back to the Land." The principals are two antipathetic Harvard graduates in New York who meet periodically at the Harvard Club. One, obviously based on Reed, is a worldly, tough-talking reporter named Josie Baldwin. The other, Vincent Strachan, is a sheltered social butterfly described by Baldwin as "neither male, female, nor good red herring." One day Strachan ventures beyond urban limits, and his ineptitude turns the trip into a disaster. (Among other calamities, he loses his money and gets thrown off a milk train.) Sharing Baldwin's glee over "Vincey's" discomfiture is Varna Stewart, an earthily attractive country Amazon.[5]

The story was sufficiently malevolent to elicit a protest from artist Bob Hallowell, Reed's classmate and close friend. Hallowell feared that such a presentation might damage Harvard's image. But Reed hotly defended his story, adding that he was thinking of changing the designation of Strachan's ultra-snobbish Harvard Club from "Bacon" (an evasion used in the text) to the real-life Porcellian.[6]

In June 1911, Reed went to Cambridge to attend his brother Harry's graduation. There they received a wire, notifying them of their father's final illness. They made it back to Portland just in time to see him before he died. At the funeral service, Jack felt mixed emotions of grief and rage. Local establishmentarians, who had treated C. J. like a pariah in his last years, hypocritically gathered at his grave to pay him an insincere final homage. This tasteless display of crocodile tears can only have added to Reed's rebellious-ness. Could a system that produced people like these be worth pre-serving?

Though C. J.'s estate was meager, his business affairs were hope-lessly tangled. Reed lingered in Portland four months to clean up the debris, not returning to New York till late October.

Back in the city, Reed plunged more into bohemianism than into radicalism. Not that the two were incompatible. Many radicals of the day were familiar figures in the Village, including Emma Gold-man, Big Bill Haywood, and the swarm of "socialists, anarchists, and single taxers" to whom Steffens had introduced Reed.

It was during this period that Reed wrote "Sangar," with its im-plied criticism of Steffens, and a joyous 1,500-line poem called "The Day in Bohemia, or Life Among the Artists." A many-faceted work, it parodies the styles of Shelley, Keats, and Whitman, cele-brates the freedom of Village life, and ridicules such pseudo-Bohemians as "the nature poet who never stirs from his steam-heated flat and the phony peasant girl wearing a $300 pastoral dress."[7]

But Reed still had not staked out a firm position on the Left. This was noted by some of his friends. Living with Reed at 42 Washing-ton Square was Edward Eyre ("Eddy") Hunt, his closest associate among the Harvard radicals. Reed had coaxed Hunt to New York and found him a position on the *American*. As late as October 1912, Hunt sensed that Reed might have some lingering attach-ment to progressive capitalism. "Don't let the Bull Moose draw you from Socialism," he wrote his friend.[8]

Hunt needn't have worried. By the end of the year Reed's com-mitment to Socialism was firm and irrevocable. In December Jack came upon a magazine that delighted him for both ideology and literary style. Up to now he had been dissatisfied in his reading. Literary magazines were depressingly divorced from social issues, while "red" journals were dull and cliché-ridden. But this publica-tion was different. Timely, sparkling, and well-researched, it was a perfect synthesis of Left thinking and right style.

The object of Jack's admiration was *The Masses*, founded in Jan-uary 1911 by an exuberant Dutchman named Piet Vlag and edited since July 1912 by Max Eastman, a conspicuously cerebral Colum-bia Ph.D. Among its contributors were Louis Untermeyer, Mary

Heaton Vorse, and the talented cartoonist Art Young. (Reed was particularly delighted by Young's two-page spread depicting establishment newspapers as fancy prostitutes and big advertisers as their clients.)

With characteristic enthusiasm he burst into Eastman's apartment and insisted in delivering a batch of his material in person. At first the low-key Eastman was turned off by the frenetic Reed—gesticulating, talking without pause, endlessly moving about, he seemed a borderline madman. But Eastman's opinion abruptly changed when he saw Reed's work. "Dear Mr. Reed," he wrote the next day, "your things are great." Eastman promised to use one of Jack's stories in the next issue.[9]

Wanting to join the staff of this wonderful magazine, Reed composed a manifesto and offered it for the masthead. It was an unnecessary gesture; Reed's work alone was good enough to get him admitted to the *Masses* family. As for the manifesto, it was turned down in favor of one proposed by Eastman. This was a wise decision. Though he became a noted revolutionary, Reed was always at his weakest as a theoretician. His proposed *Masses* manifesto, which will be analyzed in a later chapter, was as puerile and inept an effort as Reed ever produced.

Association with *The Masses* deepened Reed's commitment to social issues and, with it, his progress toward revolution. In April 1913 he completed a three-act play called *Enter Dibble*. Dibble is a young Harvard graduate who is engaged to a construction mogul's daughter. Possessed of a burning social conscience, he rejects snob values, becomes a laborer, organizes a strike against his fiancée's father, and delivers speeches about capitalist oppression and hypocrisy. Like Josie Baldwin in "Back to the Land," Dibble is a thinly disguised Reed. In Jack's fiction we witness his political evolution. Where Josie Baldwin was nothing more than a wisecracking vulgarian baiting an effete snob, Dibble militantly organizes workers against an exploiting boss.

Life at times imitates art, and *Enter Dibble* was immediately followed by a factual drama of industrial oppression in which Reed found himself a participant as well as a chronicler. In Paterson, New Jersey, 25,000 silk workers were striking for an eight-hour day. Reaction to this demand was savage—on the part of management as well as local law-enforcement agencies. Strikers were beaten and jailed; critics of police and municipal officialdom were being tried for sedition.

Reed and Eddy Hunt went to Paterson to march in a picket line. Separated from Hunt, Reed was arrested, manhandled, and sentenced by a police-court magistrate named Carroll (the infamous "Recorder Carroll") to twenty days in the Passaic County Jail.

This experience exposed Reed to another segment of the system toward which he was daily becoming more hostile: its penal apparatus. Sheriff Radcliffe, Passaic County's chief law-enforcement officer, was a relatively humane man. But he was unable to mitigate the terrible sentences handed out by Recorder Carroll—six months for begging, six days to a little boy for breaking a window.[10]

Reed described the County Jail as "a peculiar institution . . . nowhere as important as a penitentiary or state prison. It houses the petty criminals, the drunk and disorderlies, the little thieves . . . the weak outlaws of society who have neither the courage nor strength to commit state prison offenses."[12]

Unspeakable barbarities were inflicted on these hapless misfits. An Italian was thrown into a verminous dungeon for eighteen hours for dropping a chicken bone. The insane Billy Mack was put in the same dungeon for disobeying orders he couldn't understand. A little boy was confined in a cell with "a young degenerate convicted of sodomy." Eddy, an idiot, was there because his father had been jailed for beating him and there was no room for him at the state institution. A man received a sentence after his wife lodged a drunk complaint—she had a lover and wanted to be rid of him.

Equally dehumanizing were the sanitary conditions. Cockroaches abounded, vermin crawled in the food, and Charley, a syphilitic with running sores on his legs, daily *washed his bandages in the tub where they washed the dinner dishes!* (Italics in original.) The prison doctor was so inept (or indifferent) that he diagnosed Charley's ailment as "nervousness" and gave him four sugar pills.[12]

Immediately after his release, Jack went to work on a pageant, to be held in New York, that would dramatize the Paterson strike and raise money to keep it going. How the idea for this presentation was born is somewhat obscure. Mabel Dodge, wealthy salon keeper and patroness of the arts, claimed the idea was hers. She insisted that Reed's trip to Paterson was made at her behest and to get material for the production. This version is open to question because there is never any mention in Reed's letters, or those of his friends, that he went to Paterson for the sole purpose of getting material for a pageant.[13]

It was held on 8 June at Madison Square Garden, with strikers themselves taking part in the production. Though the pageant was an artistic triumph (it was directed and largely written by Reed), it flopped financially. At first it seemed as if the presentation would fulfill its goal of raising money for the strike. On that June night there was a tremendous rapport between performers and audience. In an emotion-swept display of solidarity, upper- and middle-class bohemians joined workers and radicals like Bill Haywood, Carlo Tresca, and Elizabeth Gurley Flynn in chorus after chorus of the *Internationale.*

Yet the pageant showed a $2,000 deficit—the costs of putting on a one-night production had been staggeringly high. Though attendance was excellent, many seats had gone to workers for twenty-five cents while card-producing IWW members had been admitted free.[14]

With no money coming from the pageant, strikers began returning to work. Not a single one of their demands was met and the IWW—which had fomented the strike—suffered an irretrievable loss of prestige.

Though battling in a losing cause, Reed reaped a personal harvest of kudos. Bobby Rogers, Harvard classmate and Washington Square roommate, wrote Jack an admiringly humorous letter in which he described his plight in terms of a Biblical parable: "And the prophets of Baal lifted up their eyes and saw him coming afar off, and took counsel among themselves, saying . . . 'Let us take this Dreamer and cast him into a pit, and take his shirt of many patches back into Steffens his father, saying "Lo, he is not, the System hath devoured him."'"[15] Rogers's letter, written in June, was followed by a July communication from two other Harvard radicals, Hiram Kelly Moderwell and Sam Eliot. "We've read . . . newspaper accounts of the pageant and we're damn proud of them. . . . The IWW may not offer a final state of perfection, but it is helping to stir up life more abundantly in the working class, and that's what they need."[16]

By now Reed was involved with Mabel Dodge. Though the Dodge-Reed relationship is of obvious interest to those concerned with the more intimate aspects of Reed's life, it is of secondary importance in an analysis of his development as a revolutionary. It should, however, be mentioned. Reed's road to revolution had a detour; that detour was his affair with Mabel Dodge.

Mabel Dodge was a sort of American Madame de Stael, a rich, intellectually restless woman who indiscriminately collected lovers and causes. Less clever and witty than the former Germaine Necker, Dodge was more moderator than innovator at the salon over which she presided. Her radicalism was superficial and the impression came across that she was playing at it. Reed—most unfairly—has been called the playboy of the Socialist Revolution; this lack of commitment could have far more accurately been imputed to Dodge. Once, while Reed squirmed with embarrassment, Dodge toured the Lower East Side with him in a chauffeured limousine. Reed wanted to change the system, and these Lady Bountiful gestures of condescension were completely repugnant to him.

Reed recounts that when the pageant was over, "I went to pieces nervously, and friends [read Mabel Dodge] took me abroad for the summer. The strike . . . was lost, the men went back to work dispirited and disillusioned. . . . I got diphtheria in Italy and came back to New York weak and despondent. For six months I did almost nothing. And then, through the interest of Lincoln Steffens, the *Metropolitan Magazine* asked me to go to Mexico as a war correspondent, and I knew that I must do it."[17]

Typical of Reed's meager output during this unproductive period was a story titled "Showing Mrs. Van." Mrs. Van, a bejeweled, socially pretentious gorgon, is touring Europe with two pretty daughters and her cousin Cuthbert. The latter is a fat, monocled party who fondly believes himself a raconteur in the style of Chesterton. In Paris Mrs. Van's party encounters two impecunious but resourceful young men. One, based on Reed, is American; the other is French. Volunteering to act as tourist guides, the youths fleece Mrs. Van, shamelessly flirt with her daughters, and poke fun at the fatuous Cuthbert.[18] It was not one of Reed's better efforts. Here he sacrificed militance for social satire and laid the satire on with a trowel.

Mexico put Reed back on the revolutionary track, terminating his brief tenure as idler and kept man. Dodge, with characteristic possessiveness, accompanied Reed all the way to El Paso. But she returned to New York once he crossed the border.

After Reed's return from Mexico, the affair continued fitfully. Dodge was with Reed in Europe during the early days of the First World War, where Jack was assigned as a correspondent. But she came home after the Battle of the Marne—the austerity of wartime Paris bored and depressed her.

The relationship came to an end in the fall of 1915. By then Dodge had a new lover, the painter Maurice Sterne. They were living at Finney Farm, near Croton-on-Hudson, and Reed came to pay a visit. In true Madame de Stael fashion, Dodge suggested a ménage that would include her incumbent lover, Sterne, with Reed, her ex-lover, as a guest. For a time he accepted. Reed needed a place to write and Dodge had offered the entire third floor as a studio. But Reed was too American-idealistic to continue accepting so suavely continental an arrangement. In December he boarded a train for Portland; there he met Louise Bryant. The affair with Mabel Dodge was over.

In April 1914, Reed was exposed to a drama of industrial tyranny that made Paterson seem tame by comparison. In the foothill country of southeast Colorado the Rockefeller-controlled Colorado Fuel and Iron Company reigned supreme. Operating as a state within a state, the corporation not only ran company stores but owned all houses, business establishments, saloons, and churches in the area.

Fuel and Iron was not a benevolent despot. Though Colorado had passed the eight-hour day and industrial safety laws, the company brazenly required miners to work ten hours and was so negligent in enforcing safety regulations that Colorado had an accident rate of better than 3–1 over the national average.[19]

Almost half the workers were foreigners, a circumstance that derived from deliberate company policy. Native American workers who had demanded better pay and a safer environment promptly found themselves blacklisted. Fuel and Iron then replaced them with Slavs, Italians, Greeks, and Mexicans, many of whom spoke no English. This was also deliberate. In recruiting foreigners from differing national backgrounds, the company reasoned that linguistic barriers would prevent them from getting together and fighting to improve their lot.

Unlike the Italians in Paterson, who had a tradition of syndical-ism and champions like Carlo Tresca, these foreign workers were docile and cowed. "They had come to America," wrote Reed, "ea-ger for the things that the Statue of Liberty in New York harbor seemed to promise them. . . . They wanted to obey the laws. But the first thing they discovered was that the boss in whom they trusted insolently broke the laws."[20]

Another distinguishing feature of this dispute was that "nine out of ten business and professional men in the coal district towns were violent strike sympathizers." They included "doctors, ministers, hack drivers, drug store clerks, and farmers (who) joined the fighting stri-kers with guns in their hands. . . . They are the kind of people who usually form Law and Order Leagues in times like these; who con-sider themselves better than laborers, and think that their interests lie with the employers." Said a clergyman's wife: "I don't see why they ever made a truce until they had shot every mine guard and militiaman, and blown up all the mines with dynamite."[21]

The strikers belonged to the United Mine Workers, which had established a local branch in 1911. "The United Mine Workers did everything they could to avoid a strike. They appealed to Governor Ammons to call a meeting of the operators to confer with them concerning the demands of the men; the company officials refused to meet them. . . ."[22]

The operators then began to prepare for war. To bolster their security force they imported labor goons from all over the country and swore them in as deputy sheriffs. Some of the strikebreakers were known criminals, including such unsavory figures as "Bob Lee, a notorious killer once connected with the Jesse James outlaws" and "Lou Miller, a . . . gunman with five murders to his credit."[23]

On 22 September 1913, the workers went out on strike. The union's main demand was that the operators agree to obey *existing state laws* regarding the work day and safety conditions. Fuel and Iron responded by forcibly ejecting strikers from their company-owned houses. The evicted miners—11,000 in number—built colonies of tent cities to house themselves and their families. Of these, the largest settlement was at Ludlow.

Unable to break the strike with mine guards and imported gun-men, the operators prevailed on the governor to send in the Na-tional Guard. At first the militia made a show of impartiality, fraternizing with strikers and disarming strikebreakers and mine guards as well as unionists. This was a ruse—weapons confiscated from company supporters were returned to them along with arms taken from the strikers. General Chase, the venomously anti-union militia commander, established secret military courts to try unionists. About this time a striker killed a detective attached to the Baldwin-Felts Agency (an organization, like the Pinkertons, that specialized in industrial espionage and strikebreaking). Thirty-five miners were rounded up at random and an Italian named Zancanelli was tortured into "confessing" to the slaying.

Hatred and violence escalated. General Chase personally laid open a woman's head with his saber, while in Denver a group of operators descended on the spineless Governor Ammons. "You God damned coward," said one of them, "we are not going to stand for this much longer. You have to do something about it [the strike] or we'll get you!" "Don't be too hard on me, gentlemen," was Ammons's heroic rejoinder. "I'm doing it as fast as I can."[24]

The final horror came on 20 April 1914. That evening a Greek striker named Louis Tikas went to a pre-arranged meeting with Major Hancock of the militia. The station was on neutral ground and the purpose of the meeting was to discuss a militia charge that the strikers were holding a man against his will.

But Tikas noticed something strange: the militiamen were in full battle gear and machine guns had been planted on a hill overlooking the tent city. Suddenly three bomb flares went up—it was the signal. Militia machine guns opened up on the tents and a 400-man force of mine guards and strikebreakers came pouring out of the hills. When the carnage was over, twenty-six dead bodies had been recovered.[25] Some women and children had burned alive in their tents.

After the massacre, a Red Cross team from Denver came to inspect the damage. Accompanying the group was a local minister, Reverend Randolph Cook. Arriving in Ludlow, they were greeted by General Chase with threats and obscenities. Outraged, Reverend Cook protested the general's use of such language in front of women. "Pimps, preachers, and prostitutes look all the same to me," replied the irrepressible Chase. "You get to hell out of here . . . and never come near here again."[26]

Reed arrived in Ludlow ten days after the massacre. In this passage he eloquently records the legacy of loathing left by the events of 20 April:

> Three militiamen were hurrying toward the station. They walked in the middle of the street, with their eyes on the ground, joking nervously and loudly. They walked between two lines of men on the sidewalks— two lines of hate. . . . The town held its breath. The streetcars stopped running. . . . Then the train came along and they boarded it. We straggled back. The town sprang to life again.[27]

If Reed had any faith left in capitalism, it vanished after Ludlow. He was also beginning to get a clearer picture of his enemy. In the early days, the days of naive liberalism, he was a well-intentioned young man with a developing social conscience and vague resentment against such amorphous concepts as Injustice and Oppression. He now saw his foe as a malign world force of multiple aspect, a hydra-headed monster. The beast showed different faces, but all were ugly and menacing. In Paterson and Ludlow he had witnessed industrial exploitation in its meanest form; in Mexico he had ridden against a usurper trying to re-impose a discredited regime. During the opening months of the First World War Reed found himself in England. There he encountered another head of the hydra: imperialist war.

Imperialist war, as Reed perceived it, was war started by profiteers under a cover of patrioteering slogans. It was directed by connivers but fought by ordinary men who had been duped or intimidated into the trenches. Imperialist war not only led to ghastly battlefield slaughters but unleashed domestic repression and canceled social gains.

In England, Reed saw all these processes at work. Though King George V may have been the titular head of state (and Prime Minister Asquith the official one), the real ruler was "Kitchener of Khartoum . . . Bloody Kitchener, the most complete expression of an imperial policy that has consisted of blowing men from the mouths of cannon so that you may civilize them."[28]

Kitchener served as War Minister in Asquith's cabinet. Though nominally subordinate to the Prime Minister, he wielded his vast power with an arrogance astounding even by British imperial standards. One time he was visited at his office by Lord Northcliffe, publisher of the *Daily Mail* and the most powerful media tycoon in England. Kitchener refused to see Northcliffe, requiring him to write his questions on a sheet of paper and hand them to an orderly. This impertinence was deliberate. Offended because the *Daily Mail* had published an article without submitting it to the military censor, Kitchener sent word that if the offense was ever repeated he would have Northcliffe shot. [29]

Regrettably, Kitchener's despotism was not limited to humiliating press lords. Under his direction "the authorities seized the telephone; if you said something they did not like, you were cut off. They opened your private mail; if the sentiments of your letter did not suit them, they destroyed it. Sentries . . . shot and killed civilians who failed to halt quick enough when ordered to." [30]

Nowhere was profiteering more cynical than in schemes devised by business to dragoon men into the Army. "The merchants began to discharge all their employees of serviceable age, and called upon the Labor Exchange to fill their places with old men, who would, of course, accept a much lower salary." [31]

Psychological intimidation was another weapon used to stimulate enlistment. Girls would hand out white feathers to healthy-looking men in mufti. Music-hall actresses would single out civilian males in the audience and ask them why they didn't enlist. These performers would also regale audiences with hortatory songs. As one of the worst—and most popular—Reed singles out "Fall In!", a ditty that combines, with sickening impartiality, elements of bullying, mawkishness, and sexual titillation:

> *"What will you lack, sonny, what will you lack,*
> *When the girls line up in the street,*
> *Shouting their love to the lads come back*
> *From the foe they rushed to beat?*
> *Will you send a strangled cheer to the sky*
> *And grin till your cheeks are red?*
> *Or slink away when your mate goes by*
> *With a girl that cuts you dead?"* [32]

In attacking the "monstrous hypocrisy of England," Reed denied any pro-German sentiment. His attitude was one of malevolent neutrality, bent on keeping America out of this "traders' war" and rejecting Kaiserism just as completely as he did the "democratic"

Western Allies and their Czarist partner. But he did feel impelled "to put the public on their guard against the British press campaign of lies and distortions. . . ."[33]

Jack also witnessed how the war was eroding democratic liberties in France. In Paris censorship was not only stifling but ridiculous, targeting humble vendors rather than that city's notoriously venal press magnates. "The newsboys were forbidden to cry their newspapers; they held them up mutely. 'We will be arrested if we tell you how close the German Army is to Paris, but you read the whole thing here for five centimes.' So we would buy . . . the latest official communiqué, which said: 'The strategic retreat of the Allies continues with great success.'"[34] French democracy was under constant attack, wolfishly assailed by right-wing and militarist journals which had been in eclipse before the war and were now enjoying a field day. One opined that "The pacifists and anti-militarists with their sentimental belief in the softness of the human race were almost the cause of our ruin. If this is what universal suffrage leads to, is it worthwhile to trust the destinies of France to an ignorant democracy?"[35] Another recommended that military affairs be "removed entirely from the hands of the voters, and put into the hands of experts with complete authority."[36]

As his revolutionary consciousness heightened, Reed was able to comment on issues which in those days were not directly linked to anti-imperialism or the class struggle. One of these was birth control.

On 18 January 1915, Margeret Sanger was indicted for circulating "lewd, lascivious, and obscene matter" through the mails. In a caustic attack on the indictment, Reed observed that "it was the language of the articles that made them indictable. He (the prosecutor) said that if she had allowed a medical man to go over the articles and translate plain terms into medical formulae only understood by doctors, there would have been no objection to them. . . . the fact that these articles were addressed to the general public in language that (it) could understand, constituted the crime."[37]

The year 1915 also witnessed Reed's first contact with Russia. What he saw of Czarism undoubtedly contributed to his later affinity for Bolshevism. In August Jack was in Bucharest, trying to obtain a pass to visit the Russian front. With him was Boardman ("Mike") Robinson, a convivial Canadian illustrator. Rebuffed by the Russian ambassador, Reed and Robinson obtained a document from the American Legation authorizing them to look into the welfare of Jewish-American citizens residing in Galicia and Bukovina. They were allowed to cross the border and, after some confused shuttling on the antiquated Russian railway system, they ended up in Cholm, a drab settlement in the Jewish Pale.

There—after being promised transit to the front—they suddenly found themselves under arrest. Following two weeks' confinement in an evil-smelling accommodation that passed for the town's best "hotel," they were allowed to proceed to Petrograd, then Russia's capital.

In Petrograd they encountered trouble of a different kind: indifference and downright hostility from American Embassy officials. The ambassador, George T. Marye, was a fussy, supercilious little man who could have single-handedly inspired the old GI slogan, "Don't tell me your troubles." Far from trying to help his countrymen, he responded to their distress with Buddhalike equanimity. Wrote Reed: "We are ashamed of Mr. Marye here. He is afraid to ask anything of the Russian government or to protest against the ill-treatment of Americans."[38] After frostily informing Reed and Robinson that the Czarists considered their mission to Jewish-Americans a cover for subversive activities, he declined to do anything further for them. Marye would not even intervene when the Russian Grand Duke gave Reed and Robinson twenty-four hours to be on a train to Vladivostok—an impossibility because no trains left during that period. They finally received exit visas through the efforts of the British Embassy; as a Canadian, Robinson was a British subject. On departure, Reed wrote Marye a defiant farewell note: "We are finally liberated, and free to return to Bucarest [sic] or anywhere else. . . . We owe this entirely to the British Ambassador, to whom I was forced to appeal because of the failure of the American Embassy to accomplish anything for me."[39]

An account of Reed's Russian experiences, along with those in the Balkans, was published by Scribner's in April 1916. The book, a beefed-up compilation of his *Metropolitan* articles, was titled *The War in Eastern Europe*.

For all his detestation of the Czarist system, Reed loved Russia. "Russian ideas are the more exhilarating, Russian thought the freest, Russian art the most exuberant, Russian food and drink to me are the best, and the Russians themselves are, perhaps, the most interesting human beings that exist."[40] It is not difficult to imagine how desperately Reed must have longed for revolution in Russia. Here were the people he loved best, oppressed by a hateful autocracy. Did he then, in the spring of 1916, have any inkling of how close he was to seeing his dream fulfilled?

Though Reed had by now totally rejected the American system, he was still capable of affection for some of its more well-meaning representatives. Among this number he counted William Jennings Bryan. Bryan had resigned as Wilson's Secretary of State and was now on the stump, making speeches against American involvement in the war. Bryan's view tallied with Reed's own antiwar stance. He went to Florida to interview Bryan for *Collier's*, drawing him out on the deck of a boat as they floated down the Ocklawaha River. Though he found Bryan old-fashioned and faintly ridiculous, his admiration for the old crusader keeps surfacing in the article: "He led a succession of forlorn hopes: Free Silver and Populism . . . anti-rum, anti-imperialism, anti-trust (and) each time went down in crushing defeat and each time bobbed up again, a bourgeois Don Quixote!"[41]

Reed was now living with Louise Bryant. Her fidelity to Reed's cause was total—more total, we shall see, than her fidelity to Reed. Though their radicalism was genuine, it is disturbing to note the extent to which Reed and Bryant still embraced prejudices of their day, particularly those directed against racial and ethnic minorities. Jack and Louise were prodigious correspondents and, in time of separation, their love letters flew thick and fast. In one of these communications Reed managed the improbable feat of attacking Southern racism in terms that are profoundly racist. "The bloated silly people on the train," he wrote Bryant on 11 February 1916, "throw pennies and dimes and quarters to be scrambled for by the niggers. . . . Lord, how the white folks scream with laughter to see the coons . . . scrambling over the money. . . . Have you ever seen Jim-crow cars, colored waiting rooms in stations, etc.? I hate the South."[42] Not to be outdone, Bryant wrote Reed in St. Louis about "the Jewish invasion soon to take place in Provincetown . . . it's going to be sort of a New Jerusalem at that end of town."[43]

With war fever mounting, Reed plunged headlong into the fight to keep America out of what he discerned as a sordid struggle of autocrats and profiteers. In spring of 1916 he took off on the lecture circuit and lashed out at the "preparedness" groups. He used Congressional reports to show how such organizations as the Navy League and the National Security League were dominated by owners of large shipbuilding, steel, and munitions companies which were in turn controlled by Wall Street. The workingman, warned Reed, should learn that "his enemy is not Germany (but) that 2% of the United States who own 60% of the national wealth, that band of unscrupulous 'patriots' who have already robbed him of all he had, and are now preparing to make a soldier out of him to defend their loot. We advocate that the workingman prepare to defend himself against that enemy. That is our Preparedness."[44]

In June, at the political conventions, Reed savagely attacked the man who had been his father's idol. Theodore Roosevelt, the Bull Moose standard bearer of 1912, was now being maddeningly coy with his faithful constituency. The Progressives wanted to nominate him again, but he kept putting them off. First, he wanted to wait and see who the Republicans nominated; next, he urged the nomination of Henry Cabot Lodge as a compromise candidate; finally, when the Republicans nominated Charles Evans Hughes, he said he wanted to wait till Hughes announced his position on Preparedness and Americanism. Roosevelt had become an ardent interventionist, "screaming at the top of his lungs for blood-thirstiness, obedience, and efficiency, [but this] had not dimmed their faith. . . . They were for Roosevelt; they thought that he stood for Social Justice. So they blindly swallowed what he advocated and shouted 'We Want Teddy!'"[45] The sorry episode came to an end on 26 June, when Roosevelt flatly refused the Progressive nomination.

Reed viewed the Progressives' enthusiasm with pity and contempt and saw Roosevelt's performance as a cynical sellout. "We, Socialists and revolutionists, laughed and sneered at the Progressives; we ridiculed their worship of personality; we derided their hysterical singing of revival hymns. . . ."[46] "As for Colonel Roosevelt, he is back with the people among whom alone he is comfortable, the 'predatory plutocrats.' At least he is no longer tied to democracy. For that he undoubtedly breathes a deep sigh of relief."[47]

In November of 1916 Reed was temporarily sidelined by two events:

marriage and surgery. The first, to Louise Bryant, took place on the 9th; the second on the 22nd, when he had an infected kidney removed at Johns Hopkins Medical Center in Baltimore.

By January Reed's recovery was complete, and he and Bryant were preparing to go to China. Jack would represent *Metropolitan* magazine while Louise was accredited to the *New York Tribune*.

The trip was aborted by Germany's announcement of unrestricted submarine warfare. Wilson broke relations with the Kaiser's government and United States entry into the war appeared imminent. In view of the new crisis, the idea of a massive feature on China was no longer viable. *Metropolitan's* managing editor, Carl Hovey, canceled the assignment and expressed the hope that Reed would go to Europe. America was on the verge of war and Hovey looked forward to having the conflict covered by a reporter of Reed's stature.

But Reed would have none of it: his cause was now the antiwar movement. In England, in 1914, he had seen the adverse effect of war on civil liberties and social reform. "War," he wrote in *The Masses*, "means an ugly mob-madness, crucifying the truthtellers, choking the artists, sidetracking reforms, revolutions, and the working of social forces."[48] In Washington he argued against conscription before the House Committee on Military Affairs. "I do not believe in this war," he said, "I would not serve in it." The hearing was acrimonious and Reed found himself interrupted and verbally assailed by two congressmen.[49]

Reed's antiwar activities earned him a stinging rebuke from his mother. Predictably, Margeret Reed responded to the war with attitudes of conventional patriotism mingled with nativist prejudice. "I have tried to see your point of view but I cannot," she wrote Jack. "It gives me a shock when your father's son says that he cares nothing for his country or his flag. . . . I do not want you to fight, heaven knows . . . but I do *not* want you to fight against us. . . . I think most of your friends and sympathizers are of foreign birth— very few are real Americans."[50]

A more comforting letter came at the end of May from Robert Minor, left-wing cartoonist who would later become a leading figure in the American Communist Party. Reed had congratulated Minor on his efforts to aid Tom Mooney, an anarchist convicted on questionable evidence of throwing a bomb during a Preparedness

Day parade. Wrote Minor: "Trying to avoid the attitude of hero-worship, I must nevertheless say that I have always thrilled at the mere mention of you since I came to know of . . . your remarkable achievements."[51] Minor, a forthright Texan, was not a man given to fawning. His adulation was impressive testimony to Reed's growing status in the revolutionary community.

The Masses . . . Paterson . . . Mexico . . . Ludlow . . . imperialist England . . . authoritarian France . . . Czarist Russia . . . Teddy Roosevelt's sellout . . . the antiwar movement—all were milestones on Reed's road to revolution. Coming up was the final marker, the foreign revolution he would embrace as his own and, later, act as its representative in the United States.

The Czarist system that Reed so hated fell in March 1917, when Nicholas II was pressured into abdication. But radicals hardly hailed the event as a new dawn. Prince Lvov, head of a Provisional Government, talked of continuing the war, restoring social and military discipline, and even of saving the monarchy. His only goal, it seemed, was ouster of the incompetent Nicholas.[52] In Lvov's cabinet, the sole "leftist" was a moderate Socialist lawyer named Alexander Kerensky.

If radicals were mild about this first Russian revolution, not so the establishment liberals. They had always felt foolish depicting the Entente as an alliance of noble libertarians fighting Prussian militarism. Whatever her shortcomings, Wilhelmine Germany was infinitely more democratic than Czarist Russia.

But now, insisted the pro-war liberals, everything had changed. Overnight Russia had thrown off despotism and become a worthy member of the band of nations fighting "to make the world safe for democracy."

Reed knew better. It was preposterous to believe that, with the passing of the Czar, Russia had made an instant frog-prince change from autocracy to freedom. If anything, class tension had been aggravated. "The property owning classes were becoming conservative, the masses of the people more radical. There was a feeling among businessmen and *intelligentzia* generally that the Revolution had gone quite far enough, and lasted too long; that things should settle down."[53] For these "revolutionists," revolution was a matter of cosmetics: removal of the bumbling Czar, mouthing of democratic slogans, vague promises of social justice.

Organizationally, the division between "cosmetic" and radical revolutionaries was reflected in the existence of two competing power groups. One was the Provisional Government, headed by Prince Lvov until July and by Kerensky until the Bolshevik Revolution. Lvov's resignation was brought on by rioting over continuing economic inequities and military defeat on the Galician front.

The other power center was "a certain type of parliament elected by members of working-class economic organizations."[54] These organizations, or councils, were called *soviets*. Though the term has an ineluctably Communist ring these days, its roots go far back in Russian history. The Czar's Imperial Council of State, for example, was called the *Gosudarstvennyi Soviet*. The soviets represented workers and peasants and, in this wartime year, soldiers and sailors as well.

Along with political and economic differences, another major issue dividing "cosmetic" and radical revolutionaries was the war. The former supported it, the latter opposed it, and, as tension mounted, the rightists began to accuse radical leaders of being German agents.

The Right-Left split also splintered Russia's major political parties: the Constitutional Democrats (known as Cadets), the Social Democrats, and the Social Revolutionaries. The pro-war camp generally included the Cadets, a minority faction of the SDs (known as Mensheviks), and rightist SRs. Opposing them were Left SRs and a majority bloc of SDs. This faction, known as Bolsheviks, took control of the Revolution and eventually became the Communist Party of the USSR. Relating these political groupings to the power centers mentioned earlier, it would be generally correct to identify the Left with the soviets and the Right with the Provisional Government.

The preceding, it should be emphasized, is intended as a broad rule of thumb rather than as an effort to establish hard and fast designations. Russian politics are notoriously labyrinthine, and there were many deviations and inconsistencies. The Mensheviks, for example, had a radical wing that opposed the war.

As the Revolution became more revolutionary and antiwar sentiment mounted, Reed's interest in Russia perked up. Steffens came back in June from a three-month fact-finding trip, full of enthusiasm for the Bolsheviks. This enthusiasm he imparted to Reed. Approvingly, he quoted a newsman friend named Bill Shepherd. "'Bolsheviki! We must find out enough about the Bolsheviki to carry the word. Can't you see it in the headlines? It will stick. It will crackle in everybody's mouth, ear, and brain. Bolsheviki!'"[55] Though Steffens could not stay to see the "real revolution," he wrote later that he "grasped enough to hold the key to it" and came to the conclusion that Lenin's seizure of power "saved the Russian Revolution from repeating the history of the Mexican and all known revolutions."[56]

By August Reed was fairly bursting with desire to get to Russia. Bryant had just returned from covering the war in Western Europe, and now she found herself heading for revolution in Eastern Europe. They sailed from New York on 17 August on a Danish ship improbably called the *United States*.

Following a circuitous route (by sea to Stockholm, by train and ferryboat through Sweden and Finland), they arrived in the Russian capital in mid-September. There they checked into the Hotel d'Angleterre, where Reed had stayed with Mike Robinson two years earlier.

The first news they received was not of revolution but counterrevolution. General Kornilov, strong man of the Right, had launched a military *putsch*. Rumors abounded—the coup had succeeded, it had failed, Kerensky was still in power, Kerensky was dead, the Bolsheviks were in control, the Bolsheviks had gone underground. The situation was so chaotic that Reed and Bryant had no inkling of what the situation would be when their train arrived in the capital. "We arrived in Petrograd at three in the morning," wrote Bryant, "prepared for anything. . . ."[57] As it turned out, the Kornilov counterrevolution was a total failure. His troops, infected with Bolshevism, deserted in droves. Kornilov himself was arrested by a Soldiers' Committee.

Few events have been so extensively covered as John Reed's role in the Bolshevik Revolution. Revival of interest in Reed has led, over the past years, to a motion picture, several full-length biographies, anthologies of his writings, and re-issues of *Insurgent Mexico* and *Ten Days that Shook the World*.

Another rehash of those "ten days"—and the events that preceded them—would be superfluous. The emphasis in the remainder of this chapter will be on Reed's contacts with top Bolshevik leaders, contacts that legitimized his credentials and sent him back to his native land as America's leading apostle of the Bolshevik Revolution.

The top Bolsehvik leadership during the "ten days" was the duumvirate of Vladimir Ilyich Ulyanov (Lenin) and Lev Davidovich Bronstein (Trotsky). Reed met Trotsky before he met Lenin. He was granted an interview on 30 October at the headquarters of the Petrograd Soviet in the Smolny Institute. This elegant three-story building, located in the outskirts of the city, once served as a finishing school for daughters of the nobility. "Few questions from me were necessary," wrote Reed, "he talked rapidly and steadily, for more than an hour."[58]

In the arrogant, didactic manner for which he was famous, Trotsky began with an analysis of the political situation. "The bourgeoisie completely controlled the Provisional Government, masking its control through a fictitious coalition with the *oborontsi* (moderate Socialist) parties."[59] The bourgeoisie can remain in control only by civil war, through such actions as the attempted Kornilov coup. The peasants are waiting for land distribution and the pacifists have lost all authority. The Revolution can now be saved only through direct action and imposition of proletarian dictatorship. The Soviets are "the most perfect representatives of the people" and no real power can be created without them.[60]

Turning to foreign policy, Trotsky called for an immediate armistice and an appeal to the peoples of Europe over the heads of their governments. He also advocated a United States of Europe "recreated, not by the diplomats, but by the proletariat."[61]

Trotsky gave another demonstration of his internationalism in late January of 1918, in a way that directly affected Reed. Reed was preparing to return to the United States and was afraid that valuable documents (including his manuscript of *Ten Days*) might be confiscated when he reached the United States. Trotsky seemingly solved the problem by appointing Reed Soviet Consul in New York. But the appointment was immediately withdrawn. Alexander Gumberg, a Russian-American enemy of Reed, got to Lenin and convinced him to overrule Trotsky.

Reed first met Lenin in Petrograd on 18 January 1918; they were introduced by Albert Rhys Williams, an ordained minister turned radical activist. The occasion was a tense meeting of the Constituent Assembly at the Tauride Palace. Though things were not going well for the Bolsheviks—they were able to capture only 25 percent of the delegates—Lenin found time to talk to his distinguished American supporter in a friendly and intimate manner. Among other comments, he urged Jack to improve his Russian, passing out tips on his own technique of learning languages.[62]

Reed's return trip to the United States was an even more tortuous affair than his journey to Russia. While in Petrograd, Jack had made enemies of American Ambassador David R. Francis and Edgar Sisson, delegate of Wilson's Committee on Public Information. (Reed seemed to have an affinity for alienating envoys; we recall his 1915 difficulties with Ambassador Marye.) Francis, a machine Democrat and ex-governor of Missouri, strongly disapproved of Reed's pro-Bolshevik sentiments. As for Sisson, a devious and vindictive man whom Reed called "the weasel," he had been offended by Jack's go-to-hell reaction when he tried to dissuade him from addressing the Third Congress of Soviets.

Apart from normal homesickness, Reed had another reason for wanting to return to the United States. *The Masses* had been suppressed in November and Reed was under indictment for sedition. Jack saw the coming trial as an ideal forum in which to expound his views and defend the right of dissent in wartime.

Reed left Russia in February but got no farther than the Norwegian capital of Christiana (now Oslo). Thanks to the intrigues of Francis, Sisson et al., the American Consulate in Christiana refused to visa his passport for the United States.

For two months Reed lingered in Norway. Fuming with exasperation, he worked on *Ten Days*, sold articles on Russia to local publications, and badgered the Consulate with demands that he be allowed to go home. Throughout this Kafka-esque ordeal, Jack retained his sense of humor. In a complaint to the American Minister that he was being deprived of the right to return to his own country, he submitted a request for reimbursement. The accompanying expense report was itemized down to the last laundry and cleaning bill.[63]

Clearance finally came through in April and Jack boarded the S.S. *Bergensfjord*, bound for New York. Arriving on the 28th, he was immediately exposed to the climate of fear and hostility that had gripped wartime America. His notes (including the manuscript of *Ten Days*) were confiscated, he was lengthily interrogated, and he even suffered the indignity of being stripped for body search.

Seven springs before—in the innocent year of 1911—Jack Reed had been in New York following a stay in Europe. Though the phrase "American Dream" had not been coined in 1911, Reed was both its forerunner and exemplar—joyously happy and basically in tune with a system under which he aspired to make a million dollars.

Now, in this other spring, Reed was also in New York following a journey to Europe. There the resemblance ended. Reed was returning to a society where suspicion was in control, where informers were honored patriots, and where the line between dissent and treason had all but been erased. To many of his countrymen, the amiable idealist of 1911 was now both a sinister and contemptible figure: a seditionist under indictment, a subverter of America's war effort (in an extremely popular war), an intimate of foreign terrorists, a German agent (as many believed him), and an open exponent of that terrible experiment in social engineering known as the Bolshevik Revolution.

— 5 —

Villa's Foreign Legion

IT WAS NOT BY ACCIDENT OR COINCIDENCE that most of the foreigners who participated in the Mexican Revolution came under the command of Francisco Villa. Carranza, a xenophobe, permitted non-Mexicans at his side only when he considered it vitally essential to his interests. A case in point is that of Lincoln Steffens. Though Carranza realized the value of such an influential publicist, he took Steffens on grudgingly and with reluctance. Steffens writes of "Carranza, the unapproachable, who received me but did not for months open up."[1]

Obregón followed pretty much the same policy. Though his nature was more open than Carranza's, in those days he was still trying to ingratiate himself with the First Chief. Yet this superb pragmatist did not hesitate to use foreign skills when the occasion demanded. At Celaya, a crucial battle against Villa, Obregón benefited hugely from the expertise of "the German officer, Colonel Maximilian Kloss, [who] put into use for the first time in Mexico, barbed wire, trenches and mine traps, and machine gun nests."[2] This is the comment of an American who served on the *villista* side, a Texas doctor appointed by Villa as medical chief-of-staff. Kloss, the son of a Prussian officer, was also in charge of munitions productions for Carranza and Obregón.[3]

The exclusively nativist makeup of the *zapatista* forces was more a matter of geography than top-level preference. Alone among the revolutionary leaders, Zapata operated in a landlocked sector far from any border. Foreign supporters could reach him neither by sea (as Steffens had joined Carranza in Veracruz) nor by crossing the border, as Reed and many others had done to join Villa.

The foreign presence in the *villista* forces was pretty much limited to the period between late 1910 and mid-1914. Many volunteers left with the beginning of the First World War, and by late 1915, following Wilson's *de facto* recognition of Carranza, Villa's diminished force had once more become exclusively Mexican.

The warm welcome that Villa extended toward foreign volunteers tells us a great deal about his attitude toward revolution. With his idealistic and romantic temperament, Villa rejected the narrow nationalism of Carranza. Though 1910–20 has been identified as the time of the Mexican Revolution, it would be more accurate to limit that identification to the 1910–14 period, with the other six years consumed by a power struggle among victorious revolutionaries. It was during these four years that Villa functioned *specifically* as a rebel against an oppressive order—an order represented successively by an entrenched dictator (Díaz), a traitor who sold out to the cattle barons (Orozco), and a usurper (Huerta). Then the issues were clear and the pro-American Villa (as he was at the time) expansively welcomed the aid of American friends. This was only logical. He was a frequent visitor to border towns and had a host of social and business connections with Americans. Under the circumstances, it would have been cold and unfriendly to deny his *amigos gringos* the opportunity to help him against such hated enemies as Díaz, Orozco, and Huerta.

It can, of course, be argued that Villa did not recruit foreigners to his ranks simply because he liked them or because he was an internationalist at heart. This is true to an extent. Villa's cause was greatly aided by the journalistic skills of a John Reed and the military ones of some of the experienced soldiers who rallied to his standard.

Yet he was amazingly unselective, especially if we compare his standards to the ultra-rigid ones of Carranza and Obregón. Foreign *villistas* ran the gamut from experienced professionals to vagrants and criminals. In fairness, some of these sociopaths served the Revolution well. One, whose career we will examine later, was an ex–bank robber. But all too many were, in John Reed's words, "hard, cold misfits in a passionate country, despising the cause for which they were fighting, sneering at the gaiety of the irrepressible Mexicans."[4] Reed encountered five such men sitting on a park bench in Jiménez, a city in southern Chihuahua. No dates are mentioned, but the encounter had to be between January and March of 1914. All had fought at Ojinaga, and Villa, preparing to drive on Torreón, had given them the choice of discharge with 50 pesos or accepting Mexican citizenship and remaining with his forces. This was probably a ploy to get rid of them. All five vociferously disliked "greasers" and only one, a reform-school graduate, thought of accepting Villa's offer. But he planned to do so under an assumed name and desert as soon as he had "a stake to go back to Georgia and start a child labor factory."[5] Another of the group, who had lost a leg, revealed that he was wanted on two murder charges, though he insisted that he was the victim of a frame-up. Reed's harsh judgment was that he had seen few American *villistas* "who would not have been tramps in their own country."[6]

Not all the men who joined Villa were soldiers. Some were technicians—like the man Reed describes as "a dry-as-dust scientist studying the action of high explosives in field guns." Others, like Reed, were correspondents.

Of the latter, the best-known was Ambrose Bierce. Bierce—along with Judge Crater, Amelia Earhart, and James R. Hoffa—has the unenviable distinction of being one of modern history's great *desaparecidos*, individuals who vanished without a trace but are widely believed to have died violently.

Apart from the fact that they were both writers and *villista* correspondents, Reed and Bierce furnish a study in contrast. Reed, at 26, was one of the youngest correspondents to cover a major revolution; Bierce, at 72, was one of the oldest. Reed was an idealist, Bierce was a cynic. Reed was a socialist moving toward communism, while Bierce, with his contemptuous elitism, could be described as a sort of premature fascist.

What impelled Bierce, at his advanced age, to come to Mexico? An avowed foe of radicalism, he was hardly inclined to look benignly on revolution. Yet this elderly man, who lacked for nothing in economic comfort and professional recognition, chose to risk his life in a primitive country and in association with a cause that failed to command his sympathy.

Bierce's decision was based on philosophy rather than politics.

Bierce had a deep contempt for Judaeo-Christian teaching and particularly for the tenet that suicide is a sinful and cowardly act. He agreed with his friend, Colonel Robert G. Ingersoll, that suicide is an excellent remedy and too seldom used. Beyond Ingersoll, Bierce went back to the Romans, calling for "a return to the wisdom of the ancients, in whose splendid civilization suicide had as honorable a place as any other . . . reasonable and unselfish act."[7] By contrast, Bierce denounced the Christian concept "of looking upon the act as that of a craven or a lunatic [as] the creation of priests, philistines, and women. . . ."[8] Suicide, concluded Bierce, "is always courageous."[9]

Bierce, then, had a death wish. In the fall of 1913, he expressed this sentiment more specifically in a letter to his nephew's wife: "If you should hear of my being stood up against a Mexican stone wall and shot to rags, please know that I think it is a pretty good way to depart this life. . . . To be a gringo in Mexico—ah, that is euthanasia."[10] About the same time Bierce wrote a more matter-of-fact letter to his daughter: "The fighting in Mexico interests me," he said. "I want to go down and see if these Mexicans can shoot straight."[11]

On 24 October 1913, Bierce was in New Orleans. There he first made his intention public. "I like the game," he told a reporter. "I like the fighting. I want to see it."[12]

In late November Bierce crossed the border at Juárez, where he was granted credentials as an observer with the *villista* forces. He rode to Chihuahua City on horseback, arriving on 16 December and carrying $1,500 (U.S. currency) in his saddlebags.[13]

Bierce was in Chihuahua City at least ten days. That he was aware of the precariousness of his position is apparent from a 24 December letter to a San Francisco friend named J. H. Dunnigan. "Pray for me—real hard," reads one excerpt.[14]

But Bierce's resolve was unshaken. This is apparent from a laconic 26 December message to Carrie Christensen in Washington, D.C.: "Trainload of troops leaving Chihuahua every day. Expect next day to go to Ojinaga, partly by rail."[15] This was Bierce's final word.

There are two versions of Bierce's death: that he was murdered by order of Villa and that he died in combat during the Ojinaga action.

The first account was propagated by a former *villista* officer named Elías Torres. Torres states that Villa had Bierce killed because he announced that he was going over to Carranza. He quotes Villa as saying, "Let's see if this damned American tells his last joke to the buzzards on the mountain."[16] Torres also maintains that Bierce was serving as an officer on Villa's staff.

This last claim can be viewed with skepticism. Bierce was over seventy, had had no exposure to combat since the American Civil War (which he covered as a reporter), and was accredited to Villa's forces as a journalist, not a military officer.[17]

Gregory Mason, another correspondent attached to Villa, reported that he had heard of an American with a beard serving on Villa's staff. But Bierce had no beard.[18] Also drawing a blank was George Carothers, State Department special agent who was in Mexico during the Revolution. Carothers asked Villa if he had ever heard of Bierce, and he replied that he knew of no such person. Later, State Department officials showed Bierce's picture to twelve men who had been close to Villa. None recognized him.[19] The search was taken up again in the fifties by Professor Haldeen Braddy of Texas Western University. Braddy sent questionnaires not only to surviving *villistas* but also to survivors of the Pershing expedition against Villa. Not one respondent knew anything about Bierce.[20]

A more reasonable hypothesis can be constructed from a report issued by Carranza after his accession to power. Having heard reports that Bierce accompanied Toribio Ortega's force in the attack on Ojinaga, Carranza instructed Major Gaston de Pudu to show a picture of Bierce to Ortega's officers. A captain Salvador Ibarra recognized the picture and confirmed that Bierce had accompanied Ortega's *tropa* in the Ojinaga action. Ibarra added that he lost track of Bierce during the fighting and had no idea what happened to him. If Ibarra's account is correct, Bierce was in all probability killed and dumped into a shallow grave. He may also have been carrying the $1,500 he had brought with him. If so, Bierce's killer (or burier) would have scant incentive to reveal his identity.[21]

If Bierce was killed at Ojinaga, he and Reed figure in an astounding historical juxtaposition. Since Reed crossed into Mexico during the Ojinaga fighting, it was a sequence that could have been stage-managed: exit Bierce, enter Reed.

Though Villa may have been initially careless in processing his foreign volunteers, he was quick to atone for his mistakes. The "sad sacks"—such as Reed encountered in Jiménez—were rapidly weeded out and shipped to the border. Those who remained were men like Oscar O. Creighton, Ben Turner, Edward S. ("Tex") O'Reilly, and Sam Dreben.

We have spoken of a bank robber who rendered heroic service to the rebel cause: this was Oscar Creighton. Originally from San Francisco, Creighton was so skilled at handling high explosives that he was nicknamed "the Dynamite Devil."[22] Much trite prose has been written about the love of a good woman and its redeeming effects; in Creighton's case, the worn stereotype had validity. Creighton had a fiancée who disapproved of his extralegal activities. She dissuaded him from a life of crime and at this point the stage seemed set for an early wedding. But Creighton elected to go the extra mile. The *maderista* revolution had just broken out and, as Creighton explained matters to his fiancée, his redemption would not be complete until he had made a trip to Mexico to fight tyranny. Here one may suspect that Creighton was as much prompted by an adventurous spirit as by an uneasy conscience.

Whatever his motive, Creighton crossed the border in 1911 and attached himself to a rebel unit under Villa's command. His immediate superior was Colonel Giuseppe Garibaldi, grandson and namesake of the Italian liberator. At first Garibaldi was not impressed by Creighton. "In appearance he was anything but prepossessing," he wrote. "Though tall and well-proportioned, he was homely. He had a mop of unkempt red hair, blue-grey eyes set too far apart, a small knob of a nose, and a receding chin covered by a tangled red beard."[23] These misgivings were soon dispelled by Creighton's ability and daring. He was commissioned a captain and served Garibaldi as chief scout. Garibaldi also admired Creighton's sense of duty. In early March of 1911 the rebels were defeated by a federal force at Casas Grandes, Chihuahua. Creighton had been detailed by Garibaldi to stop a train bringing enemy reinforcements. The ex–bank robber made a valiant effort, killing the engineer and several members of the crew. Still, the train got through and the troops on board were committed to the engagement against the *maderistas*. A downcast Creighton, accepting full responsibility, made a shamefaced apology to Garibaldi. But the Italian cut him short. "The fault is mine and not yours, Captain Creighton," he said. "I sent you to an objective too far away."[24]

The redemption Creighton sought came on 15 April 1911 at Estación Bauche. This railroad spur is only 10 miles south of Juárez and the engagement fought there was a prelude to the decisive battle at Juárez that led to Díaz's resignation. Creighton's heroism at Bauche is described by Garibaldi:

> Seeing a part of our line waver . . . he rushed up to steady the men . . .[and] was pumping lead from his Winchester at the advancing federals when a bullet pierced his heart. The men, seeing him fall, were so enraged that they sprang forward and charged the oncoming enemy. With this action the federal rout began. . . . Even in death the brave American captain had accomplished his purpose.[25]

Garibaldi arranged to have Creighton's body buried by the railroad track so that it could be easily located for a later, and more honorable, burial.[26]

After the fall of Juárez, Garibaldi had an interesting conversation with the El Paso Chief of Police. The Chief had been in touch with Creighton's family and fiancée, and they wanted his body brought back to the United States and buried with full military honors. But the Chief was aware of Creighton's criminal record—could he authorize such a move? His decision displayed both wisdom and compassion. If Garibaldi would prepare a favorable testimonial to Creighton's conduct as an officer, the Chief would assent to Creighton's honorable reburial in the United States. Garibaldi enthusiastically assented, and Creighton's body was disinterred and repatriated. In death, Oscar Creighton attained the respectability that eluded him the length of his stormy life.[27]

Ben Turner was a young El Paso machinist and railroad worker who had lived and labored in Mexico. He spoke Spanish fluently. In late 1913, following Villa's audacious capture of Juárez after he had been repulsed at Chihuahua, a rebel colonel named Eusebio Calzada came to the border to recruit volunteers for the *División del Norte*. A number of Americans, including Turner, joined up and then attended a banquet given by Calzada in Juárez. After the banquet, he harangued the volunteers with a fiery speech, urging them to fulfill the ideals of Madero and liberate Mexico from tyranny.[28]

Turner and his fellow enlistees were sent south the next day. Though no specific dates are given, Turner mentions having served as a machine gunner at Lerdo. Lerdo is located in the cotton-growing and industrial complex that also includes Torreón and Gómez Palacio. The date would have had to be between 22 and 27 March 1914, the period in which Lerdo and Gómez Palacio were invested in preparation for the assault on Torreón.[29]

In a later action, at Conejos, Turner encountered a wounded federal soldier sprawled in a doorway. Rousing a family who lived next door, he told them to take the wounded man in and care for him.[30]

This act of clemency almost cost Turner his life. A *villista* officer witnessed the episode and, infuriated by Turner's "softness," ordered him to be shot the next day. Confined to a hut, Turner proceeded to spend the longest night of his life. As dawn broke, he glumly awaited execution.

Then came one of the weirdest turnabouts in the history of the Revolution. The door to Turner's hut burst open, and a huge, savagely handsome man came in. Fully bearded, he brimmed with menace and animal vitality. "Who is this Texan we are going to execute?" he demanded fiercely. Then he saw Turner. For a moment he stared incredulously—then his demeanor abruptly changed. Rushing forward, he embraced Turner in a massive bear hug. "*Hola, Benito*," he cried with delight. The newcomer, a former railroad man, had worked with Turner before the Revolution, when the latter was sent to Mexico by the Southern Pacific Engineers Company. Since the ex–railroad man outranked the officer who had condemned Turner, the order was immediately rescinded.

What makes this story astounding is not the rescue but the rescuer. Turner's savior, the "good angel" who reprieved him from death, was a high-ranking Villa aide called Rodolfo Fierro. A bloodthirsty mass executioner, Fierro was known throughout Mexico as "the Butcher."[31] The next day Fierro introduced Turner to Villa, whom he had never met before.

Though Turner owed his life to Fierro, he was too perceptive to have any illusions about him. Like everybody else who had contact with him, Turner was numbed by Fierro's murderous reputation. Turner relates an incident that took place one day in Chihuahua City. Fierro and a companion were strolling down the street when a disagreement between the two developed. Fierro's companion insisted that a man, when mortally wounded by gunfire, falls backward when he dies. Fierro dissented from this view, offering to bet that a dying man falls forward. Then he pulled out his pistol and casually squeezed off a round at a passerby. The man fell forward and Fierro collected his bet.[32]

Turner was one of the few men to serve both with and against Villa. In 1916, when the *villistas* attacked Columbus, Turner was back in El Paso working as an auto mechanic. It was in this capacity that he accompanied Pershing's punitive expedition into Mexico. Serving in a civilian rather than military capacity, Turner, an excellent mechanic, was paid the then unheard-of sum of $150 a month to service the expedition's motor transport section.[33]

Though Turner and Villa ended on opposing sides, Turner's admiration for Villa never waned. Turner described Villa as "truly a crusader who never gave up on trying to help his people." Turner also has an interesting insight into Villa's religious orientation, seeing it as part of his populism. "Villa," he wrote, "was not a religious man, but he had a belief in Deity, I am sure. Once I heard Villa say, 'When you give to the people you are closer to heaven than at any other time in your life, for you are being directed by the hand of God.'"[34]

As a railroad man and skilled mechanic, Ben Turner was a *villista* volunteer of civilian background. (So, in his own way, was Oscar Creighton.) One of the military antecedents was Edward S. ("Tex") O'Reilly. O'Reilly, who grew up on a west Texas ranch, lost no time in escaping hardscrabble poverty and seeking a life of travel and adventure. Born on 15 August 1876, he joined the Army at an early age and saw action in both the Spanish-American War and the Philippine Insurrection.

The Philippines furnished an environment in which O'Reilly's ingrown prejudices were first put to the test. As a Southerner on the oppressor end of a colonial war, O'Reilly came to the Philippines with all the racist, male chauvinist, and stereotyped macho attitudes that one might expect. To have sexual relations with Filipinas was acceptable, even desirable, but, as O'Reilly sententiously points out, "There was an unwritten law among soldiers that a white man must not wed a native."[35]

Yet O'Reilly was deeply touched by the tragedy of a friend, a trooper to whom he assigns the pseudonym of "Jackson." Ostracized when he married a native woman, Jackson became morose and took to drink. One night, when in his cups, he struck a lieutenant and was sentenced to six years' imprisonment. Escaping from the stockade, he took refuge in his wife's *casa*. Then the insurrection broke out and Jackson burned his final bridges. Boiling with hatred against America's colonialist establishment, he joined the insurrectionists, thereby acquiring the double stigma of traitor and white renegade. During an engagement Jackson was mortally wounded. When his former comrades found him, he was dying in his wife's arms. Jackson died in silence—his final message to the men surrounding him a cold stare of hate. Jackson's death was followed by another tragedy. He and his wife had a son, a blue-eyed boy almost completely Caucasian in appearance. Rejecting his paternal heritage, Jackson's son would never have anything to do with Americans.[36]

Though "Jackson" violated every precept that O'Reilly was brought up to respect, O'Reilly recounts his tragedy with sensitivity and compassion. The incident had a profound effect on him. He had served with an oppressor force in the Philippines; he would never do so again.

After his tour of duty in the Philippines, O'Reilly shipped out to Shanghai as a seaman and later put in a stint as a police reporter in Chicago. O'Reilly next saw action in Venezuela, but this time on the "right" side. Along with Garibaldi, he participated in an unsuccessful rebellion against the dictator Cipriano Castro.[37]

O'Reilly was recovering from the Venezuela disaster in Texas when the *maderista* revolution broke out. He entered Chihuahua as a bodyguard to Abraham González; his favorable impression of the insurgent governor was recorded in the first chapter.

As the most experienced American volunteer, O'Reilly was elected captain of his company. Electing officers was customary, and O'Reilly had all the qualifications to be chosen captain of his unit. His first lieutenant, whose name O'Reilly doesn't recall, was a cowboy picturesquely known as Death Valley Slim.[38]

O'Reilly fought at Santa Rosalia, an action that preceded the Villa-Orozco capture of Juárez in May 1911. The following year found him in action under Villa against the *orozquistas*. In this engagement, near Parral, one of O'Reilly's machine gunners was cut off and captured. He was a New Mexican named Tom Fountain. Fountain's fate was not a pleasant one. Cruelly toying with their captive, the *colorados* subjected him to a particularly vicious application of the *ley fuga*. Feigning friendliness, a *colorado* officer handed Fountain a silver dollar. "See that *chino* restaurant down the street," he said. "Go buy your breakfast and return." The unsuspecting Fountain started toward the restaurant—and was immediately cut down by a hail of bullets.[39]

But O'Reilly survived Mexico's revolutionary caldron. Like so many Americans who had fought with Villa, this hard-bitten Texan went on to serve with distinction in World War I.

Another Texan who served in Mexico was an El Pasoan named Sam Dreben. Dreben, known as "the fighting Jew," for a time fought with Orozco. But he later transferred allegiance, contracting "his services to Villa agents on the border as a skilled machine gunner and expert in the training for that arm."[40] This must have been in 1913 or 1914. It could not have been earlier because Dreben is identified as serving with Orozco in 1912, after Orozco had gone into counterrevolution and when he and the *villistas* were contesting Parral. It is interesting that O'Reilly and Dreben fought on opposite sides during this action.

A friend of Dreben's, Louis Fischbein, had a tailor shop in Parral. When Villa rode into town, his secretary came into Fischbein's shop and told him that Villa wanted to have a riding suit made up. Fischbein took Villa's measurements and promised to go to his headquarters in three days' time for a fitting. But the day of the fitting coincided with a strong *orozquista* attack on Parral and Fischbein stayed home. The attack was repulsed and the next day Fischbein came to Villa for the fitting. Villa asked him why he had not come the day before. "There were too many bullets flying around," replied Fischbein. "Those that fly around don't hurt you," said Villa. "It's those that hit you that are the bad ones." Villa then tried on the coat.[41]

Villa never saw his completed suit. The *colorados* attacked in force a few days later and the *villistas* had to abandon Parral. The *orozquista* occupation was accompanied by a wave of looting; among the targets was Fischbein's shop. The tailor lost his entire stock, including Villa's suit.

Wandering disconsolately around town, Fischbein saw a familiar

Austin Community College
Learning Resources Center

face. "Among Orozco's followers I recognized Sam Dreben. They used to call him the 'fighting Jew.' He was sitting on some stone steps leading up from the street with about twelve other soldiers. I asked him, 'Why didn't you save our place?' Dreben said if he had known whose it was he would have done so."[42]

An unabashed admirer of Dreben was Patrick O'Hea, a courtly Anglo-Irishman who found himself in Mexico during the height of the revolution. O'Hea originally came to Mexico as a farm administrator and, when fighting broke out, he performed consular duties on behalf of England and saved many lives. He and Dreben became friends, and the normally taciturn Texan opened up to O'Hea about his colorful past. "In my chats with him," writes O'Hea, "I never peered indelicately into his background, but apparently he had fought in the U.S.A. war against Spain, in the marines in Nicaragua . . . and on a condottorei [sic] basis in other Republics of Latin America. Of medium height but of rather heavy build, in age on the happy side of the half century, there was nothing of the expected bluster and blasphemy in his mild speech. . . .[he was] the very antithesis of a swashbuckler . . . silent and diffident concerning his feats of arms, but took a sort of modest pride in his profession, as might any other artificer or master craftsman. Apparently he gave no more than a professional's thought to the men stricken by his bullets with whom, he felt, he shared an equal risk."[43]

Though Dreben was close to fifty, he volunteered for service during the First World War. Told at first that he would be assigned to training troops in the United States, Dreben complained so strongly that his request for overseas duty was granted.[44]

O'Hea lost track of Dreben until one day, in the fifties, he chanced "to read in an El Paso newspaper the announcement of the peaceful death in a hospital of that Texas border town of his birth, of Samuel Drebbin [sic], popularly known as the Fighting Jew." O'Hea's final tribute, delivered in the florid yet graceful style that characterizes his reminiscences, is particularly moving: "May Yahewe rest him for a worthy scion of those lions of Judah who, as at Masada, defiantly resisted the legions of Rome until those masters of the ancient world overwhelmed by sheer disciplined weight of numbers the resistance of gallant little Israel."[45]

Reed reported and interpreted the *villista* movement and Creighton, Turner, O'Reilly, and Dreben fought in it. Then there were the healers. Unlike other revolutionary chieftains, whose approach to field medicine was notoriously casual, Villa always placed a high premium on good doctoring. At the height of his career, when he commanded the nine-brigade *División del Norte*, he saw to it that Mexico's largest military force was serviced by well-equipped hospital trains. But Villa's concern in this area far antedated his heyday. Even when the *villistas* were a bushwhacking band of irrregulars, Villa always sought the best doctors.

To secure the expertise he needed, Villa had no chauvinist qualms about recruiting talent across the border. It was in this manner that he obtained the services of Dr. Ira J. Bush, a Texan who served for a time as Villa's Surgeon General.

Bush was an adventurous soul with a strong-minded Southern wife who did not altogether approve of his activities. A pioneer feminist, she continued to use her maiden name (Catherine Dunn) and somewhat sniffily referred to her husband's friends as "so-called dreamers."[46]

One of these "dreamers" was Abraham González, whom Dr. Bush extravagantly admired and frequently quoted. Dunn recalls an occasion "early in 1911 when González came to our home . . . one morning in quite a state. He told us that he had just received an urgent message from Pascual Orozco. . . . Orozco was then at Salamayuca, twenty-five miles south of Juárez. There had been a battle with Federals near there a few days previously. Orozco needed a doctor to go to the camp and treat the wounded."[47] Dr. Bush responded to the request immediately. Accompanied by another doctor, he crossed the border and plunged deep into the war-torn Chihuahua countryside. Under the most difficult circumstances he treated scores of wounded men. Bush's steadfastness was brought into sharper relief by the behavior of the other doctor. A "tenderfoot" (according to Dunn), he gave up after two days and returned to El Paso.

Word of Bush's skill and daring had gotten to Villa. He also sent for Bush, and this time the doctor traveled as far as Casas Grandes, over a hundred miles away. Dunn, who accompanied her husband on the trip, recalls a terrifying experience. "The only safe crossing (to Villa's camp) was over a narrow ford. We got to one side and went down into quicksand. It was a very frightening sensation. Villa himself was waiting across the river. He jumped into the river with a comple of his men and got us out."[48]

It was Madero who offered Bush the post of Chief Surgeon. His military rank was *Coronel del Cuerpo Médico del Ejército Libertador* (Medical Corps Colonel of the Liberating Army). "From then on," relates Dunn, "I practically lost my husband to the cause of the Revolution. . . . During the years that followed [he] was often involved in the revolutionary battles in Mexico."[49]

The adventurous Bush was not satisfied with mere doctoring. In El Paso's main plaza was a Civil War cannon. Though ancient, it was still serviceable. One night, in April of 1911, "my husband . . . with other members of the junta kidnapped the cannon from the very center of El Paso. With much secret plotting and several weeks of devious actions they actually managed to get the cannon and a ton of ammunition across the Rio Grande and into the hands of the insurrectos."[50]

Villa's love affair with America came to an end when President Wilson extended *de facto* recognition to his enemy, Carranza, in October of 1915. Where *gringos* had been friends, they were now targets. In March of 1916 a band of *villistas* (with or without Villa) made a cross-border raid at Columbus, New Mexico, and killed a number of American civilians. This act brought on intevention in the form of a punitive expedition under General John J. Pershing. During the chase by Pershing's troops, Villa was wounded in the leg. Despite his anti-Americanism, it is interesting that Villa, in a final act of "recruiting," sent for an American doctor to treat his wound. The source of this information is Nina Kyriacopulos, née Triolo, wife of a Greek-American gambling impresario and sister of the doctor in question.

> Everybody heard about the time Pancho Villa was wounded in the leg when General Pershing's expeditionary forces were trying to catch up with him in Mexico. There were many stories about that, but we know what actually happened then . . . because Villa sent for my brother, Dr. Jerome Triolo, to attend his injury. . . . Villa's wound was not received in battle, but it was caused by the carelessness of a young soldier who was cleaning his gun which he thought was unloaded and which went off, hitting Villa.[51]

Probably the most interesting version of the Columbus raid was furnished by another medical member of Villa's Foreign Legion. This was Dr. R. H. Ellis, of El Paso, who served as medical chief of staff under Villa.[52] Ellis, who was Villa's staunchest American supporter, went so far as to claim that Villa had been framed at the time of the Columbus attack. The raid—and the massacre of sixteen Americans at Santa Isabel, Chihuahua—"were prime examples of the vicious German-Carranza propaganda machine at work."[53] Quoting "an authoritative historian, Frank M. King," Ellis insists:

> that the Columbus raid was staged by Carranza's agents in order to turn the United States completely against Villa. King says further that . . . a man resembling Villa in size and build was actually made up to look like Pancho. Then some Mexican soldiers who didn't know him were told that this was General Villa and that they were to follow him. . . . So one more outrage was laid at Pancho Villa's door, in fact splashed across the newspapers of the world.[54]

This information should be considered with caution. Not only is Ellis fiercely partisan, but he makes serious errors of fact in other portions of his narrative. He states, for example, that John Reed wrote slanted stories and was "working with Carranza."[55] If Reed slanted his stories, the beneficiary was Villa, not Carranza. Reed, as we shall see, was almost as ardent a Villa *partisan* as Ellis himself. Possibly Ellis confused Reed with Lincoln Steffens, who was a Carranza apologist.

Ellis also states that German Foreign Minister Arthur Zimmerman (author of the famous "Zimmerman telegram") was directing anti-American activity in Mexico "as far back as 1914."[56] Yet Zimmerman did not become Foreign Minister until November 1916.[57]

However careless Ellis may have been with his facts, Villa was still fortunate in having such a loyal American supporter. He was also fortunate—and farsighted—in being the first Mexican revolutionary to dispose of an aerial arm. The popular concept of Villa's forces is one of wild riders thundering out of the Chihuahua sierra. One of the first to challenge this simplistic view would have been a Texas aviation pioneer named R. L. Andrews. Though Andrews served against the *villistas*, he admired Villa's vision and gave him full credit for adaptability to changing trends in warfare. "Early in his career as a leader of the revolution," wrote Andrews, "Pancho Villa recognized the value of airplanes and their coming importance militarily. His army was . . . the first to use planes in Mexico. Records show that he bought planes from the United States and hired American barnstorming pilots. U.S. Air Force records show that in May, 1913, Villa fliers bombed federal gunboats in the bay at Guaymas, being the first aerial bombing in the Western Hemisphere. The Villa flyers were Didier Masson and Thomas J. Dean. Records from the Air University at Alabama show that Villa had four planes: two Wright-B's, one early Christofferson Curtiss Pusher, and a Martin T model. Villa used a small park at Monterrey as a landing field, as well as a rough airstrip near town and at Matamoros."[58]

Of the barnstormers that Villa recruited, most of them came from Chicago. Some of these daredevils were as colorful in name as in reputation. No Hollywood scriptwriter could improve on such nomenclatures as Mickey McGuire, Wild Bill Heath, and Farnum T. Fish. The presence of these exotic winged specimens inspired a *corrido*:

> Pancho Villa no longer rides a horse
> And neither will his people,
> Pancho Villa owns an airplane
> And he gets them with the greatest of ease.[59]

Of the volunteers who served on the ground, two had been opponents during the Boer War. One was Ben Viljoen, an ex-Boer general, and the other was A. W. Lewis, a Canadian machine gunner who fought on the British side. A man who would attain celebrity in another field was "a thirty-year-old El Pasoan named Tom Mix, who survived the Revolution and went on to make his reputation as a Hollywood cowboy."[60]

In the coverage on Oscar Creighton, some references were made to his immediate superior, Colonel Giuseppe Garibaldi. Garibaldi is worth discussing in more detail. Though he had all his grandfather's color and dash, he lacked his ideological purity. Where the elder Garibaldi consistently fought for liberty, the grandson was a condottiere type whose commitment was more to adventure than liberation. Born in 1880, he joined the Italian Legion in 1897 to help the Greek David against the Turkish Goliath. But two years later he was on the colonialist side, serving as a British mercenary against the independence-minded Boers. Switching back again, Garibaldi's next tour of duty found him helping the Venezuelan rebels against dictator Cipriano Castro.

When he returned to Italy, Garibaldi had the ironic experience of finding himself charged with draft evasion: he had been called for military service during the time he was fighting in Venezuela.[61] By family influence, the charge was dropped.

Garibaldi next drilled for oil in Romania and then accepted a commission to investigate labor conditions among Italians working on the Panama Canal. In early 1910 he went to Chihuahua to try his hand at mining. Revolutionary sentiment was gaining ground and Garibaldi, sensing the possibility of adventure, began making inquiries. He was told to go to El Paso and look up Abraham González.

Like so many others, Garibaldi immediately came under González's spell. "His followers were devoted to him," he wrote, "and he was unquestionably one of the best men Madero had around him. Would that there had been more of his type."[62]

This last sentence can be seen as a reflection on other revolutionary leaders who, in Garibaldi's opinion, were not of González's type. One of these was Francisco Villa.

Villa and Garibaldi disliked each other from the start. Though both held the rank of colonel, Villa commanded far more men and Garibaldi, with his heritage and military record, obviously resented being in a subordinate position to an unknown ex-bandit. For his part, Villa referred to Garibaldi as a "filibuster" and expressed doubt that Garibaldi really was the grandson of "the great Italian liberal."

This was the background to the famous dispute between Garibaldi and Villa. Since both men had a flair for public relations, their versions of what happened are completely at variance. This complicates the historian's task. In the absence of more definitive information, I will submit both versions to the reader's judgment.

In his memoirs, Villa states that one of his soldiers came to his hut and complained that he had been disarmed by Garibaldi's men. Villa sent Garibaldi a polite note asking him to return the man's rifle and ammunition. If Garibaldi had a complaint against the soldier, he would be happy to hear it. Garibaldi responded with a defiant message on the back of Villa's note: if he wanted the rifle and ammunition, he could come and get it. In the confrontation that followed, Villa clubbed Garibaldi with his pistol and "the panther of a moment before turned quiet as a lamb." Villa states that Garibaldi not only returned the *villista* soldier's arms but allowed his one-hundred–man force to be disarmed by just thirty of Villa's men. When Madero heard of the controversy, he angrily sent for Villa. Garibaldi, according to Villa, had fabricated a story that put the blame on him. But Madero's anger vanished when Villa showed him the paper containing his message and Garibaldi's reply. Wishing to restore harmony, he called in Garibaldi and made him and Villa embrace. Villa then returned the arms he had confiscated from Garibaldi's men and that was the end of it.[63]

Garibaldi's version is much shorter. He relates that he was in the lobby of El Paso's Shelton Hotel when he saw Villa talking to the desk clerk. Greeting Villa, he found him in an ugly mood. It was just after the battle of Juárez and, according to Villa, two American volunteers had accused him of cowardice during the engagement. Amid a volley of curses and threats, he asked Garibaldi for the names of the offending *gringos*. Before Garibaldi could answer, Villa was jumped by three men, the El Paso chief of police and two detectives. They had overheard his tirade and wanted no incidents on the American side of the border. Disarming Villa, they hustled him unceremoniously across the Rio Grande.[64]

Following the Revolution, Garibaldi made the familiar trek to Europe and World War I. He also served in the Second World War, commanding the Italian Eighth Army on the Russian front.[65]

Another Mexican veteran who came into his own during World War II was a New Zealander named Bernard Freyberg. Some of the information about him came to me in an interesting and unusual manner.

In early 1983 I was informed by Gail Benedict, Guadalajara correspondent of the Mexico City *Daily News*, that she had been approached by a Mexico City real estate man named Emil K. Michner. Michner, who had read a reference to this work in Benedict's column, told her he had information that would undoubtedly be of interest to me. A keen student of Mexican history, Michner was also the son-in-law of Dr. John J. Sparks, British Consul in Torreón at the height of the Revolution. Following an exchange of letters and phone calls between Michner and the writer, he was kind enough to send me a body of photocopied material from his archives. This documentation included statements and affidavits from the following persons: the 85-year-old head of the *villista* veterans' organization, a New Zealand correspondent well briefed on Freyberg's early life, a former British military attaché in Mexico, a Chihuahua editor, and Freyberg's son, who lives in England.

Of these documents, the item that first caught my attention appeared in a letter written by Michner to a Mexican friend about Freyberg's departure from Mexico. World War I had broken out, and Freyberg was anxious to go to England and enlist in the Allied forces. Being short of money, he succeeded in borrowing $100 from the British Consul (Patrick O'Hea) for his passage money, to Liverpool by way of Tampico and New York. "My father-in-law told me," wrote Michner, "that . . . there was another captain waiting in the anteroom, a *compañero* named Rommel. . . ."[66]

This immediately opened a fascinating avenue of speculation. Could this man have been the future Marshal Rommel who, during one phase of his World War II career, fought against Freyberg in North Africa? Such was the opinion of two people: ex-Consul Sparks and Mario González Muzquiz, Michner's Mexican correspondent.[67] If true, this would have been one of the stories of the century.

The truth, regrettably, is more prosaic. No biography of Rommel contains any mention of a trip to Mexico. Wishing to obtain a definitive statement, I wrote Rommel's son, Mayor Manfred Rommel of Stuttgart, West Germany. In his reply, Mayor Rommel categorically denied that his father had ever visited Mexico in his life.[68]

Who, then, was the mysterious Captain Rommel waiting in the anteroom when Freyberg was borrowing the passage money? Possibly he belonged to a German-Mexican family that had reportedly settled in Chihuahua and owned a ranch in the Parral area. But not even this is certain. Rubén Rocha, managing editor of *El Correo de Parral*, is the author of a book about the region. He has stated that "in my historical research I have found no reference to the (Rommel) family" in the sector on which he has written.[69] Whoever the shadowy "Captain Rommel" may have been, we know for sure that he was not Germany's World War II hero.

If Rommel's service with Villa is in the "too-good-to-be-true" category, such is not the case with Freyberg. John Hardingham, Michner's New Zealand correspondent, writes that Freyberg took up dentistry when he left school in New Zealand and then embarked for San Francisco in early 1914. Hardingham adds that, "He was already a real adventurer and had had military training in the territorial forces in New Zealand."[70]

How did Freyberg come to Mexico to fight with the *villistas*? Here the narrative is taken up by his son:

> My father was in California up to the last few days of May 1914. He could only have been in Mexico for ten weeks at the outside. . . . There have been various descriptions of how he went to Mexico, but it is likely that he was hired as a guard of some sort—either for a bank payroll, mining company, or Villa's Transport Services, or even for a film company filming the Mexican War. . . .it seems probable that he entered Mexico at El Paso in early June 1914. He must have left Mexico within two or three days after the outbreak of World War I . . . if he was to leave New York ten days later. There was insufficient time to go overland. . . .either he went via Tampico to New Orleans by tanker . . . or he went by coaster direct to New York.

Lord Freyberg concludes with this assessment of his father's role in Mexico:

> I think it stands to reason that during the comparatively short time that my father was in Mexico, he was unlikely to have achieved much prominence in whatever organization he may have joined. He had become bored with New Zealand, and like many young men before and since, he wanted to find adventure. He was about to find it in plenty in the First World War, and Mexico was to be the hors d'oeuvre before the main dish.[71]

How did Freyberg make his way from the *villista* zone to Tampico? This is frankly a mystery. His son writes of hearing a version which he describes as "interesting, but highly suspect." This account states that Freyberg walked 300 miles to Tampico to catch the boat that took him to England. Lord Freyberg's skepticism is based on the fact "that he could not have heard the news about the outbreak of World War I before the 5th or 6th of August, 1914, and (catch) a boat in New York for the UK eight days later. It would not have been physically possible for him to walk 300 miles (which would have taken at least a week) and still make the connection."[72]

The preceding indicates that Freyberg was somewhat reticent about discussing his Mexican adventures, even with members of his own family. Fortunately for the historian and researcher, careful scrutiny of the Michner archive yields more exact information. One entry is a 1965 letter to Freyberg's son from Norman Pelham Wright, former British military attaché in Mexico City. In this letter he mentions having heard that Freyberg took part in actions at Gómez Palacio and Torreón. But this couldn't have been: Torreón was secured by 3 April and the rest of the Laguna sector—including Gómez Palacio and Lerdo—ten days later. Nor could he have taken part in the diversionary attack on Saltillo, an action that ended on 20 May. Ironically, it is the incorrect information given Pelham Wright— along with Lord Freyberg's statement that his father was in the United States as late as the end of May—that provides the decisive clue. The only action in which Freyberg could have participated was Zacatecas.

Consider the sequence of events: Freyberg entered Mexico "in early June," the approach on Zacatecas began the 9th, and the city fell the 24th. The *villistas*, owing to Villa's quarrel with Carranza, took no part in the July drive on Mexico City, and by early August Freyberg was on his way to England.

What were Freyberg's duties while fighting with the *villistas*? There is a reference in the Michner archive that "Freyberg was a machine gunner with the Mexicans."[73] Yet Michner was told by Lt. Col. Eduardo Angeles Meras, head of the *villista* veterans' organization, that Freyberg was attached to the staff of his cousin, General Felipe Angeles. General Angeles was Villa's highly talented artillery commander. The two versions do not necessarily conflict. Though this is conjecture, it is entirely possible that Freyberg joined the *División del Norte* as a machine gunner and was then recruited by the perceptive General Angeles. Freyberg may have told Angeles of his territorial service in New Zealand, a stint that could have included artillery training.

After leaving Mexico, Freyberg's rise was unchecked. In the First World War he served with General Allenby in the Near East. In World War II he commanded the New Zealand Division in North Africa. From 1946 to 1952 he was Governor-General of New Zealand and, from 1953 till his death ten years later, he was Deputy Constable and Lieutenant Governor of Windsor Castle. When he died, the former dentist and payroll guard was a Field Marshal and member of the House of Lords.

In his 1965 letter to Freyberg's son, Norman Pelham Wright commented that "Carranza was a xenophobe who accepted no foreigners in his forces."[74] Had the First Chief been in complete control during the campaign, the insurgent force would have been almost exclusively of nativist background. Instead, the Mexican Constitutionalists foreshadowed the Spanish Republicans in producing an "international brigade" that captured the world's imagination. In large part, this was the doing of Francisco Villa.

— 6 —

Insurgent Mexico
and Insurgent Mexico

JOHN REED'S ASSIGNMENT IN MEXICO has been presented as a drama of redemption: young man begins promising career, young man gets led astray; young man reclaims himself in the caldron of revolution.

This explanation is too pat. It is true that the wealthy, egocentric Mabel Dodge contributed to an unproductive period in Reed's career, and it is true that Mexico inspired a work that made him world famous. But Mexico did not terminate the Dodge-Reed liaison. It continued sporadically for over a year after Reed's return and ended mainly because the principals found new partners.

None of this detracts from the fact that *Insurgent Mexico* is a remarkable achievement. The late Renato Leduc, *villista* telegrapher turned left-wing journalist, credits Reed with writing *Insurgent Mexico* as "minutely and objectivly as he wrote *Ten Days*, but with more color, emotion and—why not say it?—poetry."[1] In view of Leduc's conspicuously Marxist bias, the fact that he rates *Insurgent Mexico* over *Ten Days* is an impressive accolade.

Barring his assertion that *Insurgent Mexico* was written "objectively" (Reed never pretended to objectivity in covering the Mexican Revolution), Leduc's comments are on target. Color, emotion, and poetry—these qualities exist in overflowing abundance but as interlocking, rather than separate, identities. The poetic quality of *Insurgent Mexico* derives directly from Reed's magnificent gifts as a descriptive writer and his burning commitment to the *villista* cause.

It is difficult to conceive of an "objective" writer producing so powerful a work.

For all that, one fact must be faced: *Insurgent Mexico* is partly a work of fiction. This is not so much a reflection on Reed as on the journalistic standards of his day. We recall William Randolph Hearst's instructions on the eve of the Spanish-American War—a conflict that he brought on almost single-handedly. ("You furnish the pictures and I'll furnish the war.") This was the era of fake atrocity stories, with credulous readers exposed to tales of Belgian babies crucified by German soldiers.

By these shoddy norms, Reed emerges as Mr. Clean. Other reporters, denied entry into the country by Mexican authorities, sat in border-town hotel rooms (or bars) and filed whisky-fueled accounts of imaginary battles.

Reed would have none of this. He crossed into Mexico in defiance of a death threat, rode with *la tropa*, interviewed Villa and Carranza, and produced a vibrant book that made contemporaries compare him to Kipling and Richard Harding Davis.

Yet *Insurgent Mexico* is a hybrid, a work that is part fact and part fabrication. Reed did not so much invent as embroider. He was not above embellishing incidents, even to the extent of creating fictitious characters and arbitrarily changing their identities when it suited his purpose.

One such case involves an article Reed published in the April 1914 issue of *The Masses*. Titled "Mac—American," it describes Reed's encounter with a fellow countryman in Chihuahua. The latter, a master mechanic named Mac, is a bigoted Southerner given to disparaging comments about "niggers," "greasers," and the immorality of Mexican women. Reed endures the loutish Mac only because he knows the country well and has promised to take him south to the combat zone. The story won high praise, including an enthusiastic telegram from Max Eastman: "MAC AMERICAN IS A PEACH."[2]

Yet, when the incident was incorporated into *Insurgent Mexico*, the racist, anti-Mexican Mac is replaced by a drunken, gringo-baiting rebel lieutenant named Antonio Montoya. He comes to Reed's room, determined to kill "the gringo in this hotel" but becomes his *compadre* and traveling companion when Jack gives him his watch.[3]

The "Mac—American"–Antonio Montoya episode is the only one where Reed was caught red-handed juggling fact and fiction. But there are many other inaccuracies and incidents that have a suspicious ring. One possible invention is the Elizabetta affair, to be discussed later. As for the factual errors, many were caused simply by Reed's faulty knowledge of Spanish.

None of these flaws vitiated Reed's ability to get at important essences. He might misunderstand an idiomatic phrase or err on dates and places. But his aim was perfect when he keyed in on major figures—Villa, Carranza, Urbina et al.

Reed was also brilliant in capturing the idealism behind a movement that many saw as a comic-opera affair. Where foreign mine owners and company representatives—the "Mac Americans"— cynically viewed the Revolution as a means whereby poor "greasers" could despoil rich ones, Reed witnessed at first hand the code of honor prevailing among these ragged men. They shared everything, and a *robavaca* (rustler) who had amply robbed rich ranchers would not steal a cigarette from his tentmate.

Reed's narrative begins in December 1913. He was then in Presidio, Texas, across the Rio Grande from the dusty Mexican town of Ojinaga. As noted earlier, the federal detachment in Ojinaga was an outnumbered and dispirited remnant, the last *huertista* force in Chihuahua. The *villistas*, well-armed and flushed with victory, were approaching and there was no doubt about the eventual outcome. Honor demanded token resistance, to be followed by a cross-river movement to the safety of the American side.

Reed wanted to interview General Salvador Mercado, commander of the doomed garrison. But his message fell into the hands of Pascual Orozco, also in Ojinaga and at the head of a diminished force. The Ojinaga detachment, numbering 3,500 men, actually consisted of two remnants, one of Federals and one of *colorados*. Orozco immediately sent Reed this chillingly courteous message: "Esteemed and honored Sir: If you set foot in Ojinaga, I will stand you sideways against a wall, and with my own hand take great pleasure in shooting furrows in your back."[4]

Reed bravely ignored the threat and waded across the river. In Ojinaga he encountered a *colorado* officer named Hernández, Orozco's chief of staff. Hernández, who apparently did not know of

Orozco's threat against Reed, made no attempt to threaten or harass him. But he did pour out a stream of abuse against Mercado, refusing to take Jack to his headquarters. "General Orozco hates General Mercado!" he shouted. "He (Mercado) is a coward. He ran away from Tierra Blanca, and then he ran away from Chihuahua."[5]

Reed eventually found Mercado, whom he described as "a fat, pathetic, worried, undecided little man, who blubbered and blustered (about alleged American aid to Villa). . . ."[6]

Though Reed's good faith is not in question, very little of this is true. It would have been impossible for Mercado to run away at Tierra Blanca "and then" at Chihuahua, because the Chihuahua engagement (which the Federals won) took place eighteen days before the action at Tierra Blanca.

Nor does Reed provide an accurate picture of Mercado. Though his looks and physique may have been unprepossessing, Mercado was an able officer with a good record. He commanded the defending force at Chihuahua, saddling the *villistas* with their only defeat in that brilliant fifteen-and-a-half-month campaign that toppled Huerta. Nor was Mercado entirely at fault for the federal collapse of Ojinaga. The doomed garrison's morale was so low that "at the first shots the officers began the most incredible and disgraceful flight. . . . This reprehensible incident is unprecedented. It is the first time in our military history that very nearly two thousand men of our forces have fled at the first shots." These words are Mercado's own, as recorded by Luis Garfías.[7]

Hernández's bad-mouthing of Mercado to Reed can be traced to mutual antagonism between *colorados* and *federales*. Mercado had attributed several *huertista* defeats to the poor leadership of Orozco's "improvised officers." Mercado had also attacked the bandit behavior of *orozquista* General Antonio Rojas, stating that "his forces, like those of Orozco . . . were threatening to devote themselves wholly to the most uncontrollable pillaging. . . ."[8]

There is no way that the inexperienced Reed could have been aware of these internecine power games. As for the impression Mercado made on Reed, a man in his completely untenable position could not be expected to cut a confident figure.

By the time Villa attacked Ojinaga, Reed was far south of the border. His destination was a sector of northern Durango, an area larger than the state of New Jersey. The region's overlord was General Tomás Urbina, Villa's *compadre* and companion from bandit days. Urbina ruled this territory as a personal fief, taking, according to Reed, half the proceeds from the land and assigning the other half to the Constitutionalist government.

Urbina's headquarters was the village of Las Nieves, and Reed hoped to catch him there before he rode off to war. In Magistral, "a Durango mountain village three days ride from the nearest railroad," Reed encountered an Arab trader named Antonio Swayfeta. The Arab, who had a two-wheeled gig, was headed for Parral by way of Las Nieves and was willing to let Reed off at the latter destination. Reed states that during the journey they "climbed out of the mountains to the great upland plain of northern Durango."[9]

This is somewhat confusing. Part VI of *Insurgent Mexico*, titled "Mexican Nights," describes events that took place before those recorded in Part I. Of the three chapters in Part VI, one is about Chihuahua City and two about communities in the Durango sierra called Villa Allegre (Alegre) and Santa María del Oro. Strangely, there is no reference in these chapters to Magistral, which is about 5 miles north of Santa María del Oro.

I stress this point because it leads to another: how did Reed get all the way from the border to the remote mountains of Durango? It is over 300 miles on a direct line from Ojinaga to the nearest point in that sierra. Since the linear route traverses some of the most forbidding country in Mexico, Reed began with a detour by way of Chihuahua City, which we know from Chapter 1 of Part VI. But how did he end up in a sierra region some 40 miles *south* of Las Nieves, his original destination? The logical approach to Las Nieves would have been from the *north*, by way of Chihuahua City, Jiménez, and Parral. Yet Reed writes of traveling with the Arab out of the mountains and onto the upland plain of northern Durango. This approach could only have been from the south, since the sierra ends where northern Durango merges with southern Chihuahua. In addition, Las Nieves is off the main road between Santa María del Oro and Parral.

Here I do not charge Reed with conscious falsification. He apparently had no maps, his knowledge of Mexico was limited, and there was a considerable language barrier between himself and the

Arab. (". . . he poured out his life's story, not one word of which I could understand.")[10]

A possible explanation is that the Arab, for business reasons, made his approach to Parral via a zigzag route. There is a railroad spur between Parral, in Chihuahua, and Orestes Pereyra, in Durango. West of this line, before sierra gives way to altiplano, is a mountainous region. The trader was selling *macuche* (a tobacco substitute), and it would have been to his advantage to detour by way of Las Nieves (and the neighboring population center of Canutillo) on his way to Parral. But this is pure conjecture; also, it doesn't clear up the mystery of how Reed ever got from Chihuahua City to a sierra region *beyond* his planned destination.

Though Reed may have been shaky in his geography, his cultural perceptions remained undimmed. On the way to Las Nieves, he and the Arab enjoyed the hospitality of a *campesino*. During the meal his relatives and *compadres* drifted in, and a lively discussion ensued. Though they were resigned to paying a quarter of their meager incomes for the Revolution, some violently objected to continued tithing to the Church. "Priests without shame," cried one man, "who have come when we are so poor and take away a tenth of what we have." . . ."Shut your mouth," shrilled the woman, "it is for God! God must eat, the same as we. . . ." Her husband, who considered himself a man of the world because he had once been to Jiménez, smiled a superior smile. "God does not eat," he said. "The *curas* grow fat on us." Reed asked them why they continued to tithe. "It is the law," said several at once. What astounded Reed was that all those people—even the anticlericals among them—were continuing in 1914 to obey a law that had been repealed in 1857.[11]

The next day they arrived at Las Nieves, where Reed and the Arab bade each other an affectionate farewell. Though Jack had expected to be charged at least 10 pesos (about $5 in those days), the trader emotionally refused to accept payment.

Reed's portrayal of General Tomás Urbina is photographic in its fidelity. He makes Urbina come alive before our eyes and shows him for the savage that he was. Yet here is something strange. Reed, having mercilessly spotlighted this brutish creature, somehow shows little distaste for him. If Reed had a weakness, it was a tendency to institutionalize his grievances, to tilt excessively in the direction of hate-the-sin-but-not-the-sinner. Too often for comfort, we detect faint notes of admiration for individual representatives of systems that Reed detested. While such tolerance may be praiseworthy in the case of William Jennings Bryan, it is far less so when its beneficiaries are vicious goons like Bob Lee, graduate of the Jesse James gang, and "Lou Miller, with five murders to his credit [sic]." Reed never lost his soft spot for the brutal macho, the colorful assassin, the legendary tough guy—as long as they had some link with the romantic tradition. (This tolerance, as we shall see, did not extend to his bureaucratic enemies.)

And so it was with Urbina. On being introduced, the General extended a limp hand but did not rise. Reed then presented his papers. "I don't know how to read," said Urbina, this declaration followed by a volley in the coarsest Spanish.[12] Urbina, as recorded previously, did not share Villa's passion for education and obviously regarded literacy as an effeminate trait.

Along with being illiterate, Urbina was vain, cruel, and mawkishly sentimental.

The General's entourage included armed men, pigs, chickens, goats, half-naked children (three of them his own), his mother, and his current mistress, "a beautiful, aristocratic-looking woman with a voice like a handsaw."[13] His vanity was immediately aroused when he noticed that Reed had a camera. Jack was put to work and over the next hour he photographed "General Urbina on foot, with and without sword; General Urbina on three different horses; General Urbina with and without his family; General Urbina's three children, on horseback and off; General Urbina's mother, and his mistress; the entire family, armed with swords and revolvers; . . . one of the children holding a placard upon which was inked: General Tomás Urbina R."[14]

Like many violent men, Urbina was extravagantly devoted to his mother. But mother love did not prevent him from taking potshots at the old lady from time to time. One such episode took place during Reed's stay at Las Nieves. Urbina's "physician," a lice-ridden ex-apothecary from Parral, explained to Reed that "there has been some little trouble. The General has not been able to walk for two months from rheumatism . . . and sometimes he is in great pain, and comforts himself with *aguardiente*. . . . Tonight he tried to shoot his mother. He always tries to shoot his mother . . . because he loves her very much."[15]

Urbina's cruelty was exceeded only by that of Rodolfo ("The Butcher") Fierro, the man who killed 300 prisoners while pausing only to rest his tiring trigger finger. In a textbook case of poetic justice, it was Fierro who killed Urbina (at Villa's order) and then died a horrible death in quicksand. Fierro died both rich and friendless. While not one of his soldiers lifted a hand to save him, his descent into the mire was accelerated by the heavy bags of gold that he carried.

Reed was itching to get into action. But Urbina dawdled and drank, posed and strutted, and deflected Reed's goading with offers of money and women.

Then one day he was ready to move. There was no hint of a plan; the entire process was a miracle of improvisation. Reed had resigned himself to another ten days at Las Nieves "when the General suddenly changed his mind. He came out of his room, roaring orders. In five minutes the house was all bustle and confusion—officers rushing to pack their serapes, *mozos* and troopers saddling horses, peons with armfuls of rifles rushing to and fro."[16]

Leaving behind a tearful mother and mistress, Urbina set forth at the head of a 100-man column. This was *la tropa*, the irregulars Reed rode with in his first taste of combat. It was during this campaign that he really saw the fallacy of anti-Mexican bigotry. "Americans had insisted that the Mexican was fundamentally dishonest. . . . Now for two weeks I lived with as rough a band of ex-outlaws as there were in the army. . . . They had not been paid a cent for six weeks. . . . I was a stranger with a good outfit, unarmed. I had a hundred and fifty pesos. . . . And I never lost a thing. But more than that, I was not permitted to pay for my food. . . . Every suggestion that I should pay for it was an insult."[17]

But they did allow him to pay the music for a dance. After the festivities he had a frightening experience—one that brought him face to face with the extremes of mindless hostility and selfless friendship that one might encounter among such men. Julián Reyes, a drunken religious fanatic with the Virgin emblazoned on his sombrero, angrily reproached Reed over his noncombatant status. Why

"EJERCITO CONSTITUCIONAL"

SERVICIO MILITAR.

SALVOCONDUCTO en favor de _John Reed_

quien por orden de este Cuartel General, puede viajar de

ésta á _C. Juárez_

Libertad y Constitución.

Chih. Feb. 2 de 191_4_

Por orden del General en Jefe,

El Teniente Coronel Jefe de E. M. G.

EL CAPITAN 1º DE E. M.

Marcial Poole

Pass issued to John Reed (2 February 1914) by the *División del Norte.*

wouldn't he fight in a just cause, Reyes wanted to know? Reed replied that his orders were not to fight.

"What do I care for orders. . . . We want no correspondents. . . . We want no words printed in a book. We want rifles and killing, and if we die we shall be caught up among the saints. Coward! *Huertista!*"[18]

Reyes's diatribe was brusquely interrupted by Gino Güereca, bravest of *la tropa's* captains. "Julián Reyes, you know nothing. This *compañero* comes thousands of miles (to) fight for Liberty. He goes into battle without arms, he's braver than you are, because you have a rifle. Get out now, and don't bother him any more!"[19]

Reed and Gino become *compadres*, Gino introduces him to his family, and they make plans to hunt for a treasure. "Tomorrow," said Gino, "I shall take you to the lost gold mine of the Spaniards. Only the Indians know of them—and I. . . . We'll be rich."[20]

Tomorrow brought not riches but the end of the dream. *La tropa*, which formed the *maderista* advance guard, was guarding a pass in eastern Durango called Puerta de la Cadena. The area was swarming with *colorados* and Reed had been amply briefed about "the bandits who made Orozco's revolution." "They were so called," he wrote, "because their flag was red, and because their hands were red with slaughter, too. They swept through northern Mexico, burning, pillaging, and robbing the poor."[21]

Twelve hundred *colorados* fell on *la tropa* at Puerta de la Cadena. In the ensuing action—a massacre—most of Jack's friends were killed. Among them was the gallant Gino Güereca, who fell after downing six *colorados.*

Abandoning camera and overcoat, Reed escaped over the desert. During his flight, which he recalled as "a page out of Richard Harding Davis," he stopped with the family of Gino Güereca. (They had not yet heard of their son's death.) Though the kindly Güerecas gave Reed food and drink, they did not dare let him stay. They feared the vengeance of the *colorados* if he were found on the premises.

Reed caught up with the stragglers at Santo Domingo, about twenty-five miles west of La Cadena. There he found *don* Petronilo, a colonel, beside himself with grief. Trying to comfort him, Reed told *don* Petronilo that he should be proud of the brave fight made by his outnumbered men. But this was not the cause of the colonel's grief. He had a more personal reason: the *colorados* had captured his wife.[22]

Reed's adventures with *la tropa* end with a story that is frankly difficult to believe. Elizabetta, the Indian mistress of a captain in *la tropa*, deserts her lover to spend a night with Reed and then returns to him the next day. Though the captain makes a blustering complaint to the colonel and reproaches Reed for his discourtesy as "the guest of this *tropa*," he takes no further action.[23]

This is the stuff of a French bedroom farce, not of the *machismo*-obsessed world of revolutionary Mexico. It is hardly believable that a tough ex-bandit who rose to a command position under Urbina would have let himself be cuckolded in front of the entire troop by an unarmed gringo.

What impelled Reed to tell such an implausible story? Here one must avoid being overly judgmental. *Insurgent Mexico*, as noted, is partly a work of fiction. With journalistic standards being what they were, and with Reed's colleagues filing fraudulent dispatches from the safety of hotel rooms, he undoubtedly felt entitled to embroider his narrative here and there. He, after all, was one of the few who had actually crossed the border and taken the risks. In addition, Reed was something of a sexual braggart. Such a tale of battlefield seduction would make good reading among Jack's raffish cronies in the Village.

Reed's adventure with *la tropa* is followed by another mysterious gap, similar to the unexplained period between Chihuahua City and his reappearance in the Durango sierra. The questionably authentic Elizabetta incident takes place in Santo Domingo, Durango. Then Jack suddenly materializes in Chihuahua City. Though he is maddeningly vague on dates, he fixes the time of his appearance there as "two weeks before the advance on Torreón."[24] That would make it early March 1914.

When did Reed and Villa first meet? This is frankly a puzzler. A Reed biographer, Robert Rosenstone, places the initial meeting as early as 26 December 1913. As a source he cites two letters of Reed's, probably written to Eddy Hunt, and dated the 21st and 26th. These letters were printed in the February 1914 *Metropolitan* under the title "With Villa in Mexico."[25]

This appears to conflict with Part II of *Insurgent Mexico,* the coverage devoted to Villa. This section is divided into eight chapters. The first, titled "Villa Accepts a Medal," contains the previously mentioned reference to "two weeks before the advance on Torreón," i.e., early March. But the chapter says nothing about an earlier meeting with Villa, nor do Chapters 2 and 3 ("The Rise of a Bandit" and "A Peon in Politics"). These chapters are devoted entirely to biographical information on Villa. The first direct Villa-Reed dialogue occurs in Chapter 4 ("The Human Side"). How does one reconcile the *Metropolitan* version of a late 1913 meeting with *Insurgent Mexico's* indications that Villa and Reed did not meet till at least the following March?

An explanation can be ventured in terms of the book's extremely haphazard chronology. Part VI predates Part I. (We know this because there are references in Part VI to episodes that precede Mercado's defeat at Ojinaga.)

It is entirely possible that Reed set the first chapter of Part II in early March and then—without informing his readers—simply introduced previous material for narrative effect. Reed was a poet and used his poetic license with abandon.

Reed captures Villa's essence as brilliantly as he did Urbina's. Yet the section abounds with factual errors. Commenting on the bandit phase of Villa's career, he places it at twenty-two years rather than sixteen. (Had Reed been correct, Villa would have turned outlaw at the age of ten.) Reed also reports that Villa was "delivering milk in the streets of Chihuahua [*sic*]" when he committed the murder that sent him to the sierra. As for the victim, he is identified as "a government official."[26]

Reed is equally shaky in describing events that took place in the early days of the Revolution. He states that Villa brought his men to El Paso and placed them "at the command of Madero."[27] It is hardly likely that the American authorities would have sat with folded arms while 700 armed Mexican revolutionaries crossed the border.

Reed also errs in references to the roles of Villa and Huerta during the Orozco rebellion. He states there was only one decisive battle in the campaign, supposedly won by Villa with an "inferior force." There were, in fact, four decisive actions in the Orozco campaign, two of them won by Huerta after Villa had been removed from the scene. (As much as he detested "*el borrachito,*" not even Villa questioned Huerta's soldierly abilities.)

Nor does Reed have his facts straight about Huerta's attempt to execute Villa. He states that "Huerta suddenly summoned Villa before a court-martial and charged him with insubordination—claiming to have wired an order to Villa in Parral, which order Villa said he never received."[28] Reed also asserts that it was Alfonso Madero who stayed Villa's execution. As we know, Villa was court-martialed for refusing to give up a mare he had taken from a wealthy rancher. And it was Colonel Rubio Navarrete and another Madero brother, Raúl, who saved Villa from the firing squad.

Also misleading is Reed's information about a posthumous tribute paid to Abraham González. Villa had ordered that the body of his old mentor be taken from its shallow grave at the bottom of Bachimba Canyon and re-buried with full honors in Chihuahua City. Reed reports that this was done "in February, exactly one year after Abram [*sic*] González was murdered by the Federals at Bachimba Canyon . . . ."[29] But González was killed in March.

How to account for these errors? The last one appears to be carelessness; the others are obviously attributable to misinformation. Reed caught Villa early in his career, when information about him was largely oral. A reliable historical record had yet to be written, and Reed obtained his data by canvassing Villa's followers. Their imprecise recollections—coupled with Reed's limited Spanish—contributed to these deviations from fact. Yet not one was total invention—Villa *had* been a bandit, he *had* killed a man in his youth, he *had* put himself and his men at Madero's service, he *had* been sentenced to death by Huerta.

Though Reed may have erred about details of Villa's past, it is a magnificently true-to-life Villa that he puts on canvas. Not only does he show us Villa's more obvious personality traits—the ferocity, the quick intelligence, the tremendous lust for life—but he also reveals characteristics overlooked by other chroniclers.

One of these is flexibility. As the product of a macho-male chauvinist culture, Villa would not be expected to have advanced views about the participation of women in public affairs. Yet he showed himself amazingly receptive to new ideas. In addition to Luz Corral (his only recognized lawful spouse), Villa had a succession of "wives" during his campaigns. These marriages were "legal" to the extent that Villa was always able to intimidate some frightened priest or civil registry official into performing the ceremony.

When Reed interviewed Villa, the incumbent was "a cat-like, slender young girl, who is the mistress of his house in Chihuahua."[30] This was probably Juana Torres, a dark-eyed beauty he had discovered in a Torreón tailor shop. Reed asked Villa how he felt about women being given the right to vote. At first Villa was skeptical. "Women seem to me to be things to protect, to love. . . . They are full of pity and softness. Why, a woman would not give an order to execute a traitor." When Reed replied that women could be crueler and harder than men, Villa called over his mistress. "Last night," he said, "I caught three traitors crossing the river to blow up the railroad. . . . Shall I shoot them or not?" The girl protested that she knew nothing about such matters, but Villa insisted on an answer. "They were traitors—Federals," he said. "What shall I do? Shall I shoot them or not?" "Oh well, shoot them," she finally replied.

Villa was delighted. With this example of heightened political consciousness, it was as if a new world had opened to him. For the next few days he went about the house, querying the cook and the chambermaid about their ideas on the presidency.[31]

This revelation may have indirectly produced a change in Villa's domestic ménage. Tiring of the docile Juana Torres, he replaced her with the infinitely more "liberated" Otilia Meraz. It was a decision he would regret. Shrewish and promiscuous, Meraz carried on affairs with a number of Villa's officers and openly taunted him with her infidelities.[32]

Reed also illuminates Villa's complete lack of personal ambition. He denied coveting the presidency of Mexico and became annoyed when Reed kept bringing up the subject. "I am a fighter, not a statesman," he explained. "I am not educated enough to be President. I only learned to read and write two years ago [not true]. How could I, who never went to school, hope to be able to talk with the foreign ambassadors and the cultivated gentlemen of the Congress?"[33] As Reed persisted, Villa's exasperation mounted. He finally threatened to have him spanked and sent to the border. But Villa's good humor was soon restored. He had acquired a genuine liking for the *chatito* (pug nose), as he called Reed. From then on, their interviews would invariably end with this facetious query from Villa. "Well, aren't you going to ask me today whether I want to be President?"[34]

Of equally high order were Reed's perceptions of Villa's role as civil administrator and political theorist, subjects that will be covered in a later chapter.

We now come to Reed's meeting with Venustiano Carranza. Carranza, then Villa's shaky ally, would soon become his implacable enemy. As usual, Reed gives no date for the meeting, which took place in the border town of Nogales. But we know that it occurred around the end of February. By early March Reed was back in Chihuahua and the main topic of the Carranza-Reed meeting was the 16 February killing by *villistas* of an Englishman named William Benton. Benton, a wealthy rancher, was enraged because Villa's men were making off with his cattle. He came to Villa and angrily (some say drunkenly) threatened him with a pistol. Villa immediately ordered his execution and he was shot (some say clubbed to death) by "The Butcher" Fierro.

Ignoring the human aspect of the Benton case, Carranza saw it entirely as a matter of protocol. Following Benton's murder, the United States had made a protest to Villa. Why, Carranza wanted to know, hadn't the protest been lodged with him, the First Chief of the Constitutionalist movement? And why had the complaint been made by the United States when Benton was a British subject? (Carranza was outraged that England still recognized Huerta.) "To the United States I say the Benton case is none of your business," he shouted. He then accused England, "the bully of the world," of using "the United States as a cat's paw."[35]

As Carranza continued to fume, Reed relates that he "tried to think that here was the voice of aroused Mexico thundering at her enemies; but it seemed like nothing so much as a . . . senile old man, tired and irritated."[36]

Though Villa was not discussed during the interview, Reed received ample exposure to Carranza's views about him through conversations with second-level *carrancistas*. Jack summarized these views as follows: We [read Carranza] have confidence in Villa because he has done well as a fighting man. But, being an ignorant peon, he should not attempt to mingle in the affairs of government. Furthermore, he has said foolish things and made mistakes that we will have to remedy. These sentiments were reinforced by this patronizing statement from Carranza's headquarters: "There is no misunderstanding between General Villa and myself. He obeys my orders without question, as any common soldier. It is unthinkable that he would do anything else."[37]

Again, Reed demonstrates his remarkable capacity for getting to the heart of the artichoke. With unfailing accuracy he shows us every facet of Carranza's complex psyche—the honesty and the vanity, the rectitude and the arrogance, the high-minded patriotism and the insufferable self-righteousness. For all Carranza's idealism, Reed records that he could never detect in him "one gleam of sympathy for, or understanding of, the peons."[38]

American reaction to Reed's reports on Mexico ran the gamut from wild adulation to disapproval of their earthy realism. We have mentioned Max Eastman's telegram on receiving "Mac—American." An equally laudatory—and far longer—message came from the normally restrained Walter Lippmann. Wrote Lippmann:

> Your first two articles [in *Metropolitan*] are undoubtedly the finest reporting that's ever been done. It's kind of embarrassing to tell a fellow you know that he's a genius. . . . I just can't begin to tell you how grand the articles are. . . . You have perfect eyes, and your power of telling leaves nothing to be desired. I want to hug you, Jack. If all history had been reported as you are doing this, Lord—I say that with Jack Reed reporting begins. . . .[39]

Dave Carb, playwright and longtime friend, opined that the material was more Reed than Mexico while the *Nation* made old-maidish references to "lurid exaggeration" and "disgusting naturalism."[40]

More complex was the reaction of Lincoln Steffens. Reed returned from Mexico in the spring of 1914. That winter, following publication of Reed's book and the outbreak of the First World War, Steffens made his own pilgrimage to Mexico. Embarking from New York, he sailed for Veracruz by way of Havana. There he attached himself to Carranza's headquarters. We have already discussed the response of Reed and Steffens to the Mexican Revolution: Reed rallying to the colorful Villa, Steffens to the staid First Chief. Steffens, as noted, considered Villa an "illiterate, unscrupulous, unrevolutionary bandit."

And that wasn't all. He also saw Villa as a *pistolero*-for-hire on the order of Pascual Orozco—but on a more dangerous level. Where Orozco had only been the creature of the Chihuahua cattle barons, Steffens saw Villa as nothing less than Wall Street's man in Mexico. "The reds in New York who were watching Mexico were on Villa's side," he wrote, "but the only reason they gave was that he was at least a bandit . . . whereas Carranza was a respectable, landowning bourgeois. Jack Reed talked that way and he went in on Villa's side."[41] Steffens claimed to have talked to people on Wall Street who preferred Villa to Carranza because Carranza was "obstinate, narrowminded, proud as hell" and "won't listen to reason."[42]

With due respect, Steffens was capable of colossal errors in judgment. Soviet Communism was the future that worked, Mussolini was the "right man" formed out of a rib of Italy by the "divine Dictator," and Stalin's genocidal kulak purge was a policy that "worked pretty well."[43]

Steffens was equally off base in his view of Villa as a closet capitalist. Villa, born a peon, accomplished outstanding social reforms while military governor of Chihuahua. Carranza, by contrast, dragged his feet on such issues as land reform and stressed political goals to the exclusion of socioeconomic ones. Steffens himself characterized Carranza as a landlord and employer who "under the strain of strikes . . . shot into and put down fighting labor."[44]

How could Steffens have made such a massive blunder? This explanation suggests itself. There was a political rivalry between Steffens and Reed, with Reed trying to stake out a position to the Left of Steffens. This may have been an effort by Steffens to undercut Reed, a move in their continuing game of redder-than-thou. What better way to bolster his radical prestige than to paint Villa, Reed's hero, as Wall Street's stooge? Whatever Steffens's motive, his plan to "whiten" Villa failed. Following publication of Reed's material, a far larger audience than "the reds in New York" saw Villa as a revolutionary hero.

Insurgent Mexico came out in 1914. The coverage on Carranza, which had first appeared in the September 1914 *Metropolitan*, was incorporated as Part V of *Insurgent Mexico*. Out of print for many years, the book is now out in two new editions.

To measure the semi-fictional *Insurgent Mexico* against the reality of insurgent Mexico in the time of John Reed, it would be a sound idea to reverse the old adage of "penny wise and pound foolish." The book is "penny foolish" for its factual flaws and partly fictive content but "pound wise" for its splendid characterization, disciplined prose, and superlative descriptive artistry. As John Dos Passos commented, it was Mexico that really taught Reed to write.

——— 7 ———

The Indispensables:
Felipe Angeles
and Louise Bryant

CONTRARY TO POPULAR LEGEND, opposites don't always attract. Feeling between them is often one of the deepest revulsion. Yet these antagonists will at times unite in loyalty to a third party. The latter are usually charismatic figures—born with the magnetism to attract mutually antipathetic followers and make them work as a team.

Such a personality belonged to Francisco Villa. His entourage included barbarians like Urbina and Fierro—and cultivated men like Abraham González. González had been Villa's good angel and, within a year of his death, Villa found another, a man with the appropriate name of Felipe Angeles. Angeles replaced González as Villa's mentor and fulfilled other functions as well. Along with being a guide and role model, he was Villa's leading military adviser and architect of his greatest victories. (The defeats came about when Villa failed to heed Angeles's advice.)

But it would be an error to conceive of this as a puppet and puppeteer partnership, with Villa an object manipulated by Angeles. Villa had scored impressive victories before their relationship began, and it was these victories that had attracted Angeles to him. They fully complemented each other and Angeles deferred to Villa as a master of improvisation and guerrilla tactics as much as Villa did to Angeles as a classic tactician and "book man." This points up an interesting irony. Villa commanded both large formations in set-piece battles and small bands in guerrilla actions. But—and this is almost unique in history—Villa's progression was not from small band to large formation but rather from small band to large formation and then *back* to small band. When he commanded big units and listened to Angeles, he was unbeatable. When he commanded big units and disregarded Angeles, he was defeated. Yet when he went back to small-scale harassment, he regained a measure of success. But it was only with the big formations and heavy artillery that he could become master of Mexico—and for that he needed Angeles. In that important respect, Felipe Angeles was Francisco Villa's Indispensable Man.

Felipe Angeles was born in 1869. His birthplace was the village of Zacualtipán, Hidalgo, and he was of predominantly Indian stock. His father, also called Felipe, was a small farmer and soldier. He served in the Mexican-American War of 1847 and French intervention of 1862, rising to the rank of colonel.[1]

Young Felipe obviously inherited his father's military gifts. At the unprecedented age of 14 he was admitted to the Colegio Militar, Mexico's West Point. There he excelled in all subjects and particularly in mathematics and the physical sciences.[2]

Following graduation he was appointed a teacher at the Colegio. This teaching stint was interrupted by two technical missions abroad, one to France in 1902 and one to the United States in 1904. During this period he was gaining recognition as one of Mexico's most promising young officers, particularly in the field of artillery. Rising rapidly in the ranks, he continued to serve on the Colegio Militar's faculty, writing textbooks on geometry, ballistics, and physics.[3]

By 1909 Angeles was a full colonel. He was again sent abroad, this time for advanced training at the École d'Application in Fontainebleau, near Paris.

Angeles was in Europe when the *maderista* revolution broke out. Madero, who had tremendous respect for his abilities, appointed him director of the Colegio Militar after his victory. At this time he was raised to the rank of brigadier-general.[4]

In 1912, when the Orozco revolt broke out, Angeles organized several battalions that took part in Huerta's successful campaign against the Chihuahua renegade. Later that year Angeles was in Morelos, campaigning against the *zapatistas*.

Though Angeles deplored Zapata's rising against Madero, he was not unsympathetic to *zapatista* demands for land reform and social justice. His conduct of the war was humane, and he refrained from killing *zapatista* prisoners or setting fire to fields of pro-Zapata *campesinos*. This had been a regular practice of General Aureliano Blanquet, commanding forces in the neighboring state of Mexico. The rebellion had spilled over into Mexico from Morelos, under the direction of a Zapata lieutenant named Genovevo de la O.[5]

In line with this humanitarian approach, Angeles severely criticized two of his predecessors in the Morelos combat zone. These were Generals Juvencio Robles and Adolfo Jiménez Castro, who had bragged of hanging a *zapatista* from every tree.[6]

These were times of great danger for Madero. The *cuartelazo* (garrison revolt) that would overthrow him was now in its final planning stage. Its leaders were Felix Díaz, the old dictator's nephew, General Bernardo Reyes, ex-governor of Nuevo León, and General Manuel Mondragón, a veteran malcontent and intriguer. Fully in sympathy with the plot was Victoriano Huerta. He was temporarily on the retired list, having been removed for misappropriating funds advanced to him during the Orozco campaign.

The insurrectionists made their first move on 9 February 1913. Failing to take the *zócalo* (main plaza), they seized the Ciudadela Fortress and dug in for a long siege. During the *zócalo* fighting Reyes had been killed and General Villar, commander of loyal forces in the plaza, severely wounded.

To replace Villar, Madero had intended to appoint Felipe Angeles. But, in accordance with a now familiar pattern, the indecisive Madero acted as his own worst enemy. He referred the matter to his ministers and they ruled that Angeles was too junior in rank to be appointed plaza commander. He was shunted off to the western sector of the city while the plaza command was given to Huerta. "And with this," wrote Roberto Blanco Moheno, "the last hope was lost."[7]

Huerta's appointment was followed, in rapid succession, by the Tragic Ten Days, Huerta's seizure of power, and Madero's murder.

As a Madero loyalist, Angeles was promptly arrested. Fortunately for him, he had friends in high places. Manuel Mondragón, Huerta's new Minister of War, was his godfather. He visited Angeles in his cell and made a wholehearted attempt to win him over to the *huertista* cause. Though Angeles rebuffed this overture, he agreed to a second Mondragón proposal: that he go on a military mission to Belgium.[8] But Huerta overruled his Minister of War and Angeles remained in confinement. The friction between Huerta and Angeles had a personal as well as political basis. Though both were of indigenous background, Huerta, with his gruff mannerisms and shaved head, evolved as a "Prussian" type while Angeles—who had lived in France and spoke the language—projected more of a "French" image. Brilliant, debonair, and immaculately groomed, he could have passed for a graduate of St. Cyr.

After Mondragón's failure to help his godson, Angeles's cause was taken up by another high-placed reactionary. This was a lawyer and *científico* (one of the technocratic elite that surrounded Díaz) named Manuel Calero. Calero persuaded Huerta to release Angeles in July; the following month he was sent on a study mission to Paris.[9]

This was a serious miscalculation on Huerta's part. Normally distrustful to the point of paranoia, he let a dangerous genie out of the bottle when he released Angeles. On reaching Paris, Angeles's first act was to offer his services to Miguel Díaz Lombardo, Carranza's representative abroad. On 17 October 1913, Angeles crossed the border at Nogales and joined the Constitutionalist forces.[10]

At first Carranza was delighted. He gave a banquet for Angeles and appointed him Secretary of War in the Constitutionalist government. But the appointment did not sit well with another important revolutionary: Alvaro Obregón. These two able men took a strong and immediate dislike to one another. Obregón lost no time in voicing his displeasure to Carranza: "If we are fighting the Federals (who treacherously murdered Madero), how is it possible that the Revolution can make a Federal Secretary of War?"[11] Obregón was a powerful man and Carranza acceded to his wishes. In a humiliating demotion, Angeles was reduced to something called "Subsecretary of War in Charge of the Office."

This demotion, added to the feeling that he was distrusted by powerful individuals in a movement he had embraced so wholeheartedly, created in Angeles a "delirium of persecution."[12] Unappreciated at Constitutionalist headquarters, he began to cast his eye in an easterly direction—to the region where Francisco Villa was operating. With admiration and astonishment, he had been observing the triumphs of the *División del Norte*. After Villa's victory at Ojinaga he sent him a laudatory telegram.

This was the beginning of one of history's most successful mutual admiration societies. Villa immediately wired Carranza, requesting that the First Chief attach Angeles to the *División del Norte*. Carranza agreed, and the next day a rapturous Villa greeted an equally delighted Angeles. "Ah, my General Angeles!" Villa exulted. "That damned old greybeard (Carranza) doesn't know how he helped the cause of the people by sending you to teach my boys how to handle artillery."[13]

Elegant Felipe Angeles and rough Francisco Villa—the Revolution's Odd Couple—lost no time in pooling their resources. Angeles joined the *División del Norte* right after Ojinaga; Villa was then preparing for the march southward to Torreón and Zacatecas. We have mentioned the role played by Angeles at Zacatecas; his expertise also contributed to *villista* victories at San Pedro de las Colonias, Paredón, Torreón, and Ramos Arizpe. The latter location, near Saltillo, was the site of that diversionary thrust ordered by Carranza to liberate the capital of his native state.

The role of Angeles as a military adviser to Villa has commanded so much attention that one tends to overlook the almost equally important role he played in the civil arena. To measure Angeles's true value to Villa, his services as a political strategist should be evaluated as carefully as those he rendered in the military sphere.

We get our first look at the political man just before the battle of Zacatecas. Though Huerta's days were numbered, there was so much dissension within the movement opposing him that it was a neck-and-neck race whether Huerta would fall before the coalition opposing him broke up.

In late May, following the capture of Saltillo, Carranza had given an interview to a journalist named Heriberto Barrón. In the interview he had not only rejected Villa's protestations of loyalty—referring to them as "the hypocrisies of that bandit"—but also attacked Madero. Telling Barrón that he would not deliver himself into the hands of the *maderistas,* he added that the "shortcomings of Madero and Pino Suárez were the cause of disaster. . . ."[14]

The astute Angeles lost no time in making capital of the situation. Madero was the saint of the Revolution and Carranza's words bordered on sacrilege. In an interview with the same journalist, he attacked Carranza's "dictatorial and absolutist tendencies" and accused him of disrespect to the memory of Madero.[15]

A more severe crisis came up just before the attack on Zacatecas.

In an effort to undercut Villa, Carranza had ordered three other generals to lead the assault. They were Pánfilo Natera, an incompetent, and the Arrieta brothers, longtime enemies of Villa. This decision was followed by an exchange of telegrams between Villa and Carranza, ending with a terse message of resignation by Villa.

Though Carranza was quick to accept, it soon became apparent that Villa's "resignation" was purely rhetorical. The *División del Norte's* generals began a telegram campaign of their own, ending with this insubordinate declaration: ". . . MORE IMPORTANT [than your desires] ARE THOSE OF THE MEXICAN PEOPLE FOR WHOM THE PRESTIGIOUS AND VICTORIOUS SWORD OF GENERAL VILLA IS INDISPENSABLE."[16]

Even more extreme was the reaction of one *División* general, a hot-headed *norteño* named Maclovio Herrera. Pointing his pistol at a trembling telegrapher, he ordered him to send this message: "DON VENUSTIANO CARRANZA, SALTILLO. YOU ARE A SONOFABITCH. SIGNED MACLOVIO HERRERA."

Herrera was restrained by the cool hand of Felipe Angeles. Angeles had signed the other telegrams and yielded to no one in his desire to cut down Carranza and Obregón. But this was not the way. "Put away your pistol," he said, "do me this favor, General Herrera. This is a time for reflection, not violence."[17] Angeles was doubtessly reflecting on the political maneuvering that would follow the fall of Huerta. It was in this arena that Carranza and Obregón could be bested.

The arena proved to be a convention, set up in October for the purpose of forming a new government. Before the convention Angeles figured in an episode, both ludicrous and ironic, in which he helped save the life of his worst enemy. In September, following Huerta's flight and Carranza's entry into Mexico City, Obregón came to Chihuahua. His purpose was to negotiate with Villa on Carranza's behalf. There he was exposed to the extremes of Villa's mercurial temperate. At first the Centaur embraced him and called him *compañerito* (little companion). Then, on intercepting a compromising telegram, he called him a traitor and ordered him shot. The decision caused a split among Villa's followers. The savages—Urbina, Fierro et al.—were vociferously in favor of the execution. But they were opposed by the more civilized *villistas*—Díaz Lombardo, whom Angeles had approached in Paris; Raúl Madero, the late

President's brother; and Angeles. As Villa's guest, Obregón was bound by the rules of hospitality. To slay him under such conditions, reasoned Angeles, would be an ineradicable black mark against the *villista* cause. Obregón was released and allowed to return to Mexico City.

The convention, held in Aguascalientes, opened on 10 October. The role of its major actors—Villa, Carranza, and Obregón—will be discussed more fully in the next chapter. Here the focus will be on the activities of Angeles. During the convention's cut-and-thrust, a severe wound to the Obregón-Carranza coalition was dealt by a cementing of relations between Villa and Zapata. In forging this alliance, Felipe Angeles played a major role.

Even before the convention, Angeles had made discreet and successful approaches to the *zapatistas*. Then, at one of the opening meetings, he read a letter from *zapatista* General Samuel Fernández. It stated that the *villistas* were in full accord with Zapata's radical Plan de Ayala (an implicit rejection of Carranza's more moderate Plan de Guadalupe) and that the *División del Norte* was authorized to represent the interests of the *Ejército Libertador* (Zapata's army) at the convention.[18] Angeles was then sent to Morelos for the purpose of inviting *zapatista* delegates to the convention.

The Zapata men, after first making a detour to confer with Villa, arrived at the convention on 26 October. Fiery oratory was followed by a nasty clash between Paulino Martínez, a *zapatista*, and Obregón. The men from the south had twenty-six delegates but wanted sixty. The rule was one delegate per 1,000 men in the field and the *zapatistas* claimed 60,000 men under arms. This declaration brought forth a sarcastic query from Obregón: if Zapata had 60,000 men, why was he unable to take Mexico City? He had captured the capital with 23,000 men, following a march of 2,500 miles. Martínez shot back that Obregón had entered Mexico City after making a deal with the Federals—a manuever the *zapatistas* would never stoop to.[19]

As a compromise candidate for provisional president, the convention elected Eulalio Gutiérrez of Zacatecas. An ex–copper-mine foreman, he had solid revolutionary credentials but no ties to either Villa or Carranza. Prior to Gutiérrez's election the delegates, by a 112–21 vote, had called on both Villa and Carranza to resign their posts by 6 P.M. of 10 November. (The Villa-Carranza rivalry was considered a major stumbling block to restoration of order in Mexico.) Villa complied but Carranza hedged (he considered Gutiérrez a tool of Villa) and let the deadline go by without obeying the resignation directive. At 6:15 the convention's Secretary of War, José Isabel Robles, declared Carranza in rebellion.[20] It was one of the Revolution's most singular ironies. Villa, the ex-bandit, had behaved with complete legality while Carranza, the epitome of bourgeois respectability, was now an outlaw.

The Villa-Angeles mutual admiration society was for a time threatened by the formation of another one: that of Villa and Zapata. Following the flight of Carranza to Veracruz, the *villistas* and *zapatistas* had marched into Mexico City. The Villa-Zapata meeting, held on 4 December, reinforced all Villa's respect for Zapata as a champion of the underdog. But there was one point on which he was reluctant to yield to the Morelos chieftain. Zapata had proposed a north-south division of the country, leaving him the right to finish off Carranza in his Veracruz stronghold. "I don't go north, you don't go south, General Villa. That way we respect each other." "But General," replied Villa, "keep in mind that these people are strong." Zapata guaranteed that he would be able to deal with Carranza. "Well, if you guarantee it," mumbled Villa. Zapata had won the argument.[21]

Shortly before Villa's decision, Angeles had strongly counseled against leaving Carranza to Zapata. "Zapata is an apostle (of revolution) but of war he knows nothing. His 'army' isn't worthy of the name. He doesn't have a single general who amounts to anything. If he asks to take charge of operations in the south don't let him. This is the time to chase Carranza to Veracruz [he was then in Córdoba] and throw him into the ocean. . . . If you give Carranza time to regroup nobody knows what will happen."[22]

Angeles proved a devastatingly accurate prophet. Though he may have been too harsh about *zapatista* military capacity (they functioned well as guerrillas in their *patria chica*), he was completely right in predicting that Zapata would never be able to handle Carranza and Obregón. Striking from their base in Veracruz, they pushed the *zapatistas* out of Puebla. In January 1915, Obregón marched into Mexico City. He now felt strong enough to confront Villa and, in April, the decisive battle took place near the *bajío* city of Celaya.

Celaya has been referred to as Villa's Waterloo. The statement is true only in the sense that it was the crucial battle of his career. If he won, he would be master of Mexico; if he lost, that opportunity would never again be given him.

On the other hand, Celaya was not a Waterloo in the sense that it was Villa's last battle. He fought other major ones, all of which he lost, and then minor ones, some of which he won. Celaya, if we pursue the Napoleonic analogy, was probably more a Moscow than a Waterloo—that is, the turning point in Villa's career.

Felipe Angeles also figured prominently in the Celaya engagement—as the man whose advice was ignored. Realizing how strong Obregón had become, Angeles counseled Villa against giving battle at Celaya. Villa should harass Obregón, make him lengthen his supply lines, draw him further into the interior, and then hit him at Irapuato, some 40 miles west of Celaya.

But Villa would not listen. "Didn't you advise me in December to march on Veracruz?" he asked. When Angeles protested that Obregón was now much stronger, Villa scorned him as a *perfumado* (perfumed one). Shortly afterwards, Angeles was approached by a member of his staff. "What do you think, general," he asked. Angeles let out a deep sigh. "He's going to his death," he replied.[23]

It was defeat rather than death that loomed ahead for Francisco Villa. There were actually two battles of Celaya, one on 6–7 April and the other from the 13th to the 15th. Both engagements were characterized by a pattern of *villista* recklessness and *obregonista* conservatism. At first, Villa's wild cavalry charges and kamikaze deployment of infantry came close to carrying the day. This was particularly true in the first engagement. But in the end it was Obregón's steadfastness that prevailed. World War I was then in progress, and Obregón had made a minute study of trench warfare tactics. How well these prevailed against Villa's suicidal *élan* is reflected in the casualty figures. Where Constitutionalist losses were 138 dead and 276 wounded, the *villistas* suffered 4,000 dead, 10,000 wounded or captured, and the loss of 32 guns, comprising all their artillery.[24]

From then on it was all downhill for Villa. After Celaya, Villa remarked that he would rather be beaten by a Chinese (he detested Orientals) than by Obregón.[25] Angeles suggested that Villa pull back to Chihuahua and regroup there; Villa again rejected his advice. Earlier on Angeles had predicted that if Villa ever suffered a major defeat it would be the end of the *División del Norte*.[26]

Now his prediction was coming true with a vengeance. Following Celaya, Villa was successively defeated at León (where Obregón lost his right arm), Aguascalientes, Zacatecas, and Torreón. The latter localities had been the scenes of his greatest victories. On 19 October 1915 the United States extended *de facto* recognition to Carranza. Recognition came on the heels of Carranza's acceptance of Secretary of State Lansing's request for a pledge that Mexico scrupulously protect American lives and property.[27] With American supplies now going to his enemies, Villa reverted to what he had been in the early days of the Revolution—a hit-and-run guerrilla raider in Chihuahua.

With the abrupt decline in Villa's fortunes, Angeles temporarily gave up the struggle against Obregón and Carranza. Crossing the border, he spent the next three years in the United States, first in El Paso and then in New York.

While in exile, this many-sided man concentrated on intellectual pursuits. In articles for exile publications, he refined his political philosophy. Liberalism, he decided, was an ideal of the past that should be replaced by what he defined as "the new liberty." This was evolutionary socialism. Though he considered Marx and Engels geniuses, he was not sure that Mexico was ready for socialism. When the 1917 Constitution was adopted, he denounced its "radical and Jacobin tendency" and saw it as the product of Carranza's "despotic ambition." In its place, he advocated a return to the 1857 Constitution (plus the Reform Laws) and adoption of "the democratic methods of Madero."[28] This represented a softening of views previously articulated by Angeles. Of conservative outlook, he had supported parliamentary democracy while espousing social concepts in the tradition of *noblesse oblige*. The prosperous had a moral duty to help the poor. At the same time, a radical transformation of the existing order was to be avoided.[29]

A faction called the Mexican Liberal Alliance was then in revolt against Carranza. Angeles joined it and returned to Mexico on 11 December 1918.

He joined Villa in northern Chihuahua, but it was soon obvious that the old magic was gone. The two men quarreled, with Villa accusing Angeles of having become *agringado* (Americanized) and Angeles protesting against Villa's inhumanity in the field.

In May 1919, Angeles broke with Villa. With only twelve men, he set out on his own. For six months he wandered about but accomplished nothing. Though a master of classic strategy, Angeles had no gift for guerrilla tactics. On 15 November he was betrayed and captured near Parral, his band having dwindled to four men.

Carranza immediately sent a telegram to General Manuel Diéguez, the area commander, decreeing a court-martial for Angeles. The result was a foregone conclusion. He was sentenced to death and executed by firing squad on 27 November. Angeles faced death with the same dignity that had characterized his life. He neatly folded his blanket, placed it on the cot in his cell, and gave his defense counsel a farewell *abrazo*. His last statement was a wish that peace be restored to Mexico.[30]

Though Villa and Angeles had not parted on good terms, Villa wept copiously when he heard of his friend's death. Later, in retirement, he kept a bronze bust of Angeles in his office.[31]

Francisco Villa's "good angels"—Abraham González and Felipe Angeles—could both have become President of Mexico. Had González evaded captivity in Chihuahua, his enormous prestige in the *maderista* camp would have made him an odds-on favorite to succeed Madero. As for Angeles, his destiny would have been altered had his advice been taken on one of two crucial occasions: when Carranza was holed up in Veracruz or when Obregón was challenging Villa at Celaya. Villa, as he repeatedly affirmed, had no presidential ambitions. Had he allowed Angeles to guide him, he would have broken the only military force capable of contesting his mastery over Mexico. His only potential rival was Zapata—but Villa and Zapata were on good terms. Even if they hadn't been, Zapata was militarily powerless outside his tropic domain in Morelos. With Villa in the position of undisputed power broker, who else but Angeles would he have raised to the presidency?

THAT FELIPE ANGELES FUNCTIONED AS AN INDISPENSABLE helpmate to Francisco Villa is beyond question. Would it be correct to assign the same role to Louise Bryant in her relationship with John Reed?

Louise Bryant has been the target of a bad press and of badmouthing by some of her contemporaries. Emma Goldman, whose generous spirit curdled in her last years, asserted that "Lincoln Steffens was right when he said about Louise (that) she was never a communist, she only slept with a communist."[32] Goldman also commented on Bryant's unhappy last years in Paris, describing a sordid scene "at the Select when two drunken Corsican soldiers carried her out of the cafe. What a horrible end. More and more I come to think that it is criminal for young middle-class American or English girls to enter radical ranks. They go to pieces. And even when they do not reach the gutter, as Louise did, their lives are empty. . . ."[33]

Also contributing to this picture of frivolity and degradation was William C. Bullitt, Bryant's second husband, from whom she was divorced in 1930. After apparently maneuvering his wife out of the country, he filed suit against her on 4 December 1929. Among other charges, he accused her of chronic drunkenness, of conducting a lesbian affair with the daughter of an English writer, and of running naked through a hotel lobby following the Harvard-Yale boat race.[34] The decree was granted on 24 March 1930, with Bullitt obtaining custody of their daughter, Anne Möen Bullitt. Bryant never saw her daughter again.

In view of this unflattering portrait, it may be at first difficult to conceive of Louise Bryant as a "Felipe Angeles" to John Reed, a strong, motivated, supportive partner who shared his ideology and aided his work. Were the attacks on her justified? What validity can we assign to the views of Goldman, Bullitt, et al.?

More positive evaluations are now emerging. An important contribution to this revisionist trend is *Friend and Lover*, a 1982 Bryant biography written by the journalist and feminist Virginia Gardner. This work, which followed a decade of research and interviews, contains the hitherto little-known information that Bryant was suffering from an incurable disease, probably contracted in 1927 and discovered in 1928. This ailment, known as Dercum's disease or adiposis dolorosa, is an affliction whose sufferers are mainly menopausal women between the ages of 35 and 50. Its features are obesity in its early stages, followed by weight loss, weakness, irritability, depression, and frequent attacks of weeping. (Hence the term dolorosa.)

There is no doubt that the disease was directly related to Bryant's disintegration. In his divorce stipulation, Bullitt states that the alcoholic pattern began in the 1926–27 period. Bryant had no previous drinking problem. Though Bohemian and sexually liberated, she was contemptuous of drunkenness. In her relationship with Eugene O'Neill, she appears almost as a Carrie Nation. She nagged O'Neill so persistently about his intemperance that Max Eastman was convinced that there was nothing more between Bryant and O'Neill "than her earnest desire to get him off the bottle." Later, "without Bryant to steer O'Neill from the bottle," he began to spend most of his time in a tough Village bar officially called the Golden Swan but known to habitués as the Hell Hole.[35]

Reed was also the target of Bryant's anti-alcoholic homilies. So much so that he sent her an exasperated letter objecting to her efforts to "censor . . . my actions . . . as you did in your letter telling me not to drink."[36] On another occasion Bryant wrote Reed about a party that had taken place in their apartment while he was recovering from surgery: "When I woke up I was all alone with many empty bottles and a terrible stale smell of booze."[37]

This much is clear: Bryant's alcohol-and-drug-related decline did not begin until at least six years after Reed's death.

Gardner has performed a useful service in challenging the myth of Bryant as a sort of super-groupie—a playgirl who attached herself to the great John Reed and claimed revolutionary credentials solely on the strength of having "slept with a communist."

Yet she goes too far in her (largely justified) hostility to the vindictive William C. Bullitt. In an Appendix, she suggests that Bullitt may have fabricated charges that one of his high-placed enemies, Under-Secretary of State Sumner Welles, was homosexual and attracted to blacks. This has been pretty well authenticated. In the early '50s an exposé magazine (copiously sued by other victims) printed a story that Welles had made sexual advances to a Pullman porter during a transcontinental train trip. Welles was alive at the time, but he neither took legal action nor denied the story. Though Gardner is right to puncture Bullitt's self-righteous posturing about Welles's "crimes," further verification can be found in a book by Bullitt's brother, Orville. (Despite the relationship, Orville Bullitt is an impartial observer.) Roosevelt, as Gardner relates, despised William Bullitt for his troublemaking; still, the President admitted "that there is truth in the allegations" and that "he was having Welles watched by a guardian (officially a bodyguard) . . . to see to it that Welles did not repeat such a performance."[38]

Gardner also criticizes the Harvard Alumni John Reed Committee, formed in 1934 for the purpose of honoring Reed. She blames the Committee for what she discerns as an effort to exclude Bryant from the ceremonies planned for her late husband. The Committee wanted some materials on Reed that were in Bryant's possession, but it definitely did not want Bryant as part of the package. Members of the Committee "had heard of the drinking, and doubtless knew of reports of the drugs. . . . What scandals she might cause if she returned to America! What an embarrassment to the Harvard men who longed to forget about her!"[39]

This seems unfair. However we may sympathize with Bryant and realize the extent to which she was victimized by her incurable disease, the fact remains that by 1934 she was so damaged by drugs and alcohol that she could well have turned the honor planned for her late husband into a humiliating disaster. On that basis, it seems that Gardner is judging the Committee too harshly.

It was a far different Louise Bryant who came to Reed in New York on 4 January 1916. The month before, in Portland, they had met and fallen in love. Bryant was then married to a local dentist, Dr. Paul Trullinger. By the standards of the Teens, especially in conservative Portland, she was avant-garde in every respect—intellectual interests, politics, life-style. She studied French, kept a studio, worked for women's suffrage, sold subscriptions to *The Masses*, and entertained Emma Goldman as a guest in her house. Though it isn't clear how Bryant and Reed first met (several people have claimed credit for bringing them together), it was a meeting that obviously produced sparks. Dr. Trullinger, an amiable, unaggressive man, was simply unable to compete with the world of adventure and commitment that Reed offered. Arriving in New York, Louise moved into Jack's Washington Square apartment. Their life together had begun.

Two areas must be examined in evaluating Bryant's services to Reed: the political and the personal.

As noted, Bryant was no revolution groupie. Along with suffragist activity and selling *The Masses*, she had become a protégée of Colonel C.E.S. Wood and his wife, Sara Bard Field. Wood, an attorney, resembled C. J. Reed in being a "traitor" to the establishment that produced him. As local hierarchs winced, Wood "contributed to *The Masses*, took IWW cases for nothing, bailed out and defended Margaret Sanger and (Emma) Goldman. . . ."[40] So Louise had a firm grounding in radical politics when she met Jack.

In some ways, Bryant was a fiercer ideologue than Reed. Jack was at times given to irony and self-mockery, even about things as sacred to both of them as the Russian Revolution. "What counts is what we do when we go home," he commented to Albert Rhys Williams. "It's easy to be fired by things here. We'll wind up thinking we're great revolutionaries. And at home? Oh, I can always put on another pageant!"[41]

Though Bryant developed her own doubts about the Soviet experiment, she expressed them in a less frivolous manner. On 11 September 1926, she gave an interview to Hearst's *New York American*. Stalin was then making his grab for power and—of Reed and Bryant's two great friends—Lenin was dead and Trotsky in decline. "I look to see Russia become one of the conservative nations of the world," she said, "and I believe all signs point . . . against any possibility of the much planned realization of the slogan, 'Workers of the World, Unite.'"

Bryant also challenged the commitment and ideological purity of Lincoln Steffens. So did Reed, but his reproaches were always more in sorrow than anger. Where Reed registered disappointment over the straying of an erring friend, Bryant's animadversions on Steffens were tinged with malice. In a letter to Granville Hicks, she furiously attacked Steffens's role in the McNamara case. "He told them (the McNamara brothers) he had the word of the authorities that they would get light sentences if they confessed. They got *life sentences*! Ask Steff how many times in the last twenty years or *if ever* he went to see those two Irish boys."[42]

This criticism was unjustified. Deeply regretting his error, Steffens was unrelenting in his efforts to obtain parole for the McNamaras. When a son was born to Ella Winter, Steffens's second wife, he received a warm letter of congratulations ending with the words "Bless you and Ella for that boy." It was signed "James B. McNamara, #25314, San Quentin Prison."[43]

Bryant also denigrated Steffens by comparing him to the Old Bolshevik Lev Kamenev, whom he physically resembled. Kamenev, of timid and vacillating disposition, was one of the two leaders who opposed armed insurrection at the time of the Bolshevik Revolution. In a venom-tipped invidious comparison, she first speaks of

Trotsky: ". . . a Marat; vehement, serpent-like, he swayed the assembly as a strong wind stirs the long grass." Then: "In striking contrast was another Bolshevik leader, Kameneff [*sic*], who reminded me of Lincoln Steffens. His way of expressing his opinions was as mild as Trotsky's was violent, sharp, and inflammatory."[44]

Also failing Bryant's ideological purity test was her sometime lover, Eugene O'Neill. O'Neill had once been an apostle of revolution but, as Bryant saw it, he couldn't stand the heat in the kitchen. His cynicism about the American working class, combined with his quietist response to revolution overseas and reaction at home, made Bryant view him as a "counterrevolutionary."[45]

The fidelity between Bryant and Reed was more spiritual and ideological than physical. Both had affairs on the side, Louise a protracted one with O'Neill and Jack a series of quick conquests. But these dalliances never really endangered their relationship. The biggest threat came from O'Neill; Bryant's physical hunger for him made her lead him on quite unfairly. "He (O'Neill) was still in love with her and she professed to be still in love with him, but her chance for adventure and personal recognition lay with Reed."[46]

In Bryant's fierce loyalty to Reed's cause, his battles became hers. An enemy of Reed was Alex Gumberg, brother of a high Bolshevik, who had been business manager of the Russian-language daily *Novy Mir* while in New York. Aloof and sardonic, Gumberg combined the functions of translator at the American Embassy and liaison with the Bolsheviks. Probably motivated by class antagonism, he saw Reed as a preppie and Ivy League dilettante playing at revolution. This unflattering evaluation stung Bryant as much as it did Reed. Reed and Gumberg quarreled frequently, and Bryant zealously took Reed's side.

Bryant also detested Gumberg for his criticism of a group she regarded as the Revolution's purest heroes. These were sailors from the naval base at Kronstadt, near Petrograd. Wrote Bryant: "Revolutionary discipline and all the intensity of that tremendous upheaval . . . known to history as the first proletariat [*sic*] revolution was largely due to the Cronstadt [*sic*] sailors." Lauding them as "true moralists," she remarked on how the sailors had forbidden drunkenness and punished thievery with death. "They cleaned first their own house," she concluded, "before they went abroad to sweep up the dirt of others."[47] During the insurrection Gumberg blamed the sailors for a delay in capture of the Winter Palace, Kerensky's last bastion in Petrograd. The Palace would have fallen earlier, he said, "if our friends the sailors had arrived here on time."[48]

Within a week of the Winter Palace's fall the Bolsheviks smashed a counterattack led by Kerensky and General Krasnov, commander of the Third Corps of Cossacks. During the fighting, Bryant had a harrowing experience. Participating in the assault was a group of Junkers, counterrevolutionary military cadets. From an armored car they fired into a crowd in St. Isaac's square. Bryant saved her life by flattening herself against a doorway. This was the closest brush with death experienced by either Bryant or Reed during the Revolution.[49]

An eloquent testimonial to Bryant's role as a revolutionary helpmate to Reed came from the late Louis Waldman, veteran labor lawyer and friend of both Jack and Louise. "[Jack] returned from Russia convinced the proletariat here was about to rise . . . and Louise was with him all the way. She always championed everything Jack said."[50]

Efforts to paint Bryant as an apolitical hanger-on also fail when one considers her grasp of tactics and the rigor of her judgments. She came, for example, to dislike anarchists and "Left-for-Left's-sake" radicals who are ever ready to sacrifice practical considerations to ideology. In a letter from Seattle, where she was on a speaking tour, she poured out her thoughts to Reed. The object of her disdain was a "silly Anarchist woman" who claimed anarchists were the only people who did anything for the Russian Revolution. "I am so sick of the Anarchists! They always pretend to be the last and final word on anything . . . . They ruin everything."[51]

Bryant was also a shrewd judge of fellow revolutionaries, at times appearing sharper than Reed. "It is interesting about Max [Eastman]," she wrote him from San Francisco. "The Russians *almost* hated him. 'This fellow is too slick—he does not touch us,' they said."[52]

One of Louise Bryant's finest hours as political activist came on 20 February 1919, when she testified before a subcommittee of the Senate Judiciary Committee chaired by Senator Lee S. Overman of North Carolina. The subcommittee was investigating "Bolshevik propaganda" and Overman, a patrioteering Claghorn, was a forerunner of Martin Dies and Joseph R. McCarthy.

In her testimony before Overman, Bryant served Reed as a shield as well as a sword.

Bryant wanted to testify. "The hearings," she wrote Reed from Washington, "are tragically funny. One feels the smell of decay and the utter impossibility of the old to understand the new." After Overman ignored a note in which Bryant volunteered to appear, she came right into the hearing and introduced herself. Overman tried to put her off but Bryant insisted. "'When will you let me know the exact day that I may testify?' He stammered and said 'Tomorrow.' So I said, 'Then I understand that you will tell me tomorrow when I will be heard?' and he said, 'yes.' And the whole room heard it."[53]

Once they had Bryant on the stand, the inquisitors' reticence vanished. Senator Nelson queried her so aggressively about her religious beliefs that she wryly commented that "it seems to me as if I were being tried for withcraft." When asked whether she believed Russia should have a Bolshevik government, she replied that it was a matter for the Russians to settle. She attacked American military intervention in Russia but denied wanting a Bolshevik government for the United States. "I do not think it would fit America at the present time," she said. High point of the hearing came the next day when Overman, with heavy gallantry, said the Committee intended to treat her like a lady. Bryant: "I do not want to be treated as a lady, but I want to be treated as a human being."[54]

Bryant's adroit and forthright performance left the senators with little stomach to take on Reed. Depleted by its two-day joust with Louise, the Committee rushed Jack through with perfunctory brevity.

Though Reed yielded to no one as an articulate communicator of his ideas, he was fortunate in having the equally articulate Bryant to render auxiliary services. These took the form of a two-month speaking tour in which she would tell "The Truth About Russia." The tour was organized by Anna Louise Strong, lifelong radical who was then on the staff of the *Seattle Union Record*. Traveling constantly, fighting off a bout of flu, she spoke in Detroit, Minneapolis, Spokane, the Seattle-Tacoma area, Everett (Washington), Ballard (Oregon), Portland, Berkeley, and Los Angeles. Bryant was a natural spellbinder and the tour proved an enormous success. In Minneapolis the overflow crowd included Sinclair Lewis. In Seattle, to an audience of longshoremen, her eloquence and fire played a major part in their refusal to load arms earmarked for the White forces of Admiral Kolchak. In Los Angeles, on 15 April, she began her talk with the dramatic message that "'Today Eugene Debs is on his way to prison.' To my happy amazement," she reported to Reed, "my whole audience burst into tears."[55]

On 17 March 1920, John Reed was arrested in Finland. Under an asumed name, he had gone to Russia the previous fall to straighten out a jurisdictional dispute between two rival American communist groups.

Though the technical charge against Reed was smuggling—he was carrying diamonds and cash—there is no doubt that the arrest had political overtones. Since January Reed had been under indictment in the United States on charges of criminal anarchy and conspiring to overthrow the government by force. Finland had a White regime and, when Reed was given permission to write, he told Bryant that he had been informed by the Finns *that I am kept in prison at the request of the United States government.*[56]

Working with furious energy, Bryant buttonholed important figures and had them send telegrams to Secretary of State Bainbridge Colby. Among the notables she corralled were Jane Addams, Arthur Garfield Hayes, Bernard Baruch, and the Republican Senator from Oregon.

Reed was freed in June, but Bryant's efforts played only a minor part in his release. He was exchanged for three anti-Soviet Finnish professors held by the Russians. The dénouement is described by Eadmonn MacAlpine, a mutual friend of Louise and Jack: "Jack returned to Russia and Lenin told him in my presence that the Finns had made a bad bargain as he would have exchanged a whole jail-full of Finns—not merely three professors—for Jack."[57]

Another example of Bryant's tenacity and devotion is the dangerous journey she undertook to join Reed in Russia after he had been released from captivity in Finland. Though the trip has been depicted in film as a hair-raising trek across ice and snow, this was artistic license. Bryant's journey took place in midsummer. She sailed from New York on 30 July and was in Petrograd before 15 September. The exact date of her arrival is unknown; the latter is the date of her reunion with Reed.

Still, the trip was hazardous enough. Her trajectory was New York-Gothenburg-Stockholm-Narvik-Vardo (on the northern tip of

Norway) and by fishing boat to Russia. She may have entered Russia at Murmansk, though this is not certain. If so, she faced an additional danger: Murmansk was held by the Allies and the Allies were supporting the Whites.

We have discussed the support Bryant rendered Reed in his capacity as a political man. Louise was also supportive of Jack in ways that had nothing to do with ideology or politics.

As much as Bryant wanted to advance Reed's career, her concern for his health was always paramount. In June 1916, Reed was covering the Republican convention in Chicago. A complaint to Bryant brought forth this anxious response: "I'm so sorry you aren't feeling well. If you *really feel* ill, Honey, run away from the silly conventions and come home. The most important thing in the world is your health. . . ."[58]

In November of that year, immediately following Reed's surgery, Bryant's concern intensified to the point of semi-hysteria: "Why was there *pus* in your wound," she wrote him at Johns Hopkins. "Please honey—tell me everything about it because I *must* know." "Must" is underlined three times.[59]

The following month, while Reed was still convalescing, she sent a letter that demonstrated not only concern for her lover but conviction that Reed's career would be best served by substituting healthful country living for an urban whirl of frivolity and dissipation. Bryant laments "the pity, the unpardonable pity that you always had to *waste* yourself with Greenwich Villages. . . . We can never take a chance like that again. That's why I think it will be so fine to do *work* out here (their rural cottage near Croton-on-Hudson). . . ."[60]

Probably the greatest tragedy of Louise Bryant's life is that she came to be judged on the basis of its final phase—the years marred by alcoholism, drugs, incurable disease, and the cruel egotism of her second husband. It was those unhappy years that created the negative image of Bryant as a freeloader on John Reed's journey to revolution. The shame of the later days completely eclipsed the luster of the early ones. Had Louise Bryant died in 1926, she would have enjoyed the same celebrity-in-her-own-right status as Eleanor Roosevelt or Krupskaya. Instead, she had the misfortune to live another ten years.

8

The Organization Men: Carranza and Obregón

HISTORY HAS RARELY SMILED ON THE ROMANTIC in his struggle against the organization man. Mark Antony, a romantic in more ways than one, dallied with Cleopatra while Octavian consolidated his power base in Rome. Bonnie Prince Charlie cut a dashing figure, but in the end it was the stodgy Hanoverians who prevailed. Trotsky, in Louise Bryant's rapturous view, may have had the ability to sway assemblies like "the strong wind stirs the long grass." But it was Stalin who had the sure, swift access to the committee chairmen and the file cabinets.

As heirs to the romantic tradition, Francisco Villa and John Reed contended with organization enemies their entire lives. But these struggles became meaningful only when Villa and Reed made their commitment to revolution. However annoying the Durango *rurales* may have been to Doroteo Arango and the Mount Auburn Street snobs to Margaret Reed's socially ambitious son, these pre-revolutionary enemies paled into insignificance when Villa and Reed moved up into the big leagues.

Both Villa and Reed faced a pair of powerful foes within the revolutionary movements they embraced. All four of these antagonists were organization men in that they operated within the revolutionary system and, whenever possible, used its bureaucratic apparatus to stifle what they considered the romantic excesses of Villa and Reed. Villa's enemies were Venustiano Carranza and Alvaro Obregón; Reed's were Grigori Zinoviev and Karl Radek.

I embraced him . . . but with the first few words we spoke my blood turned to ice. As far as he was concerned, I was a rival, not a friend. He never looked me in the eye and during our entire conversation emphasized our differences in origin. . . . There was nothing in common between that man and me.[1]

This was Francisco Villa speaking about Venustiano Carranza and, with primitive but unerring instinct, getting right to the heart of everything that separated them.

As Villa's angry reference to differences in origin indicates, Carranza had trodden a far more respectable road to revolution. Born on 29 September 1859, he was over fifty when Madero rose against Díaz. The Carranzas were of old creole stock. Colonel Jesús Carranza, the future First Chief's father, was a large landowner with properties near Cuatro Ciénegas, in northern Coahuila. His mother, María de Jesús Garza, came from one of the state's leading families. Young Venustiano studied at the exclusive Fuente Ateneo in Saltillo and, at age 15, was enrolled in the National Preparatory School in Mexico City.

But he was soon forced to drop out. His eyes were abnormally sensitive to light and, in later years, he was never seen without tinted glasses. Carranza returned to Coahuila and there devoted himself to what passed for agro-business in those days. He managed family farms at Las Animas and El Fuste, following this uneventful career until he was almost thirty.

The year 1887 brought a significant change in Carranza's life. He married Virginia Salinas and successfully ran for municipal president (mayor) of Cuatro Ciénegas. Thus began Carranza's political career, one that must ever be considered in the light of his personality and values. Though Carranza sprang from the landowning aristocracy, his mentality was completely middle-class. Robert E. Quirk describes him as "bourgeois mediocrity incarnate," a man who was "impeccably honest (but) insufferably conscious of his own rectitude."[2]

Both these traits surfaced in Carranza's first major political confrontation. When he began his term as municipal president, the state governor was his cousin, Jesús María Garza Galán. Corrupt and despotic, Garza was anxious to ingratiate himself with President Porfirio Díaz. Díaz, in the springtime of his long career, was then running a taut ship; the rot had not yet taken hold. Determined to appear in a favorable light, Garza Galán began putting pressure on state municipal presidents to falsify their *informes* (annual reports). On receiving instructions to describe conditions in Cuatro Ciénegas as "brilliant and prosperous," Carranza immediately shot back this defiant message: "In this *informe* I will tell the truth—that there is no prosperity and that municipal conditions are causing anguish."[3] Garza Galán forced Carranza's resignation and the latter, aided by his three brothers, went into rebellion.

The matter was settled in the Carranzas' favor by Bernardo Reyes, then governor of the neighboring state of Nuevo León. Using his influence with Díaz, he got Garza removed from the governorship and Carranza restored to his municipal presidency. He served in this capacity till 1898, then became a state deputy and a federal senator. In 1908 he served briefly as interim governor.

Carranza joined the *maderista* revolution and Madero made him Secretary of War and Marine in May 1911. When Madero became president, Carranza successfully ran for governor of Coahuila. Though Díaz was out of the way, Carranza had none of Madero's naiveté about the old dictator's sympathizers who surrounded the new president in Mexico City. Putting Coahuila on a war footing, he organized a militia of irregulars and made military training compulsory in schools and colleges.[4]

Carranza's precautions stood him in good stead. On 18 February, 1913, following the *cuartelazo*, he received a telegram that Huerta sent out to all state governors: "AUTHORIZED BY THE SENATE I HAVE ASSUMED EXECUTIVE POWER THE PRESIDENT AND HIS CABINET BEING PRISONERS."[5] (Madero and Pino Suárez had not yet been killed.) Carranza immediately called a special session of the legislature and repudiated Huerta. This act was followed by armed clashes, in which Carranza's irregulars were bested by federal troops. Following an unsuccessful attack on Saltillo, the state capital, Carranza and a band of supporters made for the hacienda of Guadalupe, about 60 miles north of Saltillo.

There he published the celebrated Plan de Guadalupe and appointed himself First Chief of the Constitutionalist movement, aimed at overthrowing Huerta. The Plan, containing seven points, was purely political in nature and contained no provisions for economic reform. Its gist was repudiation of Huerta, nomination of Carranza as First Chief, and a call for free elections after peace had been restored. It was, in short, a remarkably conservative document, even less radical than Madero's cautious Plan de San Luis. Madero's Plan made a passing reference to the agrarian problem; Carranza's did not.[6]

In the meantime, Villa had crossed into Chihuahua and begun his spectacularly successful campaign with the *División del Norte*. This was a development Carranza viewed with mixed feelings. Though the victories pleased him, the fact they they were being won by an ex-bandit did not sit well with one of Carranza's staid temperament and cautiously reformist views.

At the same time, he looked with approval on a man from Sonora who had also been scoring against the Federals. This was Alvaro Obregón, a 33-year-old schoolteacher, who was giving Francisco Villa stiff competition for the title of Mexico's most successful amateur soldier. Methodically cleansing the northwest of *huertismo*, he had bested the Federals at Nogales on 13 March 1913, at Cananea on 26 March, at Santa Rosa on 13 May, and at San Alejandro on 27 June. After promulgation of the Plan de Guadalupe, Obregón sent Carranza a friendly message. Wanting to meet this prodigy—a revolutionary as promising (and infinitely more respectable) than Francisco Villa—Carranza and his entourage trekked across the Sierra Madre in late summer of 1913. Their initial meeting took place in La Fuerte, Sinaloa, on 20 September.[7]

There has long been confusion about Obregón's background, some of it contributed by Obregón himself. During the Aguascalientes Convention he got into a hot verbal battle with a Leftist Zapata delegate named Antonio Díaz Soto y Gama. Both were given to hyperbole and Obregón was ridiculing Soto y Gama's melodramatic claim that when the Revolution broke out he had taken to the mountains and lived like an Indian. "Sr. Soto y Gama," he thundered, "should know that he is talking to a pure Mayo Indian, one who knows their language and can make speeches in it."[8]

Obregón's "Mayo" affiliation was rhetorical and sentimental rather than ethnic. He lived among the Mayos, he spoke their language, he fought for their rights, and he even gave the name Mayo to one of his children.

Though Obregón's ancestors were not Mayos, they may have come from a county of that name. His surname derives from an ancient

Gaelic word for "wild goose" whose first illustrious possessor was the Irish king Brian Boru. It has subsequently appeared as Bryan or, more commonly, O'Brien. There were O'Briens in the Irish regiments that served the King of Spain in Mexico. One of them, Michael, was bodyguard to the last Spanish viceroy whose name, interestingly, was O'Donojú. This officer was an ancestor of the future president. The name remained O'Brien for six generations; by the seventh it had been Hispanicized to Obregón.[9]

Obregón also had Spanish blood (his mother's name was Calido), but the Hibernian strain showed up strongly in his countenance. Stocky, fair-skinned, and snub-nosed, he had grey-green eyes and a flowing walrus mustache. In photographs, amid a sea of dark Mexican faces, he looks like a displaced Tammany politician.

Obregón was born on 19 February 1880 on the hacienda of Siquisiva, near the Sonora agricultural town of Navojoa. His father was a poor farmer and Obregón was one of eighteen children. After attending primary school, he worked on the Tres Hermanos hacienda in Huatabampo and then in a sugar refinery. At eighteen he became a schoolteacher in the village of Moroncarit. In 1903 he married Refugio Urrea and, two years later, he acquired a ranch on the Mayo river called Quinta Chilla. Widowed, he married María Tapía on 2 March 1910. Obregón had a total of nine children, seven by his second marriage.

Clever and ambitious, he successfully ran for mayor of Huatabampo in 1911. Though he took no part in the Madero revolution against Díaz, he did join the maderista campaign against Pascual Orozco. To combat the *orozquistas* he formed a unit called the 4th Irregular Battalion of Sonora, which he headed with the rank of lieutenant-colonel. Joining the forces of General Agustín Sanginés, he brought his men into Chihuahua and won victories at Púlpito Canyon, Ojitos, and San Joaquín.

Though Obregón was a more cautious tactician than Villa, this was not due to any lack of courage. At Ojitos he captured a cannon from the *colorados*, leading his men in hand-to-hand fighting.[10]

He was discharged in January 1913 but recalled to action the following month. Madero had been overthrown and Sonora was in revolt against Huerta. With the rank of full colonel, Obregón was summoned to Hermosillo and made garrison commander.

This assignment was short-lived. As the revolution rolled south-ward, Obregón was given command of three military zones in Sonora. It was from this vantage point that he rolled off the string of victories that so endeared him to Carranza. Following the Santa Rosa engagement he was promoted to brigadier; two months later, while besieging Guaymas, he became a general of brigade (a higher rank in the Mexican army).

The 20 September meeting with Carranza proved highly satisfac-tory to Obregón. The First Chief named him "Chief of the Army Corps of the Northwest." The title was something of a misnomer because his authority extended over the north-central state of Chi-huahua (Pancho Villa's territory) and the central one of Durango.

Obregón was the ideal partner for a revolutionary as tame as Car-ranza. Following the *cuartelazo*, the First Chief was in a quandary. He wanted an orderly, respectable revolution but had to depend on what the federal officer corps superciliously referred to as "impro-vised generals." Huerta's treachery against Madero and Rábago's against Abraham González had implanted in Carranza a deep dis-trust of regular officers. (We recall his treatment of Felipe Angeles.)

Up to now, his best "improvised general" had been an individual who embarrassed him profoundly: Francisco Villa. But Obregón was different. He was an ex-schoolteacher, a sound, practical man of proven ability, and he seemingly shared many of Carranza's views. Knowing how the First Chief distrusted military professionals, Ob-regón advocated that they be barred from public office. Aware of Carranza's caution about land reform, Obregón hastened to assure him that "here in Sonora we don't have any agrarians, thank God!"[11]

Obregón was an expert at telling Carranza what he wanted to hear. Though "toady" seems too harsh a word, Obregón immedi-ately sized up the First Chief's susceptibility to flattery and exploited it masterfully. Later, as his power grew, he was able to stake out a more independent position. Obregón had an infinitely warmer per-sonality than Carranza, with a wry humor and a gift for mocking self-deprecation. Though his oratory was bombastic (even by Mex-ican standards), in private he was witty and relaxed. When he came to power, one of his first acts was to incorporate all the revolution-ary "generals" into the regular army and put them on the payroll. "If a man calls himself a general, then he must be one," was his wry comment.[12] Carranza, by contrast, was as aloof and self-righteous among intimates as he was when issuing manifestos.

What united Carranza and Obregón is that they were organization men who believed in working within the system. Carranza had been an elected official under Díaz, holding posts from small-town mayor to federal senator. Even his acts of rebellion were decorous and legalistic. He prevailed over his corrupt cousin by enlisting the aid of a more powerful man. He declared for Madero because Díaz had been fraudulently reelected. He defied Huerta because Huerta had unlawfully seized power.

Obregón also acted as a defender of organization values. He withheld support from Madero, the rebel against Díaz, but extended it to Madero, the elected president under attack by Orozco. It was only natural for Obregón to rally to Carranza. As Madero's successor, Carranza represented legitimacy while Huerta was nothing more than a putschist. Obregón was also influenced against Huerta by his commander in the *orozquista* campaign, General Sanginés. During this period Huerta, Obregón, and Sanginés were all on the same side. But Sanginés took Obregón aside and warned him to expect trouble from "this Indian, Huerta."[13]

Carranza, staid and conventional, and Obregón, sensible and pragmatic, were organization men by temperament. Within their organization—the Constitutionalist movement—they were highly skilled at political maneuver and bureaucratic infighting. These abilities enabled Carranza and Obregón to cut down opponents who, at different times, enjoyed advantages of popularity, charisma, numbers, economic resources, and military strength.

The most dangerous of these enemies was Francisco Villa. In analyzing the power struggle between Villa and Carranza-Obregón, an interesting irony emerges. Though Villa had the violent macho and "wild man" image—and Carranza and Obregón the "reasonable" one—almost all the attempts at conciliation and compromise were on Villa's part. At times, goaded by his enemies' expert thrusts, he would react with disproportionate fury. All this contributed to the widely held impression of Villa as a savage whose energy Carranza and Obregón were trying to direct into useful channels but who kept getting out of hand.

One man who rejected this view was General Hugh L. Scott. He had commanded troops on the Texas border and become friends with Villa. "He had some fine qualities if you could reach them," wrote Scott, "and with all his faults I considered him to have a far better character than Carranza. He never violated his compacts with me. . . ."[14]

Here is a Mexican analysis of the Carranza-Villa relationship:

Carranza was sure that Villa and Zapata, strong arms of the people, were necessary for war but undesirable for peace. What could they know of government? What would happen to Mexico governed by these semi-literate men. . . . Carranza, at the risk of being condemned by a majority of revolutionaries but confident in his skill as a political manipulator, decided to challenge Villa, to make him fight. . . .[15]

To make him fight! Carranza's strategy was to use Villa as long as he was of military value and then unceremoniously dump him. And since a man of Francisco Villa's choleric temperament would not take kindly to being sacked like an incompetent maid, he would be bound to fight. Carranza, and later Obregón, were undeviatingly consistent in their campaign to diminish Villa. The hesitation, the attempts at conciliation and compromise, the swings between effusive friendliness and murderous rage—all came from Villa.

The opening skirmish between Villa and Carranza took place in the spring of 1913. Villa, following the *cuartelazo*, had just crossed into Mexico and was building up his forces in northwest Chihuahua. He was there visited by two Carranza delegates, Juan Sánchez Azcona and Alfredo Breceda. The envoys first explained the Plan de Guadalupe and Villa gave it his unconditional endorsement. Then they requested that he place his forces under the jurisdiction of the Northwest Army Corps, that is, under Obregón.

Though Villa refused, his answer was courteous. It would make no more sense, he explained, for his troops to be put under Obregón than "for me, a Chihuahua revolutionary, with no knowledge of [conditions in Sonora] to be put in charge of Sr. Obregón."[16]

In November 1913, just before the Battle of Tierra Blanca, Villa and Carranza clashed on land reform. Villa had suggested that some acreage be distributed to poor farmers, and the First Chief's reply reflects his basic conservatism. "Not only am I in disagreement with the distribution of land to the people but (Villa) must return to the owners lands that were distributed during the regime of Abraham González." Villa declined, telling a visiting *zapatista* that if he followed Carranza's instructions, he would have to take "lands away from widows of men who lost their lives in defense of the Revolution."[17] According to Silvestre Terrazas, black-sheep member of that baronial family who served the revolutionaries as secretary of state for Chihuahua, Villa's refusal to return the lands was a major factor in eruption of open conflict between him and Carranza.[18]

The next encounter between Villa and Carranza involved a political appointment. Villa had been serving as military governor of Chihuahua and, with the *División del Norte* poised to attack Torreón, he wanted to relinquish the post to an interim executive. When Carranza nominated Manuel Chao, Villa sent the First Chief a polite letter of protest: "Permit me to tell you with all frankness—without this indicating the slightest lack of understanding and harmony between General Chao and me—that although I consider him one of the best elements in the state he seems inappropriate to take charge under the present circumstances because he lacks the energies needed for dominating the situation. . . ."[19] But Carranza insisted. Yielding with good grace, Villa took his division to Torreón.

L'affaire Chao had by no means been settled. It surfaced again right after the Torreón victory, this time in a more virulent form. Following the city's fall, Villa ordered Chao to take an occupying force to Torreón. Apparently reluctant to leave Chihuahua, Chao tried to refer the matter to Carranza. Unfortunately for Chao, Villa found out about his plan before Chao could locate the First Chief. Infuriated by such insubordination, Villa ordered Chao shot. While awaiting the firing squad, Chao managed to inform Alfredo Breceda, Carranza's aide, of his predicament. Breceda immediately tipped off Carranza and the First Chief halted the execution. Then he invited Villa and Chao to a reconciliation breakfast. It was not a happy occasion, with a trembling Chao browbeaten by a menacing Villa. "You escaped, my boy," said Villa, "because of the Chief's order. Don't you think you ought to thank him?" Coming almost as comic relief was Carranza's marvelously bromidic remark. "We are going to breakfast in perfect harmony because I don't want anybody here but friends and patriots."[20]

However threatening he may have been to Chao, Villa continued trying to appease Carranza. On the anniversary of Carranza's repudiation of Huerta, Villa sent him a message hailing "This memorable day when you unfurled the banner of liberty against the enemies of law and the Constitution." The First Chief never replied.[21] Villa's next fulsome expression of loyalty was followed by the previously mentioned newspaper interview, with Carranza commenting sourly on "the hypocrisies of that bandit."

Carranza's petulance deepened with every Villa victory. Though Torreón was a magnificent triumph, "Carranza received (it) coldly, saying he had not ordered the attack."[22] At the same time he did everything he could to bolster Villa's two chief rivals, the bumbling General Pablo González in the northeast and the highly competent Obregón in the northwest. Villa had his eye firmly fixed on defeating Huerta; Carranza and Obregón were looking far beyond the fading dictator.

These priorities came into plain view with the American occupation of Veracruz. Eight U.S. sailors had been arrested in Tampico for entering a restricted zone. Though they were promptly released, the American fleet commander, Admiral Henry T. Mayo, ordered a number of humiliating concessions, including a 21-gun salute. The Mexicans refused and tension mounted. At the end of April marines landed in Veracruz, beginning a six-month occupation.

Huerta, with considerable justification, denounced this ill-advised exercise in gunboat diplomacy. He called for volunteers to fight the invaders and the episode had the improbable effect of making Huerta a temporary hero. Not wanting to appear less nationalistic than his enemy, Carranza also denounced the occupation.

Only Villa failed to fall in line. Wilson's action was a blow against the "little drunkard" and that was all that mattered. "The bull has wounded Huerta," he said, "and this is a matter between Huerta and Wilson, the great president of the American people."[23]

Carranza had won a psychological victory. By taking the popular side in the occupation dispute, he made Villa appear almost as an American stooge. Now only one obstacle remained. Huerta was still a factor as long as he retained Zacatecas. This arid silver-mining center, at a height of 8,000 feet, controlled the approaches to Mexico City. If the Constitutionalists could seize it, the Revolution would be won.

Though Carranza was anxious to take Zacatecas, he did not want a lion's share of the credit going to Villa. So the First Chief's plan was to relegate the *División del Norte* to a supporting role, using three other generals to capture the city. They were Pánfilo Natera and the Arrieta brothers, Domingo and Mariano. The Natera-Arrieta force would form the nucleus of a new unit, the Division of the Center, that would play a major role in the capture of Mexico City.[24] Carranza was dead set against allowing Villa to move farther south. Not only should he be denied the glory of taking Mexico City, but everything should be done to keep him from linking up with Zapata. The organization men, Carranza and Obregón, were deathly afraid of an alliance between the "wild men," Villa and Zapata. Zapata, who had even less formal education than Villa, was surrounded by a group of radical intellectuals whose programs were anathema to the conservative First Chief.

Carranza erred in thinking that the Natera-Arrieta forces could take Zacatecas, with Villa playing a secondary role. Natera was a poor disciplinarian—both over his men and over himself. A devotee of bawdy houses, he had all Huerta's love of liquor and little of his military skill. The Arrietas were violently anti-Villa, and their forces could obviously never work in harmony with the *División del Norte*.

Natera had launched an attack on Zacatecas in early June but it was foundering badly. This abortive assault was the background to the now famous "battle of the telegrams"—an encounter that shattered whatever unity remained between Villa and Carranza.

It began on 10 June with Carranza ordering Villa to send troops to reinforce Natera. The telegram contained an optimistic prediction that Natera had "good reason to expect a triumph."[25]

Villa knew better. Natera was botching the operation, and Villa requested that Carranza order him to call off the attack pending the arrival of Villa's forces.

But Carranza was not about to let Villa take credit for a rescue operation. He now ordered Villa to send 5,000 men (he had previously requested 3,000) under the leadership of General José Isabel Robles. But they would be strictly reinforcements. The hero, in Carranza's script, continued to be "General Natera (who) has occupied magnificent positions. . . ."[26]

Villa sent two replies, one the same day and the other the following morning. In the first he informed Carranza that Robles was incapacitated by wounds and that he could not move his troops before repairing the railroad line. The second was a testy after-thought. Who, he wanted to know, had ordered Natera's rash attack in the first place? (Since such an important move could not have been taken without Carranza's authorization, the question was rhetorical.) Villa also wanted to know whether he would come under Natera's command in the operation and, after the fall of the city, would he have the authority to check breaches of discipline among Natera's troops?

In a lengthy reply, Carranza departed from his rambling and cliché-ridden style long enough to take two sharp digs at Villa's military leadership. He reminded him of his failure to take Chihuahua in November of the previous year and added that Villa could never have captured Torreón without the assistance of generals that Carranza had placed under his command.[27]

Stung to fury, Villa sent the resignation message mentioned in the last chapter. This sparked the verbal barrage from Villa's generals that ended with Maclovio Herrera's aspersion on Carranza's ancestry.

Villa fought, and won, the battle of Zacatecas against Carranza's orders. No victorious general has ever been more meanly rewarded. While Villa was destroying Huerta, Carranza was planning to destroy Villa. Many generals have been treated better after defeats than Villa was for winning the Revolution's greatest victory.

Carranza's first move was made against Villa's top planner, Felipe Angeles. In a demotion from a demotion, he removed Angeles as "Subsecretary of War in Charge of the Office" as ungraciously as he had removed him as Secretary of War. Though this spiteful gesture did Villa little real harm, the next one did. To make sure Villa wouldn't move south, Carranza held up all shipments of arms, ammunition, and coal from the *División del norte.*

Villa made a final attempt to mollify Carranza. To make it appear as if he had been following the First Chief's order during the Zacatecas battle, he arranged that the victory report go out under Pánfilo Natera's name. He also named Natera military commander of Zacatecas and interim governor of the state.[28]

Carranza remained unappeased. When promotions were announced, both Obregón and the incompetent northeast area commander, Pablo González, were elevated to divisional general. Villa remained a brigadier. The units commanded by Obregón and González became corps, while the *División del Norte*—largest formation in the Constitutionalist forces—remained a division.

Up to now, Carranza has dominated the drama of Villa's tortured relationship with his organization foes. While Carranza was foisting unwanted political appointees on Villa, clashing with him on land reform and American intervention, and frustrating him at Torreón and Zacatecas, Obregón was busy fighting a war. While he obviously sympathized with Carranza's attempts to break Villa, his collaboration in these efforts was advisory and at long range.

The first instance of Obregón's active collaboration with Carranza against Villa occurred just before Zacatecas. Villa had sent Obregón a telegram, suggesting that they coordinate their drives toward Mexico City, ignoring any limitations Carranza might try and impose on them. Obregón's reply was polite and noncommittal. Far more to the point was a wire he sent Carranza, informing him of Villa's action and pledging his unconditional loyalty.

Apparently unaware of Obregón's sentiments, Villa continued to woo him. After Zacatecas, he sent him a telegram complaining of Carranza's withholding of coal and munitions. He also invited Obregón to a conference, to be held at Torreón in July. Purpose of the conference, among others, was to call a convention that would set the stage for national elections. Obregón's response was a silky-smooth message in which he urged harmony and pleaded with Villa not to repudiate Carranza. He also begged off from attending the conference.

The conference lasted from 4 to 8 July. Its decisions—some political, some military—were forwarded to Carranza. Though he agreed to the idea of a convention, he continued to slight Villa and Angeles. Villa would not be promoted to divisional general and Angeles would not be reappointed to the unprestigious post from which Carranza had fired him.

In the meantime, Obregón was on the march. While Villa dithered in Chihuahua—still hoping to patch up differences with Carranza—Obregón captured Guadalajara on 8 July. He then fanned south and east, taking the port of Manzanillo and the strategic railhead of Irapuato. Huerta resigned on 15 July and was replaced by a caretaker government under Francisco Carbajal. By now federal morale was so low that even the bungling Pablo González began to win victories. After bloodlessly securing San Luis Potosí, he routed a band of *colorados* at León. They were headed by Pascual Orozco, and this proved to be his last hurrah in Mexico. Evading capture, he fled north and crossed the Texas border. (He died in the United States, killed by Texas Rangers the following year.) González next moved into Querétaro, 135 miles northeast of Mexico City. Since Mexico narrows at this point, Obregón and González were drawing steadily closer to each other. The two armies converged on 9 August at Teoluyucán, just outside the Federal District. Six days later the Constitutionalists marched into the city. Carbajal, Huerta's caretaker successor, had been advised to surrender by Alfonso Robles Dominguez, Constitutionalist representative in the capital. Initially opposing rendition was General José Velasco, the Minister of War. But Velasco and Carbajal were dissuaded by Robles, the latter insisting that fighting might result in a march on the capital by American troops occupying Veracruz. Carbajal resigned on 12 August and followed Huerta into exile. Not only was the Constitutionalist entry bloodless but Obregón even left some federal soldiers at their posts to help defend the city against the *zapatistas*. This earned him the undying hatred of the men from the South.[29]

The first meeting between Villa and Obregón took place in Chihuahua on 24 August. A dispute had broken out in Sonora between José Maytorena, the pro-Villa governor, and two pro-Carranza military leaders, General Benjamín Hill and Colonel Plutarco Elías Calles. Villa was still trying to cultivate Obregón, and Obregón suggested to Carranza that he might be able to help mediate the controversy. So he was sent north to confer with Villa. Villa met Obregón at the train and was the soul of affability. "Look, *compañerito*," he said, "if you had come with troops we'd be fighting now. But you came alone and you have nothing to worry about. Pancho Villa is no traitor."[30]

Their meeting went fairly well. It was followed by a visit of the two chiefs to Sonora where they conferred with Maytorena on 29 August. Maytorena was first confirmed as governor but then deposed within twenty-four hours. This was at the insistence of Obregón, who was angered by a leaflet circulated by Maytorena's followers that strongly criticized him. Obregón and Villa then returned to Chihuahua. There, on 3 September, they issued a decree naming General Juan Cabral to be Maytorena's successor as governor and state military commander.[31] In the course of the negotiations Obregón and Villa went to El Paso to confer with two American officers. They were Brigadier-General John J. Pershing and his youthful aide, Lieutenant George S. Patton. The meeting also produced a memorandum, released on 3 September and signed by Villa and Obregón, calling for appointment of judges, disqualification of military men from elective posts, local elections to form town governments, and Carranza's assumption of office as interim president. Obregón then returned to Mexico City. Carranza rejected the memorandum, saying the questions it raised were of too great importance to be "discussed or approved by a small group of persons."[32]

At this point Obregón can be compared to the boy who poked a bear with a stick and, having gotten away with it, decides to poke him again. In mid-September Obregón made another trip to Chihuahua, a journey that almost cost him his life.

Following Obregón's return to Mexico City, the Sonora pot again began to boil. Villa had sent angry telegrams to Obregón accusing Hill and Calles of violating the agreement reached during Obregón's last visit.

Another motive for Obregón's second trip was espionage. The day he arrived, 16 September, is Mexico's Independence Day. Villa, whose initial welcome was friendly, invited Obregón to witness a massive military parade. While Villa's men were marching, Obregón was counting. He had a phenomenal memory and his chief aide, Lieutenant-Colonel Francisco Serrano, was helping with the count. Obregón and Serrano counted 5,200 men and 40 cannon.[33]

Trouble began the following day. Fighting had broken out in Sonora, and Villa furiously accused Obregón of having put Hill and Calles up to attacking Maytorena, who still commanded considerable forces despite his removal as governor. He called Obregón a traitor and ordered him shot.

Ironically, Obregón's life was probably saved by an enemy. On hearing that he was to be executed, Obregón made a dignified, wryly humorous statement that death would give him a personality, something he had always lacked. Several of Villa's followers were milling about and one of them, Dr. Felipe Dussart, began to childishly jump up and down, gleefully applauding Villa's decision.

(Dussart, once on Obregón's staff, had been dismissed in disgrace.)

Infuriated by this puerile display, Villa cursed Dussart and ordered him from the room. Then the glib Serrano took over. Alternately lecturing and flattering Villa, he reminded him of the rules of hospitality and expressed shock that a man of his bravery would think of shooting an unarmed guest.

The episode ended with a tearful Villa dismissing the firing squad. Putting an arm around his *compañerito*, he assured Obregón that he was not a traitor who killed defenseless men.

But Obregón was not yet off the hook. On the morning of 23 September, while on his way back to Mexico City, he was pulled off the train between Chihuahua and Torreón and taken back to Villa's headquarters. The Centaur was again in a rage. He had intercepted a message from Carranza to Pánfilo Natera, the Zacatecas commander, to tear up railroad tracks and block all southward movement of *villista* forces. When Villa protested to Carranza, the First Chief shot back a message demanding to know what had happened to Obregón. Villa replied that he had halted Obregón's return to Mexico City. In the same message, he made the rupture with Carranza final by disavowing him as First Chief.

Obregón's second escape from death has been related in the preceding chapter. This was the episode in which Villa's more civilized advisers—including Obregón's old enemy, Felipe Angeles—prevailed over the Urbina-Fierro bandit element.

In his memoirs, Obregón claims that Villa changed his mind again and planned to have him killed during the return trip. But he escaped the trap and reached Mexico City on 26 September. One of his first acts was to deny that he had perished before a *villista* firing squad.

On 10 October the Convention began its deliberations. Aguascalientes was selected because of its location, standing about midway between Villa's power center in Chihuahua and Carranza's in Mexico City. Site of the conclave was the Teatro Morelos and the presiding officer was General Antonio Villareal, a radical ex-schoolteacher who supported Carranza.

The Convention was doomed to failure. First, because differences between its most powerful factions were irreconcilable; second, because it lacked real power and quickly degenerated into a sort of political icon to whom everybody paid meaningless lip service. To insult the Convention was like attacking motherhood and God—yet no serious attempts were made to convert it into an effective political instrument.

In this context, it is interesting to observe the attitudes of Mexico's three most powerful men, Obregón, Villa, and Carranza. Obregón, with typical verbal melodrama, declared in an opening-day speech that he was willing to give up his general's rank and "enlist as a sergeant to fight anyone who rebels against this Convention." Later, when he himself went into rebellion, the Convention's newspaper caustically commented that "the Convention is waiting for Sergeant Obregón to join its ranks."[34]

Unlike Obregón, Villa was not a delegate to the Convention. But he came to Aguascalientes a few days after the opening session. His tearful, emotion-charged harangue was preceded by an oath to support and obey the Convention. In an extra touch of irony, the speech was followed by an exchange of *abrazos* with Obregón.

Though Carranza hedged on accepting the Convention's authority, he did issue a statement (read by Obregón on 29 October) that he would be "disposed to retire" as First Chief if Villa and Zapata would also step down from their posts. In what seems like a gratuitous dig at Villa (one he obviously couldn't resist), Carranza called on him to "renounce, not his candidacy for the presidency or the vice-presidency, neither of which has been offered to him, but the military command of the Division of the North. . . ."[35]

Villa was quick to return venom with venom. Following a vote demanding the retirement of both Carranza and Villa, Villa sent this message to Felipe Angeles, his leading representative at the Convention: "I propose not only that the Convention retire Carranza from his post in exchange for retiring me from mine, but that the Convention order both of us shot."[36]

We have spoken of the Convention's intrinsic weakness. Adding to this weakness was the fact that it was impossible to elect a man of national stature as provisional president. For factional reasons, Villa, Carranza, Obregón, and Zapata were all out of the running. Nor was it possible to elect second-rank *villistas* or *carrancistas* of proven ability. These included José Isabel Robles, a general in the *División del Norte*, and Antonio Villareal. The compromise president, Eulalio Gutiérrez, was a courageous man with a good revolutionary record. But he was little known and, as events would prove, passionately addicted to personal enrichment.

Villa had accepted the Convention's decision, but Carranza was still hedging. The fact that Gutiérrez was a relative nonentity undoubtedly contributed to Carranza's evasiveness. He denounced Gutiérrez as a Villa puppet (which he was not) and wrote the Convention that conditions for his withdrawal had not been met. Annoyed by Carranza's cat-and-mouse game, the Convention delivered him an ultimatum to hand over the executive power to Gutiérrez by 10 November.

Carranza's reply, published on 8 November, contemptuously referred to the Convention as a "junta" whose authority he didn't recognize. (In Carranza's view, the time for paying even lip service to the Convention had passed.) He then called on *carrancista* delegates to leave Aguascalientes before the ultimatum expired.

This led to the near-surreal situation described in the preceding chapter: the Convention as Mexico's supreme political authority; Carranza as a rebel and outlaw; and Villa commanding the forces of legitimacy. Following the election, "General Villa . . . went through the comedy of resigning as commander of the *División del Norte* and delivering his forces to Gutiérrez."[37] This authority was restored a few days later, right after the ultimatum to Carranza expired.

Now what would Obregón do? He had made fervent declarations of loyalty to the Convention (as the future "Sergeant Obregón") and he headed the commission that had informed Carranza of Gutiérrez's election. On 11 November, the day after the ultimatum expired, he wired Villa to halt his advance toward Mexico City. If Villa would step down and leave the country, Carranza would follow suit. Obregón also tried to seduce some of Villa's generals, slyly reminding them of how much Villa was in their debt. Then he wired Gutiérrez, offering to accept his authority if Gutiérrez abandoned Villa. The final message, sent on 19 November from Mexico City, was an unconditional declaration of allegiance to Carranza. Obregón had been restrained in his previous utterances; now he let his prose run wild. He would, he said, prefer to see Mexico a vast cemetery rather than live infected by the accursed trinity of Villa,

Angeles, and Maytorena.[38] Four days later the Americans evacuated Veracruz. This was an opportune development for Carranza and Obregón. Forced out of Mexico City by Villa and Zapata, they now had a base from which to launch their comeback.

They had a long way to go. As 1914 drew to a close, Francisco Villa was truly the "cock of the walk"—a designation festooned on him by the American press. He commanded the Convention armies, he was in firm alliance with Zapata, and his enemies, Carranza and Obregón, were largely reduced to running a beachhead government in Veracruz (though there were *carrancista* remnants in the north and west).

Villa's fall was as rapid and spectacular as his rise. What caused it? We have examined the military picture, the horrifying reverses Villa suffered when he failed to heed Felipe Angeles. He had twice held Obregón captive in Chihuahua; he also held him captive in Veracruz. Had it not been for his misplaced loyalty to Zapata, Villa could have easily secured that port in late 1914. Several *carrancista* generals had gone over to the Convention and Obregón's force was down to 4,000 men.[39] But he let Obregón off the hook, and the result was Celaya.

Villa's decline was also hastened by political factors. Far from bringing order, the Convention regime ushered in a period of anarchy such as Mexico had never witnessed. Villa quarreled with Gutiérrez (who resented *villista* depradations in the capital) and Gutiérrez—after helping himself to 10 million pesos from the National Treasury—moved north and set up a rump government in San Luis Potosí. He sent feelers out to Carranza and Obregón, but in the end these efforts aborted. To confuse things further, a new authority—also claiming to represent the Convention—came into being in Mexico City. Its leader, 29-year-old Roque González Garza, reappointed Villa and Zapata to their commands. (They had been dismissed by Gutiérrez.) But relations had declined between Villa and Zapata; Villa, ruefully recalling the words of Angeles, was fed up with *zapatista* military ineptitude.

The situation was so chaotic that at one point Mexico had four governments: the Constitutionalists under Carranza and Obregón; the Gutiérrez Conventionists; the González Garza Conventionists (recognized by Zapata); and a large independent authority in the north controlled by Villa. During this period of turmoil Mexico City changed hands three times in one five-day period. Of the occupiers, the *zapatistas* were the mildest, while Villa's men and Obregón's were detested with impartial fervor. Yet another *carrancista* occupation, under Pablo González, was considered fairly humane. At González's direction "the authorities began to import corn, sugar, etc. and to coin money and organize public services."[40]

This anarchic situation was the prelude to that showdown battle at Celaya, followed by the string of defeats that drove Villa steadily north.

In July, following Villa's loss at Aguascalientes, came the sole *villista* military success of that entire bleak period. It was engineered not by Villa but by his "butcher," Fierro. Leading a daring cavalry raid, he swept through central Mexico and came within striking distance of the capital. But he did not have enough men to press his advantage. Defeated by Obregón at Jerécuaro, near Celaya, he limped back to join Villa in the north.

In September Fierro figured in the killing of the *División del Norte*'s second meanest man, Tomás Urbina. Urbina had retired from the Revolution, burying a large portion of the division's war chest at his Las Nieves hacienda, where John Reed came to visit. A raiding party, led by Villa and Fierro, launched a surprise attack and Urbina was wounded. Villa, in a sudden change of heart, wanted to spare his old *compadre*. But he changed his mind again when only a small part of the booty was recovered. Leaving Fierro to finish off the wounded Urbina, Villa rode away.

Fierro's own death in quicksand took place on 15 October, when Villa was riding into Sonora to aid his old ally Maytorena. The Sonora gambit was a useless venture. On 1 November the *villistas* attacked a Carranza force under General Plutarco Elías Calles at Agua Prieta, across the border from Douglas, Arizona. Greatly contributing to Villa's defeat in this engagement was American aid received by his enemies. His men fought in the glare of searchlights from the American side and on the night of 2 November, with the issue still in doubt, three thousand *carrancista* reinforcements attacked him from the rear. The United States had by now recognized Carranza, and these troops had been transported by train across American territory. Agua Prieta marked the end of the *División del Norte* as an organized fighting force.[41]

General Pancho Villa (center) with some of his military *compadres*. To his right is General Fierro ("the Butcher"). To Villa's left are General Ortega and Colonel Medina. The men to the far right and far left are not identified. (*Courtesy of Special Collections, University of Arizona Library.*)

As if he didn't have enough difficulties, Villa was also rendered a disservice by his "ally," Maytorena. The latter, a conservative, had thwarted efforts of Villa's representatives in Sonora to bring about land reform. Next he weakened Villa militarily by instructing two Yaqui generals, Francisco Urbalejo and José Acosta, to deceive him about troops that might be placed at his disposal. He then fled to the United States, leaving a bewildered Villa to fend for himself in Sonora.[42]

Following Maytorena's flight, Villa again traversed the sierra into Chihuahua. But the noose was tightening fast. The *carrancistas* held Juárez and Villa's Christmas Day appearance in Chihuahua City marked one of the last times the *villistas* would ever hold a major population center.

Addressing a 400-man remnant—all that remained of the mighty *División del Norte*—Villa told them they were free to do whatever they wished. Then he gathered a small band and vanished into the sierra.

Carranza and Obregón were not gracious victors. On 16 December Obregón received a telegram from General Fidel Avila, a Villa negotiator:

". . . I HOLD THE BELIEF THAT GENERAL VILLA WILL RETIRE COMPLETELY FROM THE CONVENTION ARMY. IT IS ABOUT THIS IMPORTANT AFFAIR WHICH INVOLVES THE FUTURE OF MEXICO THAT I WISH WE HOLD TALKS.

Obregón's reply came the next day:

MEXICO'S FUTURE IS WRITTEN ON THE BANDIT VILLA'S BACK. HIS RETIRE-MENT NOW HAS NO MEANING SINCE WE SHALL RETIRE HIM . . . . VILLA IS AN OUTLAW.[43]

Why such vindictiveness to such a thoroughly beaten enemy? Alfonso Taracena suggests that Villa "greatly humiliated [Obregón] when he had him in his hands in Chihuahua and spared his life . . . neither Obregón nor Carranza would ever forgive Villa."[44]

There have been few more stunning reversals than Villa's 1915 annihilation by his organization enemies. In the final week of 1914 he was virtual master of Mexico while his foes, Carranza and Obregón, were proscribed rebels hanging on in Veracruz by their fingertips. Now, with Carranza and Obregón triumphant everywhere, he reverted to what he had been in the earliest days of the Revolution, a guerrilla raider in the sierra of Chihuahua.

9

The Organization Men: Zinoviev and Radek

IT IS INTERESTING HOW OFTEN SUPERPATRIOTS and enforcers of ideological or organizational conformity derive from minority backgrounds. Born ethnic outsiders, they compensate by being more royalist than the King and more Catholic than the Pope. Hitler, symbol of German nationalism in its most virulent form, was an Austrian. Stalin—among his other crimes—was such a ruthless Russifier that his own children commented that he "used to be a Georgian."

Of Francisco Villa and John Reed's organization enemies, only Carranza, with his Spanish creole antecedents, could be considered the Mexican equivalent of an old-line WASP. Obregón was part-Irish and Zinoviev and Radek were Jews. Had changes not been made to conform to the prevailing ethnic pattern, Zinoviev, Radek, and Obregón would have gone down in history under names that somehow evoke a New York law firm: Apfelbaum, Sobelsohn, and O'Brien. Reed, by contrast, was a WASP and Villa, a light-skinned *mestizo*, had an ethnic provenience that could be considered typically Mexican. In the narrative that unfolds, Obregón, Zinoviev, and Radek—all of minority origin—acted as organization stalwarts against Villa and Reed, men of nativist background in conflict with establishment pressures.

Villa's struggle with Carranza was political and military; Reed's with Zinoviev and Radek political and bureaucratic. When Villa's difficulties with Carranza and Obregón began, all were united in the campaign against Huerta. Later the coalition split, and Villa was leading his own faction (in alliance with Zapata) against a rival one led by his organization enemies. Reed, Zinoviev, and Radek, on the other hand, all remained under the umbrella of international Communism. In describing his initial encounter with Carranza, Villa records that he first embraced him but then had his blood turn cold because of the older man's aloofness and patronizing manner. Though it is doubtful if Reed ever embraced Zinoviev, his initial reaction must have resembled Villa's in every other way.

Few men as widely despised as Grigori Evseyevich Zinoviev have ever risen as high as he did. At 36, he was Chairman of the Communist International. In Lenin's inner circle, he at times outranked Trotsky and at all times outranked Stalin. On the eve of the Russian revolution, he, Lev Kamenev, and Lenin were considered the *troika* (directing triumvirate) of the Bolsheviks.

It is not uncommon for powerful men to arouse hatred; the astounding thing about Zinoviev is not the hatred he inspired but the contempt. "After Mussolini," wrote Angelica Balabanov, ". . . I consider Zinoviev the most despicable individual I have ever met."[1] Though Balabanov considered Zinoviev guiltless of the charges made against him at the Moscow Trials, this in no way changed her view that "if a tribunal existed for the . . . punishment of those who have damaged and dishonored the labor movement, who have killed its spirit, who have been responsible for the moral and sometimes for the physical extinction of its best militants, both Zinoviev and Stalin would head the list of those condemned."[2]

Robert Conquest describes Zinoviev as a

> vain, incompetent, insolent, and cowardly nonentity. Except for Stalin himself, he is the only Bolshevik leader who cannot be called an intellectual . . . he had no political sense . . . no understanding of economic problems. He was a very effective orator, but his speeches lacked substance, and were only temporarily effective in rousing mass audiences.[3]

In denigrating Zinoviev, Conquest goes too far. He may not have had political sense in the grand historical context, but he had it in abundance on the fixer and dealer level. Nor can he be rightly called incompetent. Lenin was aware of his weakness, but it was precisely for his competence in a number of vital areas that he retained him as a highly placed adviser.

Another scathing word-picture comes from Max Eastman. Yet—
for all his distaste—Eastman concedes Zinoviev's great utility to
Lenin:

> Firmly held by Lenin, this firebrand—and 'fraid cat—was of momen-
> tous use to history. But left to himself he was a vain and fluid thing of
> shifty mind and tongue. His record of switched allegiances, of turning
> and doubling on his tracks, of squirming and belly-crawling and sleekly
> gliding in and out, in the conflict between Stalin and Trotsky, would
> look like acrobatics to a water snake. Moreover he was laughless, femi-
> nine, and of sad complaisance. And his handshake was like receiving
> the present of a flattened out banana.[4]

Zinoviev was born in 1883. His birthplace was Elizavetgrad (today Kirovograd) in what was then the Jewish Pale of Settlement.
He became a revolutionary while a student in Switzerland and,
under Lenin's influence, he joined the Bolshevik faction of the
Russian Social-Democratic Party in 1903. (The Mensheviks were
the other branch.) He returned to Russia in 1906 and became a
member of the Central Committee of the St. Petersburg Bolsheviks. In June of that year the Czar dismissed his moderate Prime
Minister, Sergei Witte, and replaced him with the reactionary Pyotr
Stolypin. He also dissolved the Duma, Russia's highest legislative
body. During this period Zinoviev edited several radical newspapers
and attempted to organize a revolt of the Kronstadt sailors. In 1908
he was briefly arrested. On release, he rallied to Lenin in Switzerland. There they were joined by Kamenev, third member of the
troika. In Geneva Zinoviev and Kamenev helped Lenin edit *Prole-
tarii*, the Party journal abroad. In 1910 the *troika* moved to Paris.
There Lenin founded a school for revolutionaries at Longjumeau,
near Paris. A teacher at the school was Lenin's striking French mistress, Inessa Armand. (Completely Russified, she had escaped from
Czarist exile and become a fervent Bolshevik.)[5]

In 1911 the Czar eased up on his repressive policies. Elections
were permitted for a new Duma and *Pravda*, the Bolshevik newspaper, was allowed to resume publication. Taking advantage of this
breathing spell, Lenin and his entourage moved to Cracow, in Austrian Poland near the Russian border. From this vantage point the
troika could better monitor revolutionary currents in Russia.

In 1914, when the First World War broke out, both Lenin and
Zinoviev moved back to Switzerland. Kamenev had gone to St.

Petersburg to take over the editorship of *Pravda*. Lenin lived first in Bérne but then moved to Zurich where the library facilities were better. Zinoviev remained in Berne where he found employment as a laboratory assistant.[6]

In 1915 and 1916 Zinoviev joined Lenin in attending international Socialist peace conferences held in the Swiss village of Zimmerwald. They formed part of the Russian delegation, while Radek was one of three Polish representatives. The majority position of the conference was to call for an end to the war through concerted action of socialist parties. But there was a minority bloc, "the so-called Zimmerwald Left, which called for a sharp break with Social Democracy and revolutionary opposition to the war."[7] Lenin, Zinoviev, and Radek all belonged to this faction.

In the spring of 1917 that celebrated arrangement was made to send Lenin and a number of his followers through Germany on a sealed train. Describing the episode, Winston Churchill wrote in *The World Crisis* that "they transported Lenin in a sealed train like a plague bacillus from Switzerland to Russia." This plan, approved (and financed) by the Kaiser and the German High Command, was designed to stir up revolution in Russia and make Russia leave the war. The party that boarded the sealed train consisted of thirty-one adults and a four-year-old boy. It included Lenin, Krupskaya (his wife), Inessa Armand, Zinoviev, and Radek.

When Zinoviev and Radek boarded the sealed train, they were at the same stage of revolution as Carranza and Obregón when they began their drive to overthrow Huerta. At this point a comparison is appropriate. Carranza, Obregón, Zinoviev, and Radek had in common the fact that they were organization enemies of Francisco Villa and John Reed. But Zinoviev and Radek differed from their Mexican counterparts in interesting and significant ways. Carranza and Obregón had their faults—the former was stuffy and self-righteous; the latter could be devious and vindictive. On balance, however, they were men of principle: patriotic, courageous, and ever ready to place Mexico's interest above their own. (On two occasions Carranza opposed measures that would have improved his fortunes—the aid of American troops in 1913 and the occupation of Veracruz in 1914.[8])

The same cannot be said for Zinoviev and Radek. Zinoviev was as he has been described in the unflattering portraits of Angelica Balabanov, Robert Conquest, and Max Eastman.

And Radek? Here (in a very restricted sense) we can draw a comparison with Obregón. Just as Obregón was a more vital and interesting figure than Carranza, so was Radek than Zinoviev. In *Stalin: The Man and His Era*, Adam B. Ulam refers to him as a "likable scoundrel." This is not a unanimously held view, as there were many who failed to find Radek likable. But few would disagree with the second part of Ulam's description.

Radek has been called the Soviet Puck. A small, impish, voluble man, he had a slashing wit, a wide-ranging erudition, and a total lack of scruple. He began his career as a journalist and publicist and became one of the most brilliant of his day.

Of the "four enemies," Radek was the only one who was not an organization man by temperament. Carranza and Obregón certainly were and Zinoviev, with his water-snake acrobatics, was the bureaucrat incarnate. Radek, by contrast, was a merry iconoclast whose lack of principle enabled him to place his facile pen and luminous intelligence at the service of the most repressive orthodoxies. (In John Reed's day he served Lenin and Trotsky; he would later serve Stalin.) He was, in short, the ablest intellectual gymnast of his time and possibly of all time.

Since Reed was an iconoclast himself, under other circumstances there might have been a bond between them. But Reed, fundamentally an idealist, was repelled by Radek's cynicism. Of the four organization enemies, Obregón was the only one Reed never met. Adoring Villa, he had no great affection for Carranza. Yet his dislike of the First Chief was tempered by respect for his integrity. Reed had no such mixed feelings about Zinoviev and Radek. "No one," writes Max Eastman, "could more personify the thing in Bolshevism that Jack Reed could not tolerate than Zinoviev. Radek, because of his delightful gift of mockery and wit, was a more sympathetic character. . . . But Radek carried . . . the humorist's license to the point of unprincipled elusiveness."[9]

Angelica Balabanov, who preceded Radek as Secretary of the Comintern, described him as

a strange mixture of amorality, cynicism, and spontaneous appreciation for ideas, books, music, human beings. Just as there are people who have no perception of colors, so Radek had no perception of moral values. . . . This quality, with his quick mind, his sardonic humor, his versatility and his vast reading, was probably the key to his journalistic success.[10]

While the more idealistic types—Reed, Balabanov, Emma Goldman—looked on with distaste, Lenin would commission Radek to write an article on foreign policy for the purpose of gauging reaction abroad. Should it be unfavorable, the nimble Radek would immediately write a second article—a brilliant refutation of his first.

Radek's wit was legendary. When Russia was afflicted with a plague of lice he suggested that they be collectivized, which would cause half of them to die and the other half to run away. Though Radek later turned against Trotsky, he fundamentally liked him. But he couldn't resist poking fun at Trotsky's arrogance and posturing. One time Trotsky dramatically observed that no one could talk of the triumph of socialism in a country where babies are crying for milk. Radek quickly brought him down. "Milk," he said, "is a product of cows, not socialism."[11]

For all his puckish humor, Radek was widely disliked in many quarters. Some of this hostility was caused by his arrogance, monumental even by standards of Soviet officialdom. Once a party of high-ranking Bolsheviks, including Radek, was placed in a coach in Petrograd that was not to Radek's liking. He berated the conductor, insulting him vulgarly when the poor man turned out not to know his name. He finally declared that he would not permit the train to leave Petrograd until a better coach had been found for him and his companions. At this point a military commissar offered Radek his coach. Angelica Balabanov, who was in the party, writes that "we expected Radek to be decent enough to refuse. Instead, he accepted the offer as honor due his rank." When Balabanov objected to his conduct, Radek again flew into a rage. "It is *you* who dishonor the Soviet Union, if as a member of the government you are willing to travel under such conditions. They may be good enough for other people but not for us."[12]

Another unappealing aspect of Radek's personality was a sharp and malicious anti-Semitism. Though himself of Jewish origin, he never passed up an opportunity to pander to the latent anti-Jewish spirit of his Great Russian and Ukranian colleagues, particularly those of peasant origin in whom the pogrom tradition was still strong.

This was consistent with Radek's moral insensitivity, a quality that pushed him to "ingratiate himself with people who refused to sit at a table with him, to shake hands, or even to put their names next to his on a document."[13] If Radek sensed anti-Semitism among people he wished to cultivate, he would regale them from his seemingly endless store of anti-Jewish jokes.

Radek was born in 1885. His birthplace was the city of Lemberg (today Lvov), in what was then Austrian Poland. Though he later became a high Soviet official, he was born a subject of the Habsburg Empire. Like many revolutionaries, Radek became known in history by an appellation other than the one he received at birth. The son of a minor postal official, his given name was Karl Sobelsohn. His father, Bernhard, died when Karl was five and his mother, Sophie, took the little boy and his sister back to her home town of Tarnov. There she supported her children by teaching kindergarten.

Though Sobelsohn was an East European Jew, he had no connection with the parochial world of *Fiddler on the Roof*. His mother was thoroughly emancipated and his two maternal uncles sufficiently assimilated to have served as officers in the Austro-Hungarian army. The uncles diligently attempted to impose their values on Karl, preaching contempt for both Jewish *shtetl* culture and the culture of Polish nationalism.

While they succeeded in the first instance, they conspicuously failed in the second. Defying his uncles, he identified with such figures as General Dabrowski, who fought under Napoleon for Polish independence, and the nationalist-minded Romantic writers of "The Generation of 1831."[14] He also became an avid reader of *Naprzod* ("Forward"), a Tarnov paper that favored socialism along with nationalism. In 1901 Sobelsohn was expelled from the Tarnov gymnasium for political agitation. Three years later he joined the Social Democratic Party of the Kingdom of Poland and Lithuania (SDKPiL), a group led by revolutionary heroine Rosa Luxemburg and Felix Dzierzinski, who would later become Lenin's top secret policeman. In 1906 he was imprisoned in Warsaw for revolutionary activity. Released in early 1907, he came to Germany in 1908 and offered his services to an emigré SDKPiL group centered in Berlin. This faction was headed by Luxemburg, Leo Jogiches, and Julian Marchlewski. (Dzierzinski had elected to stay behind in Poland.)[15]

By this time Sobelsohn was calling himself Radek. There are two versions as to the origin of this *nom de carrière*. Warren Lerner, Radek's biographer, states that as a schoolboy he had become captivated by one Andzrej Radek, a character in a revolutionary novel. The fictive Radek was a nationalistic Polish student leader.[16]

According to Boleslaw Drobner, a veteran Polish Socialist, Radek never referred to himself as Sobelsohn after 1903.[17] This conflicts with the account of Ruth Fischer, a German Leftist and opponent of Radek. She claims that Radek had been expelled from the German Social Democratic Party (SPD) in 1912 for stealing an overcoat from a Party comrade. Afterwards—in what seems an amazing act of self-deprecation—he took to signing his articles "K. Radek," a form deriving from the Polish word *kradziez*, meaning "theft."[18] While dismissing most of the preceding as "fanciful," Lerner concedes that there may be truth in the purloined overcoat story.[19] It would, in fact, have been impossible for Radek to be expelled from the SDP because a Party commission ruled in 1913 that he had never been a member in the first place. In 1911, at the instigation of Luxemburg and Marchlewski, he was expelled from the SDKPiL for a scathing personal attack on the latter.[20] The commission ruled that "persons who have been expelled from a fraternal (Socialist) Party because of dishonorable actions cannot acquire membership in the (SPD) without the consent of the Party that has excluded them."[21] Though Radek consistently tried to ingratiate himself with Luxemburg, he ran up against a stone wall of hostility and revulsion. Considered "the personification of Socialist morality," she detested Radek.[22]

It was under this cloud that Radek came to Switzerland in August 1914. The First World War had broken out and he wanted to avoid conscription into the Austrian army. There he joined forces with another revolutionary, one whose influence would soon outweigh that of all Radek's enemies. This was Lenin.

The Lenin-Radek relationship was not an unbroken honeymoon. Though they had been allies in the Zimmerwald Left, in 1916 they clashed sharply on the issue of self-determination for what would today be called Third World countries. Lenin favored it but Radek—quoting, of all people, Rosa Luxemburg—described self-determination as a "petty bourgeois formula that has nothing to do with Marxism."[23] But these differences were patched up. Regarding Germany as a key operational area, Lenin had the utmost respect for Radek's knowledge of that country. By the end of January he could write to Inessa Armand of Radek that they were the closest friends. In April, when the sealed train was ready for departure, Radek was a welcome member of the "plague bacilli" who would be crossing Germany to foment revolution in Russia.

Radek greatly enlivened the trip. There were only two interesting episodes during the journey, and he figured in both of them.

For the sake of propriety Lenin had placed his mistress, Inessa Armand, in the compartment next to him rather than in his own. Also in the adjoining compartment were Radek, a couple named Safarov, and Olga Ravich, a woman with a squealing, high-pitched laugh. With jokes, anecdotes, and mimicry—at which he also excelled—Radek was in top form. The sounds of revelry finally grew so loud that Lenin could no longer stand the noise. Bursting in on the merrymakers, he took leather-lunged Olga Ravich by the hand and deposited her in another compartment. After that he slept better.[24]

The second incident was more serious. In Stuttgart, a German union leader named Wilhelm Janson boarded the train. He wanted a meeting with Lenin, but Lenin refused to see him. As a member of the German Social Democratic Party, Janson had helped destroy the Second International. Then a sudden fear gripped Lenin: that Janson might catch a glimpse of Radek. The train was deep in Germany and Radek was a military deserter from the forces of the Central Powers. Lenin was concerned that Janson, angered at being rebuffed, might report Radek to the authorities. So Radek was put in the baggage car for safety. Measures were also taken to keep his voracious mind occupied. "They gave me a survival kit of about fifty newspapers so that I should be quiet and not cause any disturbance," was his wry comment.[25]

As an Austrian subject, Radek was technically an enemy alien since Russia was still at war with the Central Powers. So he was left behind in Stockholm. Lenin's plan was to set up an overseas branch of the (Bolshevik) Central Committee. Running it would be Radek and another Polish revolutionary, Jacob Fürstenburg, alias Y. S. Ganetsky.[26]

Lenin arrived in Petrograd's Finland Station on 3 April 1917. There is a faked picture of him at the door of his railroad car, waving his hat at a crowd of cheering supporters. Directly behind him is a mustachioed, Big Brotherly individual with an expression of calm benevolence on his face: Joseph Stalin. This conveys the impression—totally false—that Stalin was a companion of Lenin on the sealed train. He spent the whole time in Petrograd, helping Kamenev edit *Pravda*.

In July, "the Bolsheviki, then a small political sect, put themselves at the head of the movement (a rising against the Provisional Government). As a result of the disastrous failure of the rising, public opinion turned against them . . . hundreds were imprisoned. . . . Lenin and Zinoviev went into hiding . . . the Bolshevik papers were suppressed."[27] This is John Reed, describing the failure of the July rising. "In July," Reed continues, "they (the Bolsheviks) were hunted and despised; by September the metropolitan workmen, the sailors of the Baltic fleet, and the soldiers, had been won almost entirely to their cause."[28] Reed goes on to point up the significance of the September municipal elections, in which the percentage of the anti-Bolshevik parties tumbled from 70 to 18 percent. Partly contributing to this astounding turnabout was the fear caused by General Kornilov's attempted counterrevolution in September; another factor was the organizing skill of the Bolsheviks.

Encouraged by this change of fortune, Lenin decided the time was now ripe for insurrection. Though most of the Bolshevik leaders supported him, there were two notable dissenters: Zinoviev, the "water snake," and "Lincoln Steffens" Kamenev, known for his timidity. Where Lenin and Trotsky expressed optimism about chances of success, Zinoviev and Kamenev made this statement to the Central Committee: "There are historical situations where an oppressed class must recognize that it is better to go forward to defeat than to give up without battle. Does the Russian working class find itself in such a situation? No, and a thousand times no!"[29] Isaac Deutscher comments that "for the rest of their tragic lives they were to burn with shame whenever they were reminded of these words."[30]

Just before the rising, Zinoviev and Kamenev took a step that drove Lenin to fury. The Central Committee had endorsed the insurrection and set a date: 20 October (3 November by the Gregorian calendar). In a last-ditch attempt to head off the rising, Zinoviev and Kamenev denounced the plan in a non-Bolshevik journal. This action, unprecedented and inexcusable, was equivalent to a general staff officer publicly revealing military secrets. Lenin savagely denounced Zinoviev and Kamenev as "strikebreakers of the revolution" and demanded their expulsion from the Party.[31] Though there were expressions of criticism, nobody in the Central Committee would go along with expulsion of the "strikebreakers" and one member—Stalin—went so far as to defend their motives.[32]

Lenin's anger abated following the success of the insurrection. A pragmatic leader, he saw no sense in dismissing two men who could be highly useful in situations where courage was not called for. But he couldn't resist a dig at Zinoviev. "He is bold when the danger is past," he commented.[33]

What was behind the antagonism between Zinoviev-Radek and John Reed? It was more than ideological. Reed had differences with other Bolsheviks (Ryazanov, Kamenev), but these were mainly political. In his feeling for Zinoviev and Radek he combined a contempt for their political stance with a visceral personal loathing.

The actual power struggle between Zinoviev-Radek and Reed will be examined in the next chapter. Here we concern ourselves with motive. Reed, as we know, despised Zinoviev and Radek for their cynicism and deviousness. What was the source of their hostility to Reed?

It is logical to assume that Zinoviev was offended by Reed's published references to his pusillanimous behavior during the Petrograd insurrection. Before publication of *Ten Days that Shook the World,* Zinoviev's hysterical opposition to the rising was pretty much a family affair. Now Reed had gone and advertised his cowardice to the world. Had *Ten Days* been an obscure tract circulating among a few radicals, it wouldn't have been so bad. But it was an instant success, a best seller reviewed favorably not only in leftist publications but in such pillars of the bourgeois press as the *Los Angeles Times,* the *Philadelphia Public Ledger,* and the *New York American.*[34] Even more pleasing to Reed—and infuriating to Zinoviev—were accolades he received from men Reed regarded as the noblest heroes of the working class. These were the IWW prisoners in American penitentiaries. Typical was a letter from a black Wobbly named Ben H. Fletcher: "For five nights after finishing my convict labors I have lived in the classical and historical time, so graphically have you written. . . . We have our Chateau Thierry, the Marne, Joffre and Woodrow Wilson but the Russian proletariat's November Revolution have made Smolny Institute, Lenin, Trotsky, and Spiridinova names that belong to the ages."[35] Such praise for a work in which he is portrayed in so mean a light obviously contributed to Zinoviev's anti-IWW stance at the Second Congress of the Communist International.

Ten Days also contained a political thrust at Zinoviev. Reed identified him, along with Kamenev and Ryazanov, as belonging to "the right wing of the Bolsheviki."[36] Zinoviev, the "water snake," was far too slippery to ever wish to be categorized as a rightist, leftist, or centrist. As the Party line twisted and turned, Zinoviev wanted to be free to twist and turn along with it. Reed also focuses on Lenin's "Letter to the Comrades," characterizing it as "one of the most audacious pieces of political propaganda the world has ever seen."[37] In this document, a scathing rebuke to the "strikebreakers," Lenin unequivocally states that "we (the Bolsheviks) either must abandon our slogan, 'All Power to the Soviets,' or else we must make an insurrection. There is no other course. . . ."[38]

A final affront to Zinoviev was Lenin's enthusiastic endorsement of *Ten Days*. This is Lenin's comment in the original, showing that his English was good but not perfect:

> I read with the greatest interest and fullest attention John Reed's book *Ten Days that Shook the World*. From the deepest of my soul I recommend this work to the workers of all country [sic]. This is the book I would like to see spread in millions of copies and translated in all languages because this book gives a true and unusually interesting account of the occurring events which have a great value [in understanding] what a proletarian revolution and the dictatorship of the proletariat means. . . . John Reed's book will undoubtedly make clear this question and this is the fundamental question of the international labor movement.[39]

Zinoviev's venom against Reed is easy to understand. But what about Radek's? Radek had been in Stockholm during the Revolution, working to organize international contacts for the Bolsheviks. Collaborating with him was Angelica Balabanov. As might be expected, they clashed frequently and acrimoniously. "We despised Radek personally," she writes, "and considered him a vulgar politician."[40] There were also political differences between Balabanov and Radek. She way trying to carve out a more independent position, while Radek's was one of adhesion to the Bolshevik power center in Russia.[41]

Shortly after the Revolution Radek came to Petrograd. At this time he joined the Bolshevik Party, a formality he had previously neglected. In Petrograd he was appointed head of the Central European Division of the Commissariat for Foreign Affairs. This was principally a propaganda unit, charged with indoctrinating German, Austrian, and Hungarian war prisoners.

It was here that Radek first met Reed. Reed, along with Albert Rhys Williams and Boris Reinstein, a Buffalo Socialist, had been assigned to the Division to turn out pamphlets and flyers aimed at inducing enemy soldiers to desert. Radek, for his part, "sponsored a Liebknecht Brigade [after Karl Liebknecht, German Communist leader killed by rightists] among Germans in Siberian camps [and] organized huge mass meetings in Moscow, where delegates from the camps declared their allegiance to the October Revolution."[42]

Though Radek never stinted where his personal comfort was involved, he was apparently a Scrooge-like employer. Reed's salary barely paid his lodgings, and he wasn't even advanced money to cable his articles to the United States. Forced to send them out by mail, he suffered the frustration of forwarding material that would no longer be topical by the time it had completed the long ocean journey to New York. He quit the Division and accepted a temporary job with Colonel Raymond Robins of the American Red Cross Mission. Though a capitalist and self-made millionaire, Robins sympathized with the Revolution and had excellent relations with the Bolshevik leaders.[43] Reed found the hearty colonel a far more congenial companion than Radek.

Radek's opposition to Reed was not based on this incident alone. He was certainly pushed by other forces: ambition, opportunism, moral insensitivity, and his cynic's aversion to a blundering—yet potentially dangerous—idealist. (Reed was in high favor with Lenin and Trotsky.) It is a measure of Radek's insensitivity that he was able to make common cause against Reed with Zinoviev, a man he disliked intensely. Their history is one of temporary alliances—first against Reed, later against Stalin—and permanent antipathy.

Their anti-Reed pact was preceded by a sharp difference of opinion over the Brest-Litovsk peace conference, which formally ended the war against the Central Powers. Radek, a delegate to the conference, opposed the harsh German peace terms while Zinoviev, a member of the Central Committee in Petrograd, advocated their acceptance. His position, which generally coincided with Lenin's, was that Russia did not have the military capacity to carry on the war. They must sign the peace, gain a breathing spell, and build up Bolshevik power within the reduced geographical area that would be left to them. (Under terms of the peace, signed on 3 March 1918, Russia gave up a third of her territory and agreed to pay a heavy indemnity in gold.)

Radek, on the other hand, called for a revolutionary war against the Germans. That Russia was militarily weak was irrelevant. Let the Germans advance, let them even capture Petrograd and Moscow. The further they penetrated into Russia, the more they would be vulnerable to guerrilla warfare and Bolshevik propaganda. There had been considerable fraternizing between German and Russian soldiers in the trenches. Radek expected the German troops to overcome their officers. Then they would unite with the Russians, form international brigades, and march west to impose Communism on all of Europe. Zinoviev disagreed with this view, on ground that the West was not ready for revolution and that the Germans might exact even more onerous terms if Brest-Litovsk was not ratified.

How valid was Radek's thesis? In the "strange bedfellows" department, he found partial support from two unlikely sources. One was John Reed and the other was General Max Hoffmann, commander of German troops on the eastern front.

In January 1919, following Germany's defeat, Reed wrote an article titled "How Soviet Russia Conquered Imperial Germany." In Reed's view, Bolshevik propaganda played a big part in sapping Germany's will to win.[44]

Hoffmann, the German officer corps's most fervent Red-baiter, gave a postwar interview to an American reporter. "Immediately after conquering those Bolsheviks we were conquered by them," he said. "Our victorious army on the eastern front became rotten with Bolshevism. We got to the point where we did not dare transfer certain of our eastern divisions to the West."[45]

Radek's differences with Lenin on Brest-Litovsk were tactical rather than personal. But he did succeed in goading Lenin into characterizing him as "a lamentable Leftist who avoided responsibility."[46] Radek got the message. He flattered himself back into favor so successfully that in November 1918, just seven months after Brest-Litovsk, he was entrusted with the vital mission of organizing Communist activity in Germany. On 12 February, after the unsuccessful Spartacist rising in Germany, he was arrested. Though he spent a year in Berlin's Moabit prison, the experience was hardly martyrdom. Radek had things going for him. Immediately following his arrest, he was given diplomatic status through being named Ukranian envoy to Germany.

At Moabit Radek's situation continued to improve. Through "secret orders" he was "given an especially large cell where he could receive friends, he had a secretary, and he was even allowed to get in touch with the Moscow government."[47] During his comfortable incarceration Radek not only helped organize the German Communist Party but also functioned as a sort of plenipotentiary, regularly receiving industrialists, diplomats, and high-ranking Army officers.

Radek was exchanged in January 1920 for a group of high-level German hostages held by the Russians. Reed was then in Russia, and it was after Radek's return that he and Zinoviev began their campaign against him, one that included betrayal, foreign imprisonment, intimidation, and public humiliation. This ordeal so weakened Reed's constitution that he fell easy prey to the typhus infection that took his life in October.

How did Zinoviev and Radek fare after they had succeeded in eliminating Reed? Had Reed been writing a morality play, he could not have fashioned a more satisfactory ending for his two enemies. But the fall did not come immediately. Zinoviev and Radek were accomplished organization men. They served successfully under Lenin but, like so many of their contemporaries, were unequal to the challenge of what followed. Yet they managed to survive Reed's death by over a decade and a half before succumbing to the most terrible organization man of them all: Joseph Stalin.

In 1921 Radek made an interesting and revealing comment on a current wave of anti-religious persecution. A group of religious leaders had been arrested on charges of aiding the Whites. Among them were two archbishops, one Orthodox and one Roman Catholic.

While Radek's tone was calm in reporting the arrest of the two Christian divines, it changed to positive *schadenfreude* when he commented on another case. With sardonic pity—"oh horror!"—he records "the arrest of a rabbi in a place called Gomel. . . ."[48]

Zinoviev and Radek split again following Lenin's death. Zinoviev went into alliance with Stalin and Kamenev while Radek backed Trotsky. In July-August of 1925, at the Fifth World Congress of the Comintern, Zinoviev presented a document that summed up ten differences between his group and Radek's. These dealt mainly with Radek's German policy, which the Zinoviev group considered disastrous.[49]

Defeated on this issue, Radek was detached from German affairs and appointed dean of Moscow's Sun Yat-Sen University in 1925. As Trotsky's power declined, Radek was expelled from the Communist Party in 1927. After two years in exile, he capitulated to Stalin. In 1931 he was named editor of *Izvestia* and, from that vantage point, became one of Stalin's most slavish flatterers.

Radek laid it on so thick that one cannot help but discerning irony in some of his effusions. Consider this passage, from his *Izvestia* article on the 1933 May Day celebration: "Waves of love flowed toward the massive figure [Stalin stood barely five feet], calm as a rock, waves of love inspired with the trust that here . . . stood the leader of the future victorious world revolution."[50]

Radek's cleverness was unable to save him. On 22 September 1936, he was arrested by the NKVD, as the secret police was then known. (Previously it had been the Cheka and OGPU; later it would be the MVD and KGB.) Radek's initial reaction was one of extreme indignation; he considered the arrest an act of monstrous ingratitude on Stalin's part.

Radek was also irked by the clumsily constructed "confession" he was expected to sign. Such was his intellectual vanity that—even in the face of death—his main concern was that he would be forced to put his name to such a poorly written document.

Stalin visited him in his cell and, on the basis of this meeting, he did an about-face and ably proceeded to supervise his own destruction. Armed with superlative editorial skills, Radek "threw all his literary talents into improving the dramatic quality of the faked confessions which were required from himself and his fellow prisoners. He introduced negotiations between Trotsky and the German government (and) wrote the version of Trotsky's directives to the conspirators which was used at the trial. . . ."[51]

Though dutifully playing his role in Stalin's Punch and Judy show, Radek was clever enough to throw out two clear signals to the outside world. One involved the use of torture. "The question has been raised here," he said, "whether we were tormented under investigation." (This was a neat thrust; the question most definitely had *not* been raised.) Then his irrepressible wit took over: "I must say that it was not I who was tormented but I who tormented them to perform a lot of useless work."[52]

In sending out the second "signal," Radek not only acted with great astuteness but performed what was probably the most decent act of his life. Radek, the most cosmopolitan of the Old Bolsheviks, had a wide circle of friends among European radicals. In a warning disguised as a denunciation, he admonished "Trotskyite elements in France, Spain, and other countries that if they do not learn from our experience, they will pay with their heads."[53] The message was clear: stay out of Russia. A number of European Communists—Bela Kun, Heinz Neumann, Edmondo Peluso—had been welcomed to the Soviet Union as heroes and then arrested and killed.

Radek got ten years, an amazingly lenient sentence by Stalinist standards. "When Radek heard the verdict his face showed relief. He turned to his fellow accused with a shrug and a guilty smile, as though unable to explain his luck."[54]

Zinoviev, following John Reed's death, resumed the acrobatics which Max Eastman and others viewed with such distaste.

Lenin died on 21 January 1924. He was succeeded by a *troika* composed of Zinoviev, Kamenev, and Stalin. All feared Trotsky and carefully moved to isolate him. Then Zinoviev's fear began to shift from the flamboyant Trotsky to the ruthless Stalin. In 1926 he joined forces with Trotsky and, with Kamenev, they formed an anti-Stalin *troika*.

But it was too late. From his position as Party Secretary Stalin had amassed enough power to prevail against any enemy. In 1926 Zinoviev was deposed from the Politburo and removed as head of the Comintern. In 1927 he was expelled from the Communist Party. He recanted in 1929, was readmitted to the Party, but expelled again in 1932. Restored the following year, he had to make an even more abject recantation. "I give my word as a revolutionary," he said, "that I will be the most devoted member of the Party and will do all I possibly can . . . to atone for my guilt before the Party and its Central Committee."[55]

On 1 December 1934, a high-ranking Party functionary named Sergei Kirov was assassinated in Leningrad. Though it is now believed that Kirov's murder was engineered by Stalin, the blame was placed on past and present members of the opposition. Zinoviev, Kamenev, and a number of others were arrested on the 16th.

The arrests were followed by an intensive softening-up period. This was done according to methods described so eloquently in such works as *Darkness at Noon* and *1984*. Along with physical and psychological pressure, Zinoviev and Kamenev were promised their lives if they would cooperate.

The trial opened on 19 August 1936. All the defendants read their lines perfectly. In his final statement, on 23 August, Zinoviev declared that "my defective Bolshevism became transformed into anti-Bolshevism, and through Trotskyism I arrived at Fascism. Trotskyism is a form of Fascism and Zinovievism is a variety of Trotskyism."[56] The following morning he was sentenced to death.

All of the "four enemies" died violently. But Carranza and Obregón perished with more dignity than Zinoviev and Radek. Obregón led a revolt against Carranza and the former First Chief was gunned down in 1920, while trying to make for Veracruz. Obregón died in 1928, assassinated by a young Catholic fanatic who opposed his religious policy.

Until the very last, Zinoviev believed that Stalin was going to keep his end of the bargain. "But when he saw the guards he at once understood. All accounts agree that he collapsed, yelling in a high-pitched voice for Stalin to keep his word. . . . the NKVD lieutenant in charge, fearing the effect of this scene if prolonged along the corridor and down into the cellar, hustled him into a nearby cell and shot him then and there, receiving an award for his presence of mind."[57]

There is a grisly aftermath to Zinoviev's death. On 20 December 1936, Stalin gave a party in the Kremlin for a group of NKVD officers. One of them, K.V. Pauker, served Stalin as a sort of court jester. "When everyone had drunk a good deal, Pauker, supported by two other officers . . . played for Stalin the part of Zinoviev being dragged to execution. He hung by their arms, moaning and mouthing, then fell on his knees and, holding one of the warders by the boots, cried out 'Please, for God's sake, Comrade, call up Yosif Vissarionovich (Stalin)'."[58] Stalin howled with laughter. Then Pauker, truckling to Stalin's anti-Semitism, decided on a variation. This time he had Zinoviev raising his hands and crying, "Hear, Israel, our God is the only God!" Stalin was so overcome with mirth that he had to signal Pauker to stop the performance.

Radek died in the Gulag, in one of the Arctic camps. Though there are several versions of his death, there is general agreement that he was killed by a fellow prisoner (or prisoners). Louis Fischer suggests that he may have been "choked to death by cell inmates for turning informer against former comrades. . . ."[59]

A more widely circulated version originates with a former Secret Police officer who defected in 1954 while serving with the Soviet Embassy in Australia. "Some time in 1938," he writes, "I decoded a telegram from one of the northern prisons—it was either Irkutsk or Novo-Sibirsk. It referred to Radek and reported that a fellow-convict who shared the same cell . . . had quarreled violently with him, and in the ensuing fight had lifted Radek into the air and dashed him down on the cement floor, causing a head injury from which death had resulted. Of course it could have been just an unfortunate accident. But Radek knew many of Stalin's most compromising secrets."[60]

10

Fatal Ambush:
Parral and Baku

ONE OF THE MOST TRAUMATIC EXPERIENCES in Francisco Villa's life was the *de facto* recognition extended to his enemy, Venustiano Carranza, by the United States. Of all the Mexican revolutionary leaders, Villa had always been the most pro-American. He had uncomplainingly accepted the occupation of Veracruz, he had allowed Americans to serve under his command, and he had always been a readily accessible source of good copy to American newsmen. But now, following a string of military reverses, his former friends had suddenly turned on him.

At least one influential American sympathized with Villa and understood his disillusionment. "The recognition of Carranza," wrote General Hugh L. Scott, "had the effect of solidifying the power of the man who had rewarded us with kicks and of making an outlaw of the man who helped us." Scott also tried to prevent rail passage of *carrancista* troops through border regions of the United States to fight the *villistas*.[1] In recognition of these efforts, Villa telegraphed Scott that he was the only honest man north of Mexico.[2]

Villa meant this quite literally. No scorned lover has ever acted with more passion or outrage than did Villa against the Americans. With the exception of Scott, every *gringo* was fair game for *villista* vengeance. (If we can credit the versions of Drs. Triolo and Ellis, related in Chapter 5, they too were exempt from Villa's anti-*yanqui* fury.) Americans were now in the same category as the hated Chinese, and it was about this time that Villa began to use the term *"chino blanco"* to refer to them.[3]

Villa had faded into the sierra just after Christmas of 1915. Less than three weeks later his anti-American mood expressed itself in unpleasantly concrete terms. On 10 January 1916, a band of *villistas* held up a train near Santa Isabel in Chihuahua. On the train was a party of sixteen Americans, miners and engineers on their way to a mine where they had a work contract. The mass slaying was ordered by Pablo López, the most gringophobic of all Villa's commanders.[4]

Santa Isabel was followed by what is considered by many to be Villa's most celebrated exploit. This was the 9 March 1916 raid across the border into Columbus, New Mexico. Villa's main reason for attacking Columbus was because he believed Carranza had signed a secret pact that would have made Mexico a virtual United States protectorate. (This assumption was completely false.) He was certain the attack would provoke American intervention and that such a move would strengthen his hand against Carranza. If Carranza allowed American troops to cross the border, he would look like a U.S. puppet. If he resisted, his troops would have to ease up on the hard-pressed *villistas* to meet the new threat from the north.

Villa had two other reasons for planning the Columbus raid. First, he was angered by the failure of a local merchant, Sam Rabel (or Ravel), to deliver a consignment of arms that had been paid for. Second, he wanted to attack the encampment of a nearby military unit, the 13th Cavalry, to replenish his store of arms and supplies.[5]

Unfortunately, it was the innocent who suffered rather than the guilty. Rabel was away at the time, being treated in El Paso for sinus trouble.[6] American casualties, twenty-six in all, were predominantly civilian. Though the 485-man *villista* raiding party lost a quarter of its effectives, the Mexicans did bring back "more than a hundred of the 13th Cavalry's horses and mules along with a heavy load of rifles and machine guns. . . ."[7]

In a peculiar aftermath, Villa found himself defended in the United States and denounced in Mexico. "I have always believed," wrote General Scott, "that Villa came up to the border for the purpose of going to Washington and [when the plan aborted] his men . . . naked and hungry, got out of hand and started to loot the town against Villa's will."[8]

In sharp contrast is the view of Roberto Blanco Moheno that the Columbus raid was the act of "a maddened gang leader . . . who, in his hate for the politicians in Washington, decided to take his vengeance on old people, women, and children. It is a crime that is as repugnant as it is stupid . . . a crime more against Mexico than the United States."[9] Yet both Scott and Dr. Ellis (see Chapter 5) specifically exculpate Villa from personal complicity in the Columbus attack. Scott and Ellis were apparently unaware of Villa's belief in Carranza's "secret pact" with the United States—and how that belief pushed him in the direction of authorizing the Columbus attack.

What angered Mexicans was that Columbus provoked the 11-month Punitive Expedition under General John J. Pershing. When President Wilson first informed Carranza that he was sending troops south of the border, Carranza countered with the suggestion that they revive an old agreement, dating from the days of the Apache raids, permitting both sides to pursue marauders and bandits across the border. To Carranza's intense annoyance, Wilson interpreted this proposal as a green light for the punitive expedition.[10] Carranza and Obregón, whom he had had installed as Minister of War, were probably more angry at Villa for having brought the Americans into Mexico than they were at the Americans for being there. Following six months of negotiations—held in New London, Atlantic City, and Washington—Pershing's troops evacuated Mexico in February 1917. The *Kansas City Journal* wryly commented that Villa, at various times, had been reported dying in a cave, being killed in a ranch-house brawl, being shot while on a wild ride, and being assassinated by one of his own band.[11]

Far from damaging Villa, the Punitive Expedition made his stock rise sharply. He became a symbol of national resistance to foreign invasion. His new-won popularity even extended to Carranza's troops. The situation got so bad that Obregón instructed his commander in Chihuahua to shoot any soldiers caught shouting "Viva Villa!"[12]

While playing hide-and-seek with Pershing, Villa was stinging the *carrancistas*. Though unable to mount a major rebellion against Carranza and Obregón, his ability to harass them was undiminished. The centaur had been reduced to a horsefly, but a viciously persistent and annoying one.

On 28 March 1916, Villa routed a *carrancista* garrison at Ciudad Guerrero, Abraham González's birthplace. It was around this time that he received his wound and was treated by Dr. Triolo. He was back in action by July, and on 16 September he was briefly able to seize Chihuahua City. There he harangued the townspeople from the balcony of Government Palace. He also emptied the jails of *villista* prisoners and was able to add 1,500 recruits to his forces.[13]

The *villistas* stormed Parral on 5 November of the same year, thundering into town amid cries of "We are going to kill *gringos!*" Not finding any, they had to make do with some members of the city's Chinese community. The luckless Orientals were hanged on poplar trees by the Parral River.[14]

During most of this period Villa's opponent in the field was General Francisco Murguía, an ex-photographer who disliked shooting prisoners. Considering this procedure a waste of ammunition, Murguía hanged so many *villistas* that he became known as Pancho *Reatas* ("Pancho the Rope").[15] Sometimes winning, sometimes losing, Villa clashed with Murguía at Horcasitas, Estación Reforma, Jiménez, and Parral. In November 1917, Murguía was replaced by General Jesús Agustín Castro.[16]

Later that month Villa lost one of his best commanders at Hecienda de Rubio, between Ojinaga and Chihuahua City. Baudelio Uribe has been described by an admiring commentator as "a typical *norteño*, generous, intrepid . . . filled with ideals for the redemption of his people [who] never amassed a fortune" and "died poor but immaculate."[17] Nobody is perfect, and this paragon had one disconcerting characteristic: he was given to cutting off the ears of his captives.[18]

By now a discernible pattern was beginning to emerge. Carranza and Obregón, Villa's organization enemies, were no more able to bring Villa to earth in his Chihuahua sanctuary than he was able to begin a new march on Mexico City. But his campaign was successful enough to revive interest in his fortunes north of the border. In March 1917, Villa received a message from Charles Hunt, a representative of New Mexico Senator Albert B. Fall. Hunt wrote Villa that Fall and his associates would be willing to "meet you at any place you desire to confer upon a plan by which we can assist you in any legal manner." In return, Villa would guarantee the protection of "all foreign property within your jurisdiction." Villa declined the offer—he was successfully financing his movement from the territory he controlled and wanted no strings-attached American aid. Besides, Fall was known as one of the most grasping representatives of the oil interests.[19]

The years 1918 and 1919 followed closely the pattern of the preceding two years: Villa waging successful guerrilla warfare, being less successful in pitched battles, occasionally capturing large towns but not having the strength to hold them for more than a day.

The only break in the pattern came in 1919, when Villa was briefly reunited with Felipe Angeles. But the old magic was gone. Villa had no large forces or artillery formations to place at Angeles's disposal, and Angeles had neither the taste nor the talent for hit-and-run warfare. The final reunion was quickly followed by the final break. Angeles wandered off into the wilderness with his twelve men, and the miracle was that he evaded capture for as long as he did.

This stalemate might have gone on indefinitely had it not been for a major rupture on the other side, one involving figures of no less magnitude than Venustiano Carranza and Alvaro Obregón.

Carranza had become president on 1 May 1917, following a March election in which he was the only announced candidate. Obregón had nothing to do with the new administration, having resigned as Secretary of War to return to Sonora and raise chick peas. But he was a young man—still in his thirties—and he looked ahead to 1920, when Carranza's term would expire.

Carranza had no intention of making Obregón his successor. Obregón suffered the disability of being too good for his own good. With his military ability he had put Carranza in power. Now Carranza feared that he might be overshadowed by such an able and ambitious subordinate. Moreover, he considered Obregón too radical. In February 1917, a new constitution had been adopted. At the convention, held in Querétaro, Obregón had emerged as the hero of a left-wing faction that called itself the Jacobins. Gone were the days when Obregón felt he had to ingratiate himself with Carranza by telling him how few agrarians there were in Sonora. He advocated far-reaching land reform, he had recruited "red battalions" to fight against Villa, and he organized political discussion groups among his officers to study the aims of the Revolution.[20]

Though Carranza paid lip service to liberal principles, his basic conservatism continued to assert itself. Typical was the brutal manner in which he broke a general strike in the summer of 1916. In a 1 August decree he mandated the death penalty for those inciting strikes in factories or industrial plants providing public services.[21] In addition, Carranza disbanded Obregón's "red battalions" and returned all confiscated properties to José Yves Limantour, most influential of Porfirio Díaz's inner circle.[22]

Carranza also presided over a corrupt and privileged "new class" in revolutionary Mexico. Lincoln Steffens points out that "Carranza did not, like Madero, give the land, the mines, and other privileges to the old privileged class but [to] his revolutionary leaders . . . and, of course, these privileges did corrupt the new possessors of them into a privileged class with a privileged class psychology. He did not . . . close up the sources of corruption . . . . His 'good' men became 'bad' men. They turned against the aims of the revolution."[23] Steffens of course errs about Carranza not favoring the old elite. But he is on target about the new elite. One of its most lamentable representatives was a "revolutionary" general who established himself in the vicinity of a sugar plantation in the state of Veracruz. The property was owned by a rapacious American named Sewell Emery who kept his workers in a state of debt slavery. The general, in return for a share of the profits, protected the plantation and saw to it that the exploited peons did not get out of line.[24]

Yet none of these scandals ever touched Carranza himself. Even his worst enemies agreed that he was personally honest. But Obregón, who led a relatively clean movement, did not hesitate to use his political power in Sonora to amass a fortune in the chick-pea business.[25]

Though Carranza was constitutionally barred from succeeding himself, he wanted to continue ruling through a pliable figurehead. That automatically let out the ambitious and radicalized Obregón.

Carranza's choice as his successor must rank with the consular appointments of Caligula. The nominee was a man named Ignacio Bonillas, then serving as Mexico's ambassador in Washington. Bonillas, an MIT-trained engineer, had spent most of his life in the

United States and was totally unfamiliar with Mexico's problems. Though this is probably exaggeration, Carranza's political enemies claimed that "Meester" Bonillas (as he was known) even had difficulty speaking the language of his ancestors. Whether real or assumed, Bonillas's unfamiliarity with Spanish made him a nationwide laughingstock. Typical of this mood was a satirical skit put on by students at the University of Puebla, in which this line is spoken to an actor playing the part of Bonillas: "Mr. Bonillas, meet Mr. Ibañez [Spanish writer Vincente Blasco Ibañez], whose books you have read in English. Maybe in a few months you'll be able to read them in Spanish, as we understand you are now studying that language."[26]

Such a ludicrous choice pushed Obregón into announcing his own candidacy, which he did on 1 June 1919. Unconsciously echoing Lincoln Steffens, he announced in a manifesto that Mexico must liberate herself from her liberators. This declaration launched a political campaign that was vicious even by Mexican standards. There was a third candidate, General Pablo González, who turned out to be no more successful as a politician than he had been as a soldier. But his failure was not due to any lack of effort. González had surrounded himself with a particularly brutal camarilla. One of its members was General Jesús Guajardo, the man who had gained Zapata's confidence and then lured him into a fatal ambush. Guajardo shot two officers when they disobeyed his instruction to cry "Viva González!"

Carranza realized that his most dangerous opponent was Obregón. Along with the radicals, Carranza was supported by a powerful segment of the military and (especially in Sonora) by the newly rich "new class" of bourgeois revolutionaries.[27]

At Carranza's direction a reign of terror was launched against *obregonista* political workers. Some were shot while others were arrested and held incommunicado. Obregón replied in kind. His supporters, the railroad workers, arranged delays of Bonillas's campaign train and caused him to miss speaking engagements. This enabled Obregón propagandists to spread the rumor that "Meester" Bonillas had had to cancel his speeches because he was busy studying Spanish.[28]

What had begun as a political campaign ended in open rebellion. Target of this rebellion was a structure that was rotten to the core. So Carranza's fall came with breathtaking speed. By the end of February 1920, the state of Sonora was in open revolt against him. On 30 April, in Chilpancingo (Guerrero), Obregón declared that it was no longer possible to continue the political campaign and that the only solution was force of arms. Pablo González went into rebellion on 4 May and the following day the capital was under shellfire.

Carranza's response was to organize a 31-car train convoy which he planned to take to Veracruz. It was from there that he launched his comeback in 1915. But things were different this time. Instead of having the military genius of Obregón at his side he now had a claque of 10,000 parasites who looted the city clean in preparation for the trip. From the National Treasury to the light fixtures in the National Palace, everything of value was loaded onto the "Golden Train."

The convoy left on 7 May, but rebel attacks forced Carranza and a small band of diehards—including "Meester' Bonillas—to abandon the train a week later. The party headed north, into the Puebla sierra, where it was received with exaggerated protestations of loyalty by a local cacique named Rodolfo Herrero. Herrero lodged Carranza and his reduced following in a miserable cluster of shacks. That night—20 May—Herrero's men crept up to Carranza's hut in the pouring rain and fired a fatal fusillade of bullets at the sleeping president. Herrero, a double turncoat who had only recently declared for Carranza, announced that the former First Chief had committed suicide. Obregón denied complicity in the slaying and even had Herrero brought to trial. He was acquitted. A dissident general later tried to implicate Obregón but his charges, never substantiated, were believed to have originated with Carranza's son-in-law.[29]

How did all this affect Villa? One of his organization enemies had now devoured the other. But he would have been in error to derive too much comfort from this fact. The survivor, Obregón, was a far more dangerous enemy than the fallen First Chief.

Yet better times were ahead. A national election was scheduled for 5 September, with Obregón as the odds-on favorite. On 24 May, in a special session of Congress, Adolfo de la Huerta was chosen provisional president. De la Huerta, a former governor of Sonora, was an amiable and conciliatory man who wanted to bring peace to Mexico after a decade of constant turmoil. In this aim he had considerable success. The *zapatistas* went back to their fields and, following an amnesty for his followers, the veteran counterrevolutionary Felix Díaz was allowed to go into exile.

That left only Villa. Working with tact, patience, and sensitivity toward Villa's paranoid suspicion of Mexico City *politicos*, de la Huerta persuaded him to sign a peace treaty on 28 July 1920. Under the terms of this accord, Villa "pledged himself to lay down his arms and retire to a hacienda called Canutillo, in . . . Durango. This hacienda . . . was bought for 636,000 pesos. In addition, he was given 35,926 pesos to cover the wages owing to the troops Villa had surrendered with. He was allowed $120,000 (U.S. currency) with which to buy agricultural implements, 48,000 pesos monthly to pay the guard he was authorized to have, and 5,000 pesos monthly to help the widows and orphans of the *División del Norte*."[30]

Though the hacienda was located across the Durango line, the focus of Villa's activities continued to be the southern Chihuahua city of Parral. He made his purchases there, bought a downtown hotel, and regularly attended cockfights. He also installed one of his "wives," Soledad Seañez, in a Parral apartment. (The incumbent, Austroberta Rentería, was with him at Canutillo.)[31]

Though Villa considered himself at peace with his enemies, the feeling was not reciprocated. Villa's antagonists fell into two categories: (1) personal foes who had a grudge against him; (2) highly placed figures who still feared his revolutionary potential. This was the background to the 23 July 1923 ambush at Parral, where the personal and impersonal enemies joined forces and worked as a team.

Of the personal adversaries, the key figure was a cattle dealer named Melitón Lozoya. Villa's hacienda at Canutillo had previously belonged to a rich family called Jurado. Fleeing the Revolution, they had authorized Lozoya to sell all movable stock and equipment and keep half the proceeds for himself. When Villa heard of the transaction he flew into a rage. Though Lozoya protested that the deal had gone through prior to Villa's acquisition of the hacienda, Villa angrily gave him thirty days to replace the equipment that had been removed. Lozoya was unable to do so. Though the deadline passed without Villa taking action, Lozoya dreaded his violent temper and saw Villa as a constant threat. This made him a logical candidate for the conspiracy.

Villa spent the night of the 19th at the house of a woman friend. The next morning, accompanied by six followers, he set off for Canutillo in his big Dodge touring car. The party drove down Calle Juárez, then turned right on Gabino Barreda, the street leading across the Río Parral bridge and back to Canutillo. As the car was making the turn into Barreda, a volley of shots rang out from a two-story house. Inside were Melitón Lozoya and an eight-man assassination team he had assembled.

Of Villa's party, five out of seven were killed. The dead included Villa, Manuel Trillo, his second-in-command, Rosalío Rosales, his chauffeur, Daniel Tamayo, and Claro Hurtado. Managing to escape, though wounded, were Rafael Medrano and Ramón Contreras. One of the attackers, José Guerra, was also killed as was an unidentified passerby.

Nobody ever believed that this was just a revenge killing by Melitón Lozoya and his low-level associates. Lozoya's original claim that he was the "intellectual author" of the assassination was also ridiculed.[32] The Parral ambush was an operation planned from above, the work of Francisco Villa's organization enemies.

On 27 July, a week after the murder, President Obregón announced to the press that "the mysterious assassination of Fransciso Villa will soon be clarified."[33] It is difficult to see how this was anything but a cue. The man being prompted was a Durango congressional deputy named Jesús Salas Barraza. Salas Barraza wrote a full "confession" and delivered it by hand to General Abraham Carmona, Chief of Artillery in the Secretariat of War and Marine. Carmona released it to the press and the "confession" appeared in the 9 August issue of every newspaper in the capital.

Here the plot thickens. Carmona was in Durango when Salas gave him the "confession." It was written prior to 5 August, the date Carmona returned to Mexico City to release it to the press. Also on hand was Juan Serrano, Inspector of the National Telegraph system. All three men—Salas, Carmona, Serrano—were close friends and all belonged to a Masonic lodge in Durango.[34] This clearly indicates that Serrano and Carmona were not only emissaries from Obregón but that they may have even helped compose the letter written ostensibly from Salas to Carmona.

In agreeing to take the rap, Salas Barraza was hardly acting as a sacrificial goat. After less than a year in the Chihuahua penitentiary, he was pardoned by Ignacio Enriquez, the strongly anti-Villa state governor. He subsequently received an Army commission and was re-elected to Congress. He died insisting that he was the sole "intellectual author" of the assassination.

The "confession," far from being an expression of remorse, reads like an Emile Zola polemic. Pouring invective on "the bandit Doroteo Arango," Salas Barraza accuses Villa of causing hardship to the local population by blowing up an electric plant, of killing a friend of his named Catarino Smith, and of shooting thirty *soldaderas* (camp followers) in Camargo. In a "synthesis," Salas Barraza declares that there was so much ill-feeling against "the *latifundista* of Canutillo" that he "accepted the leadership of a band of brave men" and "took the irrevocable resolution . . . to bring about the result we all wished for: the death of the hyena."[35]

All this adds up to a finger pointing at Obregón. Was he the sole initiator of the assassination? There is reason to believe otherwise. Another powerful and ambitious organization man was now in the picture: Plutarco Elías Calles. As secretary of *gobernación* (the powerful Interior Ministry), Calles was Obregón's heir apparent. He planned to run for the presidency when Obregón's term was up and Obregón had openly given him his blessing.

Villa and Calles detested each other. Villa had never forgotten how Calles, a mediocre commander, had defeated him in 1915 with the help of American aid. Calles, for his part, was skeptical of Villa's claim that he had forever retired from public life. Calles's only potential rival for the presidency was Adolfo de la Huerta, whom Obregón had appointed Secretary of the Treasury. Though de la Huerta disclaimed presidential ambitions, Calles was disturbed by his friendshp with Villa. His peace of mind was not improved by an interview Villa gave to a group of American newsmen. When they asked him if he would ever take arms again, he said he would do so only under two circumstances: if the United States invaded Mexico or if de la Huerta ever needed his help.[36] Calles was an abnormally suspicious man, but in this case his suspicions were well founded. As if to prove that paranoids have real enemies, de la Huerta did go into rebellion at the end of 1923.

Calles had both the motive and the desire to eliminate Villa. The allegations against him began almost immediately after the assassination. They began as a whispering campaign, followed by a newspaper cartoon of dinosauric subtlety. It showed two men in the street, one asking the other "Who killed Villa?" "*Calle . . . se, amigo* ['be quiet, friend'],"* was the reply.[37]

Fuel was added to the flames by an astoundingly indiscreet interview given to a man named Justino Palomares by General Felix Lara. Lara, as a colonel, had commanded the garrison at Parral the day Villa was killed. Lara told Palomares that "a few months before [the assassination] I was called to Mexico City by General Calles whose first instructions were that we eliminate the new Cincinnatus of Canutillo because he was a great danger to the country. [Calles] knew that he had a great quantity of arms that he could use at any time." Lara was then instructed to seek out leading local enemies of Villa and then shelter them in the barracks after the killing—which he did.[38]

One of Lara's military colleagues, General Alfredo Rueda Quijano, was shocked by his indiscretion. "What a fool you are, Felix," he said. "Don't you know that Palomares was Villa's secretary and at the first opportunity is going to publish everything you've blabbed."[39] This is exactly what happened. Shortly after the Lara interview, Palomares published an article titled "The Truth About the Death of Francisco Villa."[40]

An interesting addendum is furnished by one of the assassins. "Each of us received 300 pesos," said Librado Martínez, "even Melitón." He added that the money was delivered to them at La Cochinera, a nearby village, by Josefita Solís, Lozoya's mother-in-law.[41] This damages Lozoya's claim (which nobody believed anyway) that he was "intellectual author" of the crime. It also casts doubt on Salas Barraza's assertion that the assassins were "a band of brave men" fighting tyranny.

In fixing responsibility for Francisco Villa's killing, all available evidence points directly to his organization enemies. Yet, in terms of abstract justice, this strong evidence weighs exactly the same as scant evidence or no evidence at all. So strongly was Mexico's revolutionary establishment tilted against this lonely rebel that Obregón and Calles would not have been brought to justice if they had been discovered by Villa's corpse with smoking pistols.

Francisco Villa had the satisfaction of seeing one of his organization enemies swallow the other. He also had the misfortune of seeing Carranza replaced by Plutarco Elías Calles, a younger, abler, and more ruthless man. The result was that fatal ambush at Parral.

JOHN REED'S "FATAL AMBUSH" was a more subtle one than Francisco Villa's. But it was no less lethal and involved infinitely more physical and spiritual torment. Though Reed actually died in Moscow, his constitution was fatally undermined in the course of a 2,600-mile round-trip train journey between Moscow and Baku. He made the trip in reduced health and in the company of his two bitterest political enemies.

With the recklessness for which he was famous, Reed made some notable contributions to his own destruction. Though his physical condition was poor, his sense of duty forced him into taking the long and wasting trip to Baku. While on the trip, he showed an almost suicidal disregard for health and safety. A picture taken of Reed at Baku is a shocker: gaunt face, hollow cheeks, a gaze of misery and exhaustion. (In sharp contrast, sitting at a table, is a sleek, well-fed Zinoviev.) During the return to Moscow the train was attacked by bandits. Despite his illness, Reed accompanied the Red Army train guard in pursuit of the attackers.[42] In Daghestan, near Baku, Jack shocked his companions by taking a big bite out of a watermelon in the colorful marketplace. This rash act has given rise to theories that this was how he contracted the microorganism that killed him.

Reed had returned to Russia in late fall of 1919. Under the name of "Jim Gormley," he shipped out from New York on a Scandinavian freighter in September. Debarking at the Norwegian seaport of Bergen, he made it overland to Russia with the aid of Bolshevik sympathizers.

Reed was on a political mission. After an acrid parliamentary dispute, two Communist factions had emerged in the United States. Reed's group, the Communist Labor Party, was drawn mostly from

John Reed at the Baku Conference. Contrast the gaunt,
emaciated Reed (in white shirt, standing behind the
bearded man in dark clothing) with the sleek, well-fed
Grigori Zinoviev (in dark suit, seated at table). (*By
permission of the Houghton Library, Harvard University.*)

native Americans, while the rival Communist Party, under Italian-born Louis C. Fraina, had a membership of principally foreign extraction. Both parties were seeking recognition from the Communist International.

This was the situation that prevailed in early 1920: Zinoviev was Chairman of the Comintern; Radek, following his return from Germany, was Secretary; both men were hostile to Reed. (Radek had replaced Reed's ally, Angelica Balabanov, as Secretary following a quarrel between her and Zinoviev.) But Reed's position was buttressed by his friendship with Lenin and Trotsky. It was at this time that Lenin wrote the laudatory introduction to *Ten Days*. As for Trotsky, then serving as War Commissar, he gave Reed an interview in which he expounded plans for transforming the Red Army into a postwar labor force that would develop virgin lands in remote regions of the Soviet Union.[43]

Reed's political problem was temporarily solved when the Comintern agreed to a convention, to be held at a future date, for the purpose of unifying the two Communist parties. Jack was now anxious to return to the United States. For one thing, he missed Louise; for another, he wanted to go back and face charges of criminal anarchy that had been brought against him and thirty-seven other CLP leaders. Attorney General A. Mitchell Palmer, the McCarthy of his day, had launched a witch-hunt against radicals and it was in keeping with Reed's confrontational nature to meet the challenge head on.

According to Benjamin Gitlow, then a top-ranking American Communist, Zinoviev tried to prevent Reed from leaving Russia.[44] Reed, a natural showman, could have greatly increased his prestige in the radical community with a round of courtroom heroics. This was the last thing Zinoviev wanted.

Reed rejected Zinoviev's directive and prepared to return home. Commissioned a courier, he was given 102 small diamonds (total worth about $14,000), $500, 60 English pounds, 10,000 German marks, 2,400 Swedish crowns, 900 Finnish marks, and 500 Danish crowns.[45] This bounty, to be used to foment Communism in the United States, was authorized by the Comintern. In view of Zinoviev's attitude, it is safe to assume that the donation originated with Lenin.

Leaving Moscow, Reed went to Petrograd and there had a meeting with Emma Goldman. In accordance with a Mitchell Palmer directive, she was one of 249 radicals who had been deported from the United States on the S.S. *Buford*, more popularly known as the "Red Ark."

The Reed-Goldman meeting began as an affectionate reunion but ended in sharp disagreement. "Wonderful, marvelous, isn't it, E.G.," Goldman reports Reed as saying. "Your dream of years now realized in Russia . . . made real by the magic wand of Lenin and his band of despised Bolsheviks." Goldman replied that more credit belonged to "the Russian people, preceded by a glorious revolutionary past." She grew increasingly restive as Reed, "almost bloodthirsty," advocated extermination of "treacherous gang [of] Black Hundreds, Jew-baiters, the ducal clique. . . . I have learned one mighty expressive word, *razstrellyat* (execute by shooting)." This was too much for Goldman. "Stop, Jack, stop! The word is terrible enough in the mouth of a Russian. In your hard American accent it freezes my blood." The argument escalated as Reed offhandedly dismissed the shooting of five hundred counterrevolutionaries as a "stupid blunder on the part of overzealous Chekists." "You call it a stupid blunder," replied the distraught Goldman. "I call it a dastardly crime—the worst ever committed in the name of revolution."[46]

The dispute is interesting for the way it demonstrates the response of two idealists to revolution. While Goldman remained in the humanitarian tradition, Reed had developed the chilly fanaticism of an *apparatchik*.

As Reed prepared to leave Russia, Zinoviev continued playing his devious games. In February Reed made two attempts to get out. Both failed. Though Reed just put it down to bad luck, Benjamin Gitlow states that his efforts were deliberately sabotaged by Zinoviev.[47] No group on earth was more skilled in smuggling agents across borders than the Comintern. So this sudden ineptitude is difficult to understand—especially with a Communist as important as Reed.

Reed tried again in March, this time entering Finland. He was accompanied by a Russian sailor, whom he later learned was an agent of Zinoviev. It was the sailor who betrayed him to the Finnish authorities.[48]

Reed was arrested in the hold of a freighter docked at the port of

Abo. Though he at first insisted he was the seaman Jim Gormley, the arresting party scoffed at his story. He admitted his real identity when the diamonds and currency were discovered.

During detention Reed blamed the United States for his troubles. As he wrote Louise Bryant, the Finns told him he was being kept in prison "at the request of the United States government." It was only in June, following his return to Russia, that he learned how Zinoviev had set him up.[49]

Reed emerged from Finnish captivity in an alarmingly weakened state. Though the Finns were relatively humane captors, his health suffered through solitary confinement in a small, dank cell and a miserable diet of bread and dry, salted fish.[50]

It was in this diminished condition that Reed faced Zinoviev and Radek at the Second Congress of the Communist International. For symbolic and propagandist reasons, the conclave opened in Petrograd on 19 July. It moved to Moscow on the 23rd, and all the serious business was conducted there until adjournment on 7 August. The Congress was "aimed unambiguously at the most precise coordination of (foreign) Communist parties with the Moscow center."[51] To achieve this end, Twenty-One Conditions were laid down governing the entry of foreign Communist parties into the Comintern. The Twenty-One Conditions were generally directed against reformist (evolutionary socialist) leaders like Ramsay MacDonald in England, Morris Hillquit in the United Staes, and Karl Kautsky in Germany.

Though Reed had no objection to the radical and centralizing aspect of the Twenty-One Conditions, it was Condition 9 that proved to be the great bone of contention between himself and the Zinoviev-Radek faction. This article stipulated that "Every party desirous of belonging to the Communist International shall be bound to carry on systematic and persistent Communist work in the trade unions, cooperatives, and other organizations of the working masses."[52]

Zinoviev and Radek interpreted this to mean that American Communists were to infiltrate the American Federation of Labor. This decision infuriated Reed. He favored the industrial unionism of his beloved IWW and detested the conservative craft unionism of AFL president Samuel Gompers. Gompers, a furious foe of Bolshevism and supporter of the war, represented everything about the American labor movement that Reed wanted to destroy. And now Zinoviev and Radek were slighting the militant IWW and advocating Communist entry into an organization that Reed saw as no different from "the National Association of Car Manufacturers."[53]

Though tired and rundown, Reed fought Zinoviev and Radek every inch of the way. During the Congress he was appointed to the ECCI (Executive Committee of the Communist International). But the appointment did not give him enough political strength to effectively counter Zinoviev and Radek on the labor question. They successively engineered defeat of motions that the trade-union question be considered first and that English be made one of the official languages of the Congress. When the question came to a vote, Reed was trounced by a humiliating 57–8 margin. Reed stubbornly fought on, reviving the issue at a debate on the Comintern constitution and, later, at an ECCI meeting to examine admission applications to the Comintern. Radek responded with venomous sarcasm and Zinoviev with a combination of florid oratory and parliamentary bullying, refusing to answer questions and silencing opponents. The meeting ended with Zinoviev and Radek having successfully steamrollered an embittered Reed.

Antagonism was even sharper in their private discussions. One of these conversations, as Reed revealed it to him, is recorded by Max Eastman: "Zinoviev and Radek got him aside, and Zinoviev said to him: 'Reed, you can't afford to do this—we'll destroy you. You can't fight the organization. We'll destroy you, Reed.' And Jack said: 'It hasn't worried me when American capitalists threatened to destroy me, I'm not afraid of you either—go ahead and do your worst.'"[54]

We now come to the most puzzling and controversial episode of the entire period: Reed's brief, and quickly retracted, resignation from the ECCI. Mystery surrounds both *when* and *why* Reed resigned.

Part of the confusion comes from a statement by Max Eastman that Reed quit the ECCI just before his death, i.e., *after* the Baku Conference that followed the Second Congress of the Comintern. He was allegedly disgusted with Zinoviev and Radek's behavior on the trip and during the conference.[55]

This claim is challenged by Angelica Balabanov, Granville Hicks (Reed's first biographer), and—later—by Eastman himself.

Eastman's reversal is phrased in a curiously roundabout way. Apparently accepting Hicks's version of the resignation having taken place "during one of the sessions of the executive committee (of the Second Congress)," he then shifts the topic and asks *why* Reed resigned. From this we may assume that Eastman simply made an error in placing Reed's resignation after Baku.

The *why* is indeed a more provocative question than the *when*. In his biography, Hicks attributed Reed's resignation to opposition to "Zinoviev's decision on an organizational question."[56] Eastman attacked this statement as "vague and noncommital" and, in a letter to a magazine, Hicks conceded that "we do not know all the facts involved in Reed's resignation from the ECCI."[57] A later biographer, Robert Rosenstone, comments as follows: "Annoyed by a series of unwarranted gibes . . . Jack's growing frustration one day exploded into a rage that ended with his resignation."[58]

After careful scrutiny of available data, I feel the most plausible explanation is Theodore Draper's. It involves Louis Fraina, head of the Communist faction that rivaled Reed's. In early 1920 Fraina was accused of being an agent of the Bureau of Investigation (a forerunner of the FBI). He was tried and acquitted by three Party courts, one in the United States and two in Russia.[59] Fraina later changed his name to Lewis Corey and became an anti-Communist. Under this new identity he made a full statement to the FBI in 1952. He deposed that Reed, at an ECCI meeting, brought up the matter of the Party trials. Though he professed belief in the innocence of Fraina (as he was then), Reed recommended that he be suspended from Party functions because of the unfavorable publicity that surrounded him. Other ECCI members angrily rejected Reed's proposal, a heated argument ensued, and this was the cause of Reed's brief resignation.[60] If this is true, Reed's resignation (offered and withdrawn before Baku) had nothing to do with the disillusionment he suffered on that disastrous trip.

Reed went to Baku with the greatest reluctance. Louise Bryant states that Reed didn't want to go because his health had been weakened in Finland. This view is supported by Emma Goldman's declaration that Reed "had begged Zinoviev not to insist on his going (to Baku) because he had not yet recovered from his experience in Finland. But the chief of the Third International was relentless. Reed was to represent the American Communist Party at the Congress. . . ."[61]

Zinoviev and Radek had their way. But Reed's decision to go had nothing to do with his being intimidated by these enemies. It was based on his strong sense of duty, a quality that went hand in hand with his reckless idealism. When Reed felt a commitment, self-preservation went out the window. An appreciation of this characteristic comes from Reed's onetime adversary, Fraina-Corey, with whom he died reconciled. "Could you not make more of Reed's illness?" Corey wrote Granville Hicks. "It . . . illustrated the finest of Reed's qualities. I saw the contrast between him and an English delegate [who was] interested in nothing but his chances of recovery. . . . Reed, on the contrary, was Reed to the end."[62]

Less obvious than the reason for Reed's decision to go to Baku was the one behind Zinoviev and Radek's passionate desire to get him there. Unlike Villa's enemies at Parral, they had no plans to murder Reed. Their intention, rather, was to work on this weakened man, to kill him spiritually, and to mold him into a malleable puppet. (They possibly sensed subservience in Reed's agreeing to go to Baku in the first place.) It is ironic that they succeeded in killing the body rather better than they did in killing the spirit.

But wasn't this a case of overkill? Zinoviev and Radek had thoroughly trampled Reed at the Second Congress. How could he continue to be their rival in what Max Eastman described as "the organization they so arrogantly controlled"?[63]

Eastman in fact overestimates the degree of control that Zinoviev and Radek exercised in the Comintern. The ultimate authority rested with Lenin, and both men were under a cloud: Zinoviev for his "strikebreaking" prior to the October Revolution and Radek for his oppositionist position at Brest-Litovsk and general wisenheimer reputation.

A third Comintern functionary joined Zinoviev and Radek on the trip to Baku—a man in even greater disfavor with Lenin than they were. This was Béla Kun, leader of the short-lived (21 March–1 August 1919) Hungarian Soviet Republic. Kun, against Lenin's advice, had moved too fast in socializing the land and abandoned the independent position of Communist cadres. Though Kun was given refuge in Russia following the collapse of his regime, his errors were thrown up to him at a Comintern meeting.[64]

Reed, by contrast, stood high with Lenin—despite the beating he had taken at the Second Congress. So Zinoviev and Radek had every reason for wanting to further diminish Reed. This is less true of Béla Kun. He and Reed seem to have got on well and, shortly before his death, Reed introduced Kun to Louise Bryant.

This brings us to another episode that has become shrouded in controversy: the alleged participation of Zinoviev, Radek, and Béla Kun in a mobile orgy during the trip to Baku. While the countryside was gripped by starvation, with Whites and bandits roving freely, Zinoviev, Radek, and Kun were accused of loading up the train with the finest food and wines. On arrival in the Caucasus their car was boarded by prostitutes. What followed was a round "of drunken lasciviousness in which Radek was the central figure."[65]

Though several Reed biographers (and other commentators) confirm the story, it is labeled a fabrication by Virginia Gardner. Gardner's skepticism derives mainly from her lack of confidence in two writers who have presented the story as fact. One, Benjamin Gitlow, was an ex-Communist who became a professional anti-Communist during the witch-hunts of the '40s and '50s. The other, Jacob H. Rubin, made, in his account, the patently mendacious claim that Reed considered Stalin his best friend.[66]

Gardner has done some painstaking literary detective work, especially in the two historical appendices to her book. Still, one is puzzled by her certainty that the "train orgy" story was a fabrication. It *could* have been invention—but it just as easily could have been true. Since all principals and witnesses are dead, the matter becomes one of conjecture. In this context, one has to consider probabilities. Would such behavior (callous high living in the midst of misery and danger) be consistent with the personalities of Zinoviev, Radek, and Béla Kun? The answer is a resounding yes.

This is particularly true of Radek, alleged "central figure" of the festivities. Train escapades seem to have played a big part in his life. We recall his arrogant outburst when he was placed in a coach in Petrograd that he did not consider worthy of his position. We also remember his high jinks on the sealed train through Germany, when he and his fellow merrymakers were curbed only by the intervention of Lenin. Though Radek was probably the most boisterous of the trio, neither Zinoviev nor Béla Kun (a drug user, according to Angelica Balabanov) belonged to the tradition of great revolutionary ascetics. (Olga Ravich, whose screeching exuberance so annoyed Lenin on the sealed train, was Zinoviev's second wife.)[67] Given this background, a more likely "fabrication" would have involved Zinoviev, Radek, and Béla Kun abstaining from frivolity and behaving throughout the trip with conspicuous rectitude.

Accounts of Reed's reaction to all this also show him behaving in a manner consistent with his values. Max Eastman describes him as "shocked by the luxuries enjoyed by the delegates on the way to Baku and back—luxuries that necessitated pulling down the blinds as they passed through towns where men were all but starving."[68] Though a convivial soul, and free of sexual puritanism, Reed's idealism made him react with disgust toward his companions' Marie Antoinette-ish behavior.

The Baku Conference—officially known as the Congress of the Peoples of the East—opened on 1 September 1920. Among the 1,891 delegates, mostly Moslems, were 235 Turks, 192 Persians and Parsees, 8 Chinese, 8 Kurds, and 3 Arabs. There were also 157 Armenians and 100 Georgians from the Soviet Caucasus.[69]

This congress represented the Comintern's most serious attempt to exploit the anti-imperialist and anti-colonialist aspects of the world struggle against capitalism. It also had racial, religious, and regional overtones, inflaming Asians against Europeans, Moslems against Christians, and East against West. But only the capitalist West. In the struggle of anti-colonialist Orientals against oppression, occidental Marxists would be their allies. Lenin described the situation as one in which "the infantry of the East will reinforce the cavalry of the West."[70]

The Baku Conference afforded Zinoviev the opportunity to give full reign to his superb oratorical gifts. Along with another unpleasant man, Adolf Hitler, Zinoviev was an inspired rabble-rouser. Max Eastman describes him as "the very incarnation of a demagogue. He became excited to inebriation by his own oratory, and by the hypnotic effect that his high tenor, half-chanting, madly lucid utterance had upon his auditors."[71] Sometimes Zinoviev had to be restrained. "Lenin would say: 'Now for God's sake, hold yourself in and say nothing but what you have been instructed to say by the Central Committee.' But he always came home repenting of some act of drunken eloquence."[72]

Zinoviev had had to hold himself in at the Second Congress of the Comintern. The delegates were sophisticated Westerners and much of the time was consumed with procedural and bureaucratic maneuvering. But at Baku he could let himself go. Addressing an assembly of primitive people—many wearing turbans and carrying scimitars—Zinoviev pulled out all stops in lashing them into an anti-imperialist frenzy. "The Communist International," he chanted, "turns today to the people of the East and says to them, 'Brothers, we summon you to a Holy War, first of all against British imperialism.'"[73]

Reed heard these words with outrage. As a devout Marxist, he rejected religion and demagogic pleas for holy wars. After Zinoviev's speech, he and Reed had a heated exchange. "I do not think a real revolutionist would talk that way," said Reed contemptuously.[74] When it came his own turn to speak, Reed pointedly avoided any proselytizing on a religious basis. His address was a dose of unadulterated Marxism. Reviewing the record of American oppression in Cuba, the Philippines, and Santo Domingo, he ended by urging the delegates to "follow the Red Star of the Communist International."[75]

Reed also resented Zinoviev's opportunism in inviting Enver Pasha to the conference. An "anti-imperialist" of very recent vintage, Enver had been Ottoman War Minister and played a sinister part in organizing the 1915 massacre of Armenians in Turkey. Zinoviev's ploy backfired as Enver found himself ostracized by both the Turkish and Armenian delegations to the conference.[76]

Baku finished Reed. His heroics on the return trip—when he mounted a machine gun cart and helped the train guard pursue bandits—may have been linked to a death wish. "From Baku," recalls Angelica Balabanov, "he returned a totally broken man, even physically. What he saw or heard there was the last blow."[77]

This feeling was shared by Louise Bryant, who had arrived in Moscow while Reed was in the Caucasus. When she first saw him, on 15 September, the joy of their reunion was blunted by her shock over his gaunt and wasted appearance. At this time she experienced a "supernatural premonition" that he might be suffering from a typhus infection.[78]

The premonition proved all too accurate. Within a week to ten days after his return from Baku (accounts differ) Reed took to his bed suffering from dizziness, a burning temperature, and an agonizing headache. The illness was first thought to be influenza, but, as he grew worse, he was taken to Moscow's Marinsky Hospital. It was there that his ailment was diagnosed as typhus.

While in the hospital, Reed found himself the victim of some not-so-benign neglect. None of the Bolshevik leaders came to visit him and Louise Bryant had to go directly to Lenin to procure top-quality medicines and doctors for her husband.[79] But by then it was too late. Reed continued to decline although, according to Bryant, he was spared the horrible hallucinations that afflict many typhus victims. On 17 October he died.

The malice of Reed's organization enemies pursued him beyond the grave. Its target was his best-known work, *Ten Days That Shook the World*. Lenin died in 1924 and was succeeded by the *troika* of Zinoviev, Kamenev, and Stalin. Each of the three had a strong incentive for wanting to suppress *Ten Days*. We have discussed Zinoviev's reason; Kamenev, the Revolution's other "strikebreaker," had a motive identical to Zinoviev's. As for Stalin, his megalomania was affronted by the meager attention he received in *Ten Days*. He is mentioned only twice, and then as his name appears on proclamations. To add insult to injury, the sacred name is subjected to casual variations in spelling. On page 136 he is identified as "I. V. Djougashvili (Stalin)" and on page 230 as "Yussof Djugash-vili-Stalin." Theodore Draper comments that *Ten Days* "became one of the storm centers in the struggle between Stalin and Trotsky. At one point . . . Trotsky had found confirmation in Reed's book. Stalin counterattacked by charging that Reed had been 'remote' from the Bolshevik Party, that he had picked up hostile gossip from enemies, and had spread . . . 'absurd rumors.' It is hard to imagine Reed rallying to the defense of Stalin . . . who was moreover allied with Zinoviev against Trotsky, whom Reed knew intimately and had portrayed as one of the great heroes of the Russian Revolution."[80]

John Reed mastered his enemies better in death than he did in life. Zinoviev and Radek, who engineered the Baku "ambush," died in disgrace under Stalin. Stalin, who banned *Ten Days* throughout his reign, was massively demythologized after his death. *Ten Days* is again respectable Marxist reading while Stalin's turgid works—required literary fare during his dictatorship—are almost forgotten.

— 11 —

Villa and Reed
as Revolutionaries:
An Assessment

How can Francisco Villa and John Reed be evaluated as revolutionaries? A responsible assessment should thoroughly explore two areas: their role as representatives of the romantic tradition and their success—or lack of it—as practitioners of revolution.

The term "romantic"—with its many meanings and nuances—is one that invites imprecision. So clarity must be our goal in defining Villa and Reed as romantic revolutionaries. For purposes of this study we will focus on the definition that classifies the romantic as "passionate, adventurous, and idealistic." This category certainly embraced Villa and Reed. Both men approached revolution with passion, idealism, and a high sense of adventure. It was precisely this approach that made them the supremely appealing and charismatic figures that they were and have remained.

At this point we must deal with a persistent misconception about the romantic revolutionary: that his charisma and personal appeal somehow make him "softer" and more humane than his organization counterpart. There is nothing in history to sustain such a view. The dashing rider who thunders through mountain passes can be just as cold and pitiless to enemies as the office-bound bureaucrat who supervises wholesale deportations to Arctic camps. "Hard" and "soft" revolutionaries are found on both sides of the romantic-bureaucratic divide and, if anything, the romantics probably have an edge over the bureaucrats in producing ruthless killers. Urbina and Fierro were in the romantic tradition, as were the Colorado strikebreakers Bob Lee and Lou Miller.

Villa and Reed definitely belonged to the "hard" romantic faction: romantic without being sentimental and idealistic without being mushy. True, Villa frequently gave way to tears and vacillated when he had Obregón in his power. But these lachrymose outbursts can be put down to temperament. They certainly never made him shrink (as Madero, a less tearful man, often did) from shedding blood. As for his indecision over Obregón, it was based more on *machismo* than humanitarianism. (This quality was cleverly exploited by Francisco Serrano, Obregón's aide, when he asked Villa how a soldier of his proven bravery could ever shoot an unarmed man.)

Though Reed was not on the shooting end of revolution, he in no way yielded to Villa in advocating "final solutions" for enemies. We recall his dialogue with a softer revolutionary, Emma Goldman, and her shock over Reed's lust to exterminate such antirevolutionary elements as the Black Hundreds and the ducal clique. In the same conversation, we also recall Goldman's anguish over Reed's infatuation with *razstrellyat* ("execute by shooting") and the nonchalant manner in which he dismissed the shooting of 500 innocent people as a "stupid blunder."

Another facet of Reed's "hard" romanticism was the sneaking admiration he retained for such brutes as Urbina, Fierro, Lee, and Miller. Reed could never work up the same hatred for men who had ridden with Pancho Villa and Jesse James that he could for such pompous and prissy figures as Edgar Sisson and George T. Marye.

Recognition of this "hardness" is the key to any successful analysis of Villa's and Reed's roles as romantic revolutionaries. This quality was by no means unique in Villa and Reed. Far from being an aberration among romantics, it is closer to a norm. "The romantic hero," writes Camus, "considers himself compelled to do evil by his nostalgia for an unrealizable good."[1] Camus also speaks of the "Lucifer-like" quality of romantic rebellion.[2] Both Villa and Reed had grandiose dreams: Villa of an illiteracy-free Mexico based on a network of military-industrial colonies and Reed of an apple-pie American Communism founded on the power of his beloved IWW. (Of these utopias, Villa's was more realizable and practical than Reed's.)

The "hard" romantic can also be considered in terms of Arthur

Koestler's yogi-commissar analogy. The yogi, according to Koestler, "believes that nothing can be improved by exterior organization and everything by individual effort from within," while the commissar believes that "all the pests of humanity, including constipation and the Oedipus complex, can be cured by Revolution [and] this end justifies the use of all means. . . ."[3]

While the dreamy "soft" romantic may conform to the yogi pattern, "hard" romantics are emphatically in the camp of the commissar. Reed, the energetic master of agitprop, and Villa, the pistol-point social reformer, have nothing in common with mystics and navel contemplators. One should never confuse romanticism with spirituality, and the fact that the bureaucratic type may be an unromantic figure does not invest the romantic with yogi's credentials.

With this insight into the role of Villa and Reed as romantic revolutionaries, we can now consider the question of their achievement. Again, we must be precise. How does one define a successful revolutionary? Mohammed Naguib and Ahmed Ben Bella were key figures in overthrowing King Farouk in Egypt and French colonial rule in Algeria. Yet today everyone identifies the Egyptian and Algerian revolutions with Gamal Abdel Nasser and Houari Boumedienne, subordinates who displaced Naguib and Ben Bella shortly after victory. The names of Naguib and Ben Bella are today almost forgotten. Can they be considered successful revolutionaries?

At the other end of the scale are Miguel Hidalgo and José María Morelos. Neither man lived to see the triumph of the rebellion he helped organize. Yet—though they died in defeat and disgrace— Hidalgo and Morelos (along with Juárez) are a revolutionary trinity as revered in Mexico as Marx, Engels, and Lenin are in Communist countries. In an ironic historical process, the "losers" Hidalgo and Morelos could be considered more successful revolutionaries than the "winners" Naguib and Ben Bella, who went straight from victory to obscurity.

Voltaire and Rousseau are rated the spiritual and intellectual architects of the French Revolution. Yet both men predeceased the fall of the Bastille by eleven years. Could they be considered "revolutionaries" in a revolution they never witnessed?

Once more, the crying need is for clarity. In evaluating the success of Villa and Reed as revolutionaries, responsible scholarship demands an analysis of mathematical precision. The author's task is to rigorously define the qualities of an ideal, or paradigmatic, revolutionary and then measure the performance of Villa and Reed against that standard.

After careful study, the conclusion that emerges is that a paradigmatic revolutionary must have three principal attributes: capacity as an activist, capacity as a theoretician, and capacity as an organization infighter.

Let us further define these categories. By activist, I refer to an individual who promotes revolution through military, political, conspiratorial, literary, oratorical, or spiritual means—or any combination of these. Villa and Obregón, Lenin and Trotsky, Reed and Robespierre, Jesus, Gandhi, and St. Paul—all were gifted revolutionary activitists. More often than not, revolutionary activists are persons of eclectic accomplishment. Trotsky was an outstanding military leader, a superlative orator, and a literary stylist who "wrote history as he made it."[4] Lenin, also a writer, was probably the greatest political strategist of all time. Paul, who universalized Christianity, did so through a formidable combination of talents that were both spiritual and practical.

The successful revolutionary must also have a sound grounding in theory. It is not enough for a revolutionary to excel as a soldier, conspirator, parliamentarian, or pamphleteer—he must have a principle in which he believes and the ability to expound it clearly. The revolutionist's constituency should have the feeling that he stands for something—a doctrine or plan that make him readily identifiable in the political spectrum. If such identification is absent, the revolutionist will lose credibility. At best, people will think him a vague, muddle-headed figure who, though probably meaning well, lacks the intellectual rigor to articulate principles for which he enjoins others to fight. At worst, they will ascribe his doctrinal imprecision to opportunism—like Pascual Orozco who fought for Madero in 1911 and sold out to Terrazas in 1912. No successful revolutionist has ever left potential supporters in doubt as to where he stands. Sometimes, when dealing with an uneducated populace, complicated philosophies have to be reduced to simple, appealing slogans and catch phrases. Great revolutionaries have always understood this. Compare the doughy platitudes of Carranza, a less successful revolutionary, with such heady wine as "Liberty, Equality, Fraternity" and Lenin's message of "Peace, Bread, and Land" to a war-weary peasantry.

Finally, the ideal revolutionary must be highly skilled at organizational infighting. This important area, more prosaic than the others, has been widely overlooked. Yet few of history's truly successful revolutionaries were lacking in this quality. A man notably lacking in it—and who, on this account, must be numbered among the Great Failures—was Trotsky. For all his brilliance in other spheres, his ineptitude as a bureaucratic maneuverer resulted in that fatal tortoise-hare race with the plodding Stalin.

Here an interesting parallel can be drawn between Trotsky and a more successful revolutionary who, in background, temperament, and personality, resembled him in many ways. This was Paul of Tarsus. Both were born Jews, both rejected Judaism, both changed their names, both embraced new ideologies that they had originally opposed,* both were magnificent orators and brilliant communicators, both died violent deaths in foreign lands, both were of high intelligence and strong character, both were supremely self-confident, and both had rather abrasive personalities that alienated contemporaries and laid them open to charges of arrogance.

Yet Trotsky ended as a heretic commanding a splinter faction of world Communism, while Paul succeeded in transforming a small, Jewish-oriented sect centered in Jerusalem into a global religion. Paul's superiority to Trotsky as an organizational infighter plays a large part in this triumph. Where Trotsky made error after error in his struggle against Stalin, Paul consistently outmaneuvered the unsophisticated "kosher Christians" of Jerusalem in his brilliant design to broaden Christianity and bring it to the Gentiles.

Of history's most successful revolutionaries, Lenin was another who excelled at organizational infighting. He ruled the Bolshevik Party by intellect, force of will, and his superb strategic instinct. In Lenin's day, before Stalinist absolutism took over, there was considerable freedom of discussion within the Party. In many of his most cherished designs, Lenin faced powerful opposition—and this meant that he had to use organizational skill to get his way. He launched the October Revolution over the "strikebreaking" obstruction of

*Paul, as Saul, persecuted Christians while Trotsky, as Bronstein, was an anti-Marxist *Narodnik.*

Zinoviev and Kamenev and engineered signing of the Brest-Litovsk peace treaty in the face of 48–15 opposition among delegates to the Third Congress of Soviets.[5] Up until 9 March 1923, when he suffered his third stroke, Lenin was still in effective charge of the Soviet state. That a man who had suffered a shooting and two strokes could maintain supremacy over such as Stalin (already making his grab for power) is eloquent testimony to what mastery Lenin attained in the Bolshevik organization.

How do Villa and Reed measure against this triple standard? The answer, which will be expounded more fully, can be summarized in this diagram:

	Activist	Theoretician	Organizational Infighter
Villa	Good	*Surprisingly good*	Poor
Reed	Good	Poor	*Surprisingly good*

Obviously, both Villa and Reed rate high marks as activists. Villa operated as a soldier and civil administrator; Reed as a writer, publicist, and political organizer.

We have amply discussed Villa's military career; it is now time to focus on his activities in the civil area. Villa functioned as military governor of Chihuahua from the end of 1913 up till March 1914, when he led the *División del Norte* in the Second Battle of Torreón. It was at this time that he bowed to Carranza's directive and reluctantly turned over the governorship to Manuel Chao.

Though Villa's career as a civil administrator was brief, it was remarkable for its accomplishment. This achievement was apparent in both the economic and political sectors.

When Villa took over in Chihuahua, he encountered an economic disaster area. Chihuahua City had never been a great manufacturing center, and what few factories there were had closed down. Unemployment was rampant and, with no money circulating, farmers and ranchers were withholding food from the capital's markets and burying their reserves of silver and Mexican bank notes. Unless conditions were immediately improved, economic stagnation would yield to famine.

To alleviate the situation, Villa's advisers suggested that State bonds be issued bearing 30 or 40 percent interest. Villa immediately rejected the proposal. "I can understand why the State should pay something to people for the rent of their money," he said.[6] But he thought the rates were far too high. Since only the affluent could afford to buy the bonds, he saw the plan as a gimmick to allow the rich to get richer.

Then Villa offered his own plan: he would simply print new currency, using the force of his authority to back it up. As expected, his advisers threw up their hands with horror. They were educated men and saw Villa's move as the typical reaction of a primitive who lacked the slightest knowledge of economics. No money in circulation? Well, let's just print some.

Villa's advisers, like many of his enemies, underestimated their man. In issuing the new bills, Villa was shrewd enough to realize that he would have to contend with three competing currencies: existing money, Mexican bank notes, and silver coins. So his task was clear: to create public confidence in the *dos caras* (so-called because they bore likenesses of Madero and Abraham González), he would have to discredit the rival currencies.

What happened next was a shrewd exercise in benevolent despotism. Villa began his economic reforms by fixing prices: beef at 7¢ a pound, milk at 5¢ a quart, and bread at 4¢ a loaf.[7] Then he found himself faced with another problem. The big merchants, leery of the *dos caras*, were posting one price list for the Villa money and a lower one for the competing currencies. Villa solved this problem with customary directness: sixty days imprisonment for any merchant discriminating against the *dos caras*.

Now the only obstacle was the silver and bank notes hidden in the countryside. In late January 1914, Villa issued a decree that silver and bank notes could be redeemed at the State bank for *dos caras* any time up till 10 February. After that they would be considered counterfeit. Though most citizens complied with the directive, a minority of speculators and local capitalists saw the decree as a bluff and continued to hold out. They were monumentally chagrined by another decree, issued on the morning of 10 February, that all persons trying to pass bank notes or silver coins would be jailed sixty days for counterfeiting. These simple but effective measures produced an economic miracle, causing an American observer to comment that "Chihuahua City prospers as never before in its history."[8]

Equally impressive were Villa's political reforms. Chihuahua City at the time had a population of 40,000. Giving full reign to his obsession with education, Villa commissioned the building of fifty schools during his tenure as military governor.[9]

Happily for students of this era, Villa's term as Chihuahua military governor coincided with Reed's mission to Mexico. So Reed had a first-hand opportunity to observe, and report on, Villa's innovative regime. "No sooner had he taken over the government of Chihuahua," wrote Reed, "than he put his army to work in running the electric light plant, the street railways, the telephone, the water works and the Terrazas flour mill. He delegated soldiers to administer the great haciendas he had confiscated. He manned the slaughterhouse with soldiers, and sold Terrazas beef to the people for the government. A thousand of them he put in the streets of the city as civil police, prohibiting on pain of death stealing, or the sale of liquor to the army. A soldier who got drunk was shot . . . . 'The only thing to do with soldiers in time of peace,' said Villa, 'is to put them to work. An idle soldier is always thinking of war.'"[10] There is an interesting similarity between these views and those of Leon Trotsky. We recall how Trotsky told Reed of plans for transforming the Red army into a postwar labor force.

Reed's role as activist has been amply reviewed in previous chapters. Since the two men operated in different spheres, an absolute comparison between Reed's activism and Villa's would be like matching apples and oranges. But this much can be said: John Reed, as writer-propagandist, and Francisco Villa, as warrior-administrator, were both revolutionary activists of daunting prowess.

In his approach to land reform, Villa steered a shrewdly pragmatic middle course between the conservatism of Carranza and the radicalism of Zapata. Carranza opposed land reform, while Zapata immediately distributed expropriated land to peasants. But Villa placed the lands he seized under state control. This gave him a source of revenue to finance his military operations.[11]

Turning to theory, we encounter a big surprise. It would be expected that a Harvard-trained intellectual and man of letters would have far more impressive theoretical credentials than an ex-peon and sierra bandit. Yet exactly the reverse is true. Theory, as we shall see, was Reed's weakest point.

Villa, on the other hand, had a concise and eminently logical theory of the society that he wished to create in Mexico. This society, combining elements of socialism, nationalism, and populist militarism, would be composed of a complex of military-industrial colonies staffed by veterans of the Revolution. These colonies would receive grants of agricultural land from the central government. The colonies would also contain industrial plants. Three days a week would be devoted to work and three to military training. "When the Patria is invaded," said Villa, "we will just have to telephone from the palace in Mexico City, and in half a day all the Mexican people will rise from their fields and factories, fully armed, equipped and organized to defend their children and their homes."[12] Villa disliked standing armies, seeing them as a step toward institutionalized militarism and dictatorship. The colonies would act as a constant source of trained citizen-soldiers. Thus Mexico would have a means of self-defense without running the risk of having to rely on a federal army run by an entrenched military caste.

Since Villa's theory was never put into practice, no one can tell whether it would have worked. Yet, for neatness and clarity, the concept was one of almost geometric beauty.

Villa's ideology also had a pronounced meritocratic bias. Where Zapata distributed lands indiscriminately, Villa made it clear that preference in acquiring (or keeping) land would go to those who had "earned" favored treatment through their services in the Revolution.[13]

In sharp contrast to the precision of Villa's theoretical thinking was the muddle and confusion of Reed's. In Chapter 4 I referred to a manifesto Reed prepared for *The Masses* at the end of 1912. Max Eastman, in his editorial wisdom, gently eased Reed out of the theoretical area and into assignments that gave the fullest play to his superb reportorial skills.

It is now time to consider that manifesto more closely. There is no other specimen of Reed's writing that more completely bares his meager talent as a theoretician. Here follow some significant excerpts: "It is humiliating to promise great things and not to fulfill them. . . . Our aspirations are great, but we refuse to commit ourselves to any course of action except this: *to do with The Masses exactly what we please!* . . . The broad purpose of *The Masses* is a social one; to everlastingly attack old systems, old morals, old prejudices—the whole weight of outworn thought that dead men have saddled upon us; and to set up new ones in their places. . . . So, standing on the common sidewalk, we intend to lunge at spectres—with a rapier rather than a broadaxe, with frankness rather than innuendo. We intend to be arrogant, impertinent, in bad taste, but not vulgar. We will be bound by no one creed or theory of social reform, but will express them all, providing they be radical. We shall keep a running destructive and satirical comment upon the month's news . . . . And if we want to change our minds about it—well, why shouldn't we?"[14]

Let us take these points in order. Singularly appropriate is the opening line, in which Reed states that it is humiliating to promise great things and not fulfill them. This passage could serve as a leitmotif for the entire manifesto because promising and not fulfilling is exactly what it does. Reed begins by talking of "great aspirations" but then turns right around and makes the anarchic statement—underlined in the original—that the only commitment of *The Masses* should be to do "exactly what we please." Yet, in the very next sentence, he defines the magazine's broad purpose ("a social one") and goes on to list a number of specific criteria—to attack old systems, old morals, old prejudices, etc. Then comes the weakest part of all, the section where Reed pledges *The Masses* to "lunge at spectres—with a rapier rather than a broadaxe, with frankness rather than innuendo." Considering their substance—or lack of it—what orderly intelligence could possibly advocate "lunging at spectres"? The next clause features tangled metaphor, with Reed seemingly equating a rapier with frankness and a broadaxe with innuendo. Nor is the following sentence any more logical. To follow Reed's mandate and draw a line between vulgarity and bad taste would tax the powers of a Jesuit. Reed next commits *The Masses* to expressing every creed or theory of social reform, as long as it is radical. Since few creeds of social reform are apt to be conservative or reactionary, this is something like Henry Ford's famous directive that his workers could buy cars of any color as long as it was black. The manifesto's final sentence—"And if we want to change our minds about it—well, why shouldn't we?"—is another gem. A manifesto, by definition, is a public declaration of serious intention. Yet Reed sees fit to add this nonchalant tagline. It's as if Marx and Engels had breezily ended the Communist Manifesto with "Let's try another if this won't play in Peoria."

Apart from theoretical weakness, what astounds readers is the poor quality of the manifesto's prose. As a chronicler of war, revolution, and social unrest, Reed was second to none. Yet, when he turned to theory, he was on such unfamiliar ground that even his writing ability seemed to desert him.

Reed wrote the *Masses* manifesto in 1912, at the beginning of his career. He had just embraced Socialism but the great events that impelled him to Communism—Mexico, Colorado, the First World War—were still in the future. Did Reed's theoretical ability improve as he became more committed to Marxism?

There is no evidence to support such a view. Interestingly, one person aware of Reed's theoretical weakness was Reed himself. "I have no idea what I shall be or do one month from now," he wrote in the late summer of 1917. "Whenever I have tried to become someone or something, I have failed; it is only by drifting with the wind that I have found myself, and plunged joyously into a new role."[15] It is significant that this statement was made in 1917, almost five years after the sophomoric *Masses* manifesto and at a time when Reed was deeply committed to revolutionary Socialism. He was able, in Orwell's term, to "bellyfeel" Socialism, to grasp it emotionally and intuitively, but with a total lack of theoretical rigor. His more perceptive contemporaries were quick to note this failing. "Reed was a great talent," wrote Walter Lippmann, ". . . but as a descriptive, romantic writer, not a political thinker. He was Byronic. But he was not a politically oriented man."[16] A modern biographer, Robert Rosenstone, comments that "the revolutionary impulse in John Reed was deeply rooted in premises he never clearly articulated."[17]

We now move to the arena of organizational infighting. Though a skilled and innovative civil administrator, Villa remained the anti-Organization Man incarnate. In Chihuahua—where he *was* the organization instead of a man marching in it—he brought about a miracle of political stability and economic recovery. But working in harness with the stubborn, self-righteous Carranza and the clever, ambitious Obregón was quite another matter. How completely Villa was outmaneuvered and then destroyed by his organization foes has been amply related in previous chapters.

And Reed? Again we're in for a surprise. The Harvard graduate who failed so miserably in articulating theoretical concepts showed an unexpected talent for organizational cut-and-thrust.

Reed demonstrated this skill at three important conclaves, two in America and one in Russia. The first was a June 1919 conference of the Left Wing of the Socialist Party, held in Chicago. Reed had joined the Socialists shortly after his return from Russia in the spring of 1918. He quickly aligned himself with the Left Wing, and on 15 February 1919 he was elected to its 15-man City Committee in New York. He also accepted the Left Wing's nomination to the post of International Delegate.

Some of Reed's Party work was literary. In November 1918, the Left Wing established a magazine called *Revolutionary Age*. It was edited in Boston by Louis Fraina, Reed's future rival, and Reed served as a contributing editor. In April 1919, Reed became managing editor of a New York weekly called *Communist*.

Reed's organizational work was, of course, aided by having two magazines from which to trumpet his views. Reed had been sidelined with influenza and the Left Wing's April victory in the Socialist Party elections had a distinctly tonic effect on him. His faction captured twelve of fifteen Executive Committee seats and four of five International Delegate positions. One of these delegates was Reed.

The Left Wing's growing power provoked the Right Wing into an act of political suicide. On 24 May the Socialist Party's National Executive Committee expelled 70,000 out of its 110,000 membership, leaving the "parent" faction a powerless splinter.[18] Though external factors—notably a wave of anti-Socialist repression—were also involved, Reed played an important part in maneuvering the rightists into this act of political hara-kiri. Doing what he did best, he produced a hilarious parody of *Socialist*, the Party's official organ. This spoof, which even included a satire on the magazine's attack on Reed, played no little part in inducing the National Executive Committee's self-destructive rage.

On 21 April the Left Wing called for a June conference. It opened in New York on the 21st. There Reed showed skill at organizational infighting that would have done credit to a Tammany sachem. A minority faction, most of its members foreign-born, proposed the organization of a Communist Party. This plan was opposed by a Reed-led majority, committed to taking over the Socialist Party for revolutionary Socialism. The secessionists then announced their intention of holding a convention in Chicago to organize their new party.

At this point Reed had to contend with an act of betrayal. The National Council of the Left Wing entered into negotiations with the secessionists and on 28 July issued a statement supporting their advocacy of a Communist convention. Angry and defiant, Reed and his associates went among the rank and file. Wheedling, cajoling, and arm-twisting, Reed used all his persuasive powers in an effort to counteract the National Council's treachery.

The confrontation came on 30 August. Reed's opponents had scheduled their convention on the second floor of Machinists' Hall. Reed boldly led eighty of his delegates to the meeting but was stopped by the chairman of the credentials committee. A scuffle ensued and order was finally restored by the police. Reed's group then moved to a room downstairs. Following unsuccessful negotiations, Reed and his supporters moved to the IWW hall and proclaimed themselves the Communist Labor Party of America. Reed was elected to the post of International Delegate which made him, in effect, the CLP's ambassador to the Comintern. This was the background to the jurisdictional dispute that sent Reed back to Russia. His rivals, who called themselves the Communist Party, sent Louis Fraina to challenge the CLP's right to be recognized by the Comintern.

Though Reed failed to attain recognition as America's No. 1 Communist, he had reason to be proud of his organizational work. In April of 1918, on his return from Russia, he was nothing more than a propagandist without party affiliation of any kind. Now he was a leading figure in an organized Communist group and its representative of the Comintern. In this capacity, he committed the CLP to a bold revolutionary program. It was pledged to IWW-style industrial unionism, rejection of bourgeois democracy, and undeviating loyalty to the Soviets. Delegates who thought this program too radical were defeated by a better than 2–1 vote. The following passage reflects Reed's militancy and confidence: "Either the one (social reformism and parliamentarianism)," he wrote, "or the other (Dictatorship of the Proleteriat) must dominate the Party. Compromise there can be none."[19] "WONDERFUL CONVENTION," he wired Louise Bryant. "EVERYTHING IS GOING FINE."[20]

Reed's activity at the Second Congress of the Comintern was

discussed in the last chapter. Though ill and fighting in a losing cause, his skill and tenacity drove his two enemies, Zinoviev and Radek, to near frenzy. In debate over the labor question, Reed's parliamentary deftness succeeded in shattering the aplomb of the normally unflappable Radek. Abandoning mockery for anger, the "Soviet Puck" furiously accused Reed of sabotage. Equally riled, Zinoviev darkly predicted the collapse of the Comintern if Reed's pro-industrial unionism position were adopted.[21]

Reed's success as an organizational infighter becomes even more impressive when one reflects that this was an acquired, rather than inborn, skill. Drawing a provocative comparison, Max Eastman writes that "Lafayette was a natural swordsman; and John Reed was not a natural organizer. . . . He had to change his nature and mode of life. . . ."[22]

A final evaluation. Villa surprises us with his unexpected strength as a theoretician no less than Reed does with his unlooked-for skill as an organizational infighter. Yet both men were damaged by off-setting weaknesses. Though Villa and Reed hold impressive revo-lutionary credentials, these flaws prevented them from attaining the stature of such mega-revolutionaries as Marx and Lenin, Mao and Gandhi, Jesus and Paul. But their accomplishment need never be held cheaply. Francisco Villa and John Reed were, *par excellence*, popularizers and showmen of revolution. Though theirs may have been a barker's role, with dash and charisma exceeding expertise, it is precisely this imbalance that made revolution attractive to future generations of dissidents. Can Che Guevara fail to have been influ-enced by Villa or the militants of the '60s by Reed? While both these romantics failed in their goals—Villa to build a Mexico of military-industrial colonies, Reed to create a Bolshevik America—their enduring achievement was the extent to which they made rev-olution a metaphor for romance.

Notes to Chapters

1. The Mentors: Abraham and Lincoln

1. William H. Beezley, *Insurgent Governor: Abraham González and the Mexican Revolution in Chihuahua*, p. 158.
2. Ibid., p. 159.
3. Ibid., pp. 159–60.
4. Ibid., p. 160.
5. Daniel Moreno, *Los hombres de la revolución*, p. 64.
6. José Fernandez Rojas and Luis Melgarejo, *La revolución mexicana*, p. 202.
7. Beezley, *Insurgent Governor*, p. 136.
8. Ronald Atkin, *Revolution: Mexico 1910–20*, p. 67.
9. Beezley, *Insurgent Governor*, p. 136.
10. Moreno, *Los hombres*, p. 65.
11. Ibid., p. 62.
12. Edward S. ("Tex") O'Reilly, *Roving and Fighting*, p. 288.
13. Moreno, *Los hombres*, p. 62.
14. John Reed, *Insurgent Mexico*, pp. 136–38.
15. William W. Johnson, *Heroic Mexico*, p. 40.
16. Moreno, *Lox hombres*, p. 63.
17. Ibid., p. 64.
18. Ibid., p. 64.
19. Roque Estrada, *La revolución y Francisco Madero*, p. 167.
20. Martín Luis Guzmán, *Memorias de Pancho Villa*, p. 49.
21. Moreno, *Los hombres*, p. 64.
22. Charles C. Cumberland, *Mexican Revolution: Genesis Under Madero*, p. 95.
23. Alfonso Taracena, *Historia extraoficial de la revolución mexicana*, pp. 41–42.
24. Johnson, *Heroic Mexico*, p. 44.
25. Ibid., p. 159.
26. Guzmán, *Memorias de Pancho Villa*, pp. 44–45.
27. Estrada, *Revolución y Francisco Madero*, pp. 327–28.

28. Ibid., p. 390.
29. Ibid., pp. 366–67.
30. Ibid., pp. 475–76; Johnson, *Heroic Mexico*, pp. 63–64.
31. Francisco R. Almada, *Diccionario Chihuahuense*, p. 230.
32. Johnson, *Heroic Mexico*, p. 165.
33. Beezley, *Insurgent Governor*, pp. 157–58.
34. Ibid., p. 157.
35. Ibid., p. 158.
36. Roberto Blanco Moheno, *Crónica de la revolución mexicana*, pp. 154–55.
37. JRP (HL), pamphlet reprint of Lincoln Steffens 11/3/1920 *Freeman* article with introduction by Clarence Darrow.
38. Ibid., pp. 28–29.
39. Justin Kaplan, *Lincoln Steffens: A Biography*, p. 167.
40. Robert A. Rosenstone, *Romantic Revolutionary: A Biography of John Reed*, p. 45.
41. Kaplan, *Lincoln Steffens*, p. 170.
42. Barbara Gelb, *So Short a Time: A Biography of John Reed and Louise Bryant*, p. 31.
43. Rosenstone, *Romantic Revolutionary*, p. 78.
44. Ibid., pp. 75, 80–81.
45. JRP (HL), Lincoln Steffens to John Reed. 6/14/1912.
46. Kaplan, *Lincoln Steffens*, p. 190.
47. Ibid., p. 193.
48. Ibid., p. 194.
49. Lincoln Steffens, *The Autobiography of Lincoln Steffens*, vol. 2, p. 690.
50. Ibid., vol. 2, p. 727.
51. John Reed, *Insurgent Mexico*, p. 241.
52. Kaplan, *Lincoln Steffens*, p. 227.
53. John Reed, "Almost Thirty," *New Republic*, 4/29/1936, p. 333.
54. LSP (BL), clipping in Steffens's scrapbook.
55. Ella Winter and Granville Hicks, *The Letters of Lincoln Steffens*, p. 419.
56. Charles Seymour, ed., *Intimate Papers of Colonel House*, vol. 3, p. 89.
57. Virginia Gardner, *"Friend and Lover": The Life of Louise Bryant*, p. 133.
58. Rosenstone, *Romantic Revolutionary*, p. 316.
59. JRP (HL), 6/17/1918 letter from Lincoln Steffens.
60. LSP (BL), 6/29/1918 letter from John Reed.
61. Kaplan, *Lincoln Steffens*, p. 248.
62. JRP (HL), 3/21/1919 letter to Louise Bryant.
63. Lincoln Steffens, *Lincoln Steffens Speaking*, pp. 307–10.
64. LSP (BL), 11/7/1934 letter to Granville Hicks.

2. 1910: The End of the Beginning

1. *Enciclopedia de México*, vol. 12, p. 800.
2. Ibid., p. 800.
3. Guzmán, *Memorias de Pancho Villa*, p. 9.
4. Ibid., p. 10.

5. Edgcumb Pynchon, *Viva Villa! A Recovery of the Real Pancho Villa*, p. 14.
6. Guzmán, *Memorias de Pancho Villa*, p. 10.
7. Ibid., p. 11.
8. Ibid., p. 11.
9. Luis Garfías, *Verdad y mito de Pancho Villa*, p. 14.
10. Celia Herrera, *Francisco Villa ante la historia*, p. 11.
11. Reed, *Insurgent Mexico*, p. 130.
12. Hugh Thomas, *The Spanish Civil War*, p. 444.
13. Reed, *Insurgent Mexico*, p. 125.
14. Garfías, *Verdad y mito*, p. 45.
15. Almada, *Diccionario Chihuahuense*, p. 535.
16. Garfías, *Verdad y mito*, p. 16.
17. Ibid., p. 16.
18. Guzmán, *Memorias de Pancho Villa*, p. 11.
19. Johnson, *Heroic Mexico*, p. 159.
20. Guzmán, *Memorias de Pancho Villa*, p. 17.
21. Ibid., p. 20.
22. Ibid., pp. 23-24.
23. Ibid., pp. 15-16.
24. Almada, *Diccionario Chihuahuense*, p. 564.
25. Guzmán, *Memorias de Pancho Villa*, p. 29.
26. Ibid., p. 25.
27. Ibid., p. 26.
28. Ibid., pp. 31-33.
29. Ibid., p. 41.
30. Rosenstone, *Romantic Revolutionary*, p. 12.
31. Gelb, *So Short a Time*, pp. 26-29.
32. JRP (HL), "The Charge of the Political Brigade," 1910.
33. Rosenstone, *Romantic Revolutionary*, p. 55.
34. JRP (HL), "The Cattle Boat Murder," p. 7, 1911.
35. Rosenstone, *Romantic Revolutionary*, p. 64.
36. Ibid., p. 68.
37. Ibid., p. 68.
38. JRP (HL), 9/1910 letter to Bob Hallowell.
39. JRP (HL), from "A Dash Into Spain," p. 15.
40. Ibid., pp. 47-48.
41. Ibid., p. 53.
42. Ibid., p. 54.
43. Ibid., pp. 19-20.
44. Ibid., pp. 35-36.
45. Rosenstone, *Romantic Revolutionary*, p. 73.

3. Villa's Road to Revolution

1. Guzmán, *Memorias de Pancho Villa*, p. 44.
2. Ibid., p. 44.
3. Ibid., p. 45.

4. Ibid., p. 45.
5. Ibid., p. 46.
6. Ibid., p. 46.
7. Ibid., p. 48.
8. Ibid., p. 49.
9. Ibid., p. 49.
10. Ibid., p. 50.
11. Ibid., p. 52.
12. Ibid., p. 52.
13. Garfías, *Verdad y mito*, p. 25.
14. Guzmán, *Memorias de Pancho Villa*, p. 53.
15. Ibid., p. 53.
16. Ibid., pp. 54–55.
17. Garfías, *Verdad y mito*, p. 25.
18. Guzmán, *Memorias de Pancho Villa*, p. 57.
19. Ibid., p. 58.
20. Ibid., p. 59.
21. Ibid., p. 61.
22. Ibid., p. 65.
23. Ibid., p. 65.
24. Ibid., p. 72.
25. Garfías, *Verdad y mito*, p. 27.
26. Guzmán, *Memorias de Pancho Villa*, p. 75.
27. Ibid., p. 76.
28. Ibid., p. 77.
29. Ibid., p. 82.
30. Ibid., pp. 82–83.
31. Johnson, *Heroic Mexico*, p. 161.
32. Guzmán, *Memorias de Pancho Villa*, pp. 83–84.
33. Johnson, *Heroic Mexico*, p. 59.
34. Ibid., p. 59.
35. Garfías, *Verdad y mito*, p. 30.
36. Johnson, *Heroic Mexico*, pp. 60–61.
37. Atkin, *Revolution*, p. 84.
38. Ibid., p. 103.
39. Johnson, *Heroic Mexico*, pp. 87–88.
40. Friedrich Katz, *The Secret War in Mexico*, p. 159.
41. Eugenio Toussaint Aragón, *Quien y como fué Pancho Villa?*, p. 58.
42. Ibid., p. 58.
43. Ibid., p. 59.
44. Ibid., p. 64.
45. Ibid., p. 67.
46. Johnson, *Heroic Mexico*, p. 165.
47. Garfías, *Verdad y mito*, p. 50.
48. Ibid., p. 50.
49. Ibid., p. 51.

50. Atkin, *Revolution*, p. 170.
51. Johnson, *Heroic Mexico*, p. 170.
52. John Reed, *Insurgent Mexico*, p. 30.
53. Garfías, *Verdad y mito*, p. 69.
54. Ibid., p. 71.
55. Luis Garfías, *La revolución mexicana*, p. 130.
56. Johnson, *Heroic Mexico*, p. 208.

4. Reed's Road to Revolution

1. Granville Hicks, *John Reed: The Making of a Revolutionary*, p. 63.
2. Lincoln Steffens, *Autobiography*, vol. 2, p. 653.
3. JRP (HL), "Almost Thirty," p. 17.
4. Hicks, *John Reed*, p. 73.
5. JRP (HL), "Back to the Land," 1911.
6. JRP (HL), 3/9/1912 letter to Robert Hallowell.
7. Rosenstone, *Romantic Revolutionary*, p. 95.
8. JRP (HL), 10/28/1912 letter from Eddy Hunt.
9. JRP (HL), 12/2/1912 letter from Max Eastman.
10. JRP (HL), "Sheriff Radcliffe's Hotel," *Metropolitan*, September 1913, p. 1.
11. Ibid., p. 1.
12. Ibid., pp. 1–3.
13. Rosenstone, *Romantic Revolutionary*, p. 126.
14. Ibid., p. 130.
15. JRP (HL), 6/13/1913 letter from Bobby Rogers.
16. JRP (HL), 7/14/1913 letter from Hiram Moderwell and Sam Eliot.
17. JRP (HL), "Almost Thirty," p. 19.
18. JRP (HL), "Showing Mrs. Van," *Smart Set*, December 1913.
19. Reed, *Education of John Reed*, "The Colorado War," p. 92.
20. Ibid., p. 90.
21. Ibid., p. 90.
22. Ibid., p. 93.
23. Ibid., p. 99.
24. Ibid., pp. 107–8.
25. Rosenstone, *Romantic Revolutionary*, p. 173.
26. Reed, "The Colorado War," p. 120.
27. Ibid., p. 89.
28. JRP (HL), "Rule Britannia," 1914.
29. Ibid., p. 11.
30. Ibid., p. 10.
31. Ibid., p. 7.
32. Ibid., p. 6.
33. Ibid., p. 30.
34. JRP (HL), "With the Allies," *Metropolitan*, December 1914, p. 11.
35. Ibid., p. 20.
36. Ibid., p. 20.

37. JRP (HL), "Comment on Margaret Sanger's Arrest," 1915, typed sheet in collection.
38. JRP (HL), "No Americans Need Apply," July 1915, p. 4.
39. JRP (HL), 6/19/1915 letter to George T. Marye.
40. Rosenstone, *Romantic Revolutionary*, p. 234.
41. JRP (HL), "With Bryan on the Ocklawaha." Published in 5/20/1916 *Collier's* as "Bryan On Tour."
42. JRP (HL), 2/11/1916 letter to Louise Bryant.
43. JRP (HL), 6/12/1916 letter from Louise Bryant.
44. Rosenstone, *Romantic Revolutionary*, p. 244.
45. Reed, *Education of John Reed*, "Sold Out," p. 161.
46. Ibid., p. 162.
47. Ibid., p. 166.
48. Rosenstone, *Romantic Revolutionary*, p. 265.
49. Ibid., p. 265.
50. JRP (HL), 4/5/1917 letter from Margeret Reed.
51. JRP (HL), 5/31/1917 letter from Robert Minor.
52. Isaac Deutscher, *The Prophet Armed: Trotsky 1879–1921*, vol. 1, p. 251.
53. John Reed, *Ten Days that Shook the World*, p. 29.
54. Ibid., p. 24.
55. Steffens, *Autobiography*, vol. 2, p. 761.
56. Ibid., p. 761.
57. Louise Bryant, *Six Red Months in Russia*, p. 33.
58. Reed, *Ten Days*, p. 68.
59. Ibid., p. 68.
60. Ibid., p. 68.
61. Ibid., p. 69.
62. Rosenstone, *Romantic Revolutionary*, p. 312.
63. Ibid., p. 316.

5. Villa's Foreign Legion

1. Steffens, *Autobiography*, vol. 2, p. 717.
2. Jessie Peterson and Thelma Cox Knoles, *Pancho Villa: Intimate Recollections by People Who Knew Him*, p. 142.
3. Katz, *Secret War*, p. 428.
4. Reed, *Insurgent Mexico*, p. 157.
5. Ibid., p. 157.
6. Ibid., p. 158.
7. Richard O'Connor, *Ambrose Bierce: A Biography*, p. 300.
8. Ibid., p. 300.
9. Ibid., p. 300.
10. Ibid., p. 299.
11. Ibid., p. 299.
12. Ibid., p. 301.
13. Ibid., p. 302.

14. Ibid., p. 302.
15. Ibid., p. 302.
16. Ibid., p. 305.
17. Ibid., p. 305.
18. Ibid., p. 306.
19. Ibid., p. 307.
20. Ibid., p. 307.
21. Ibid., p. 304.
22. Haldeen Braddy, *Cock of the Walk: The Legend of Pancho Villa*, p. 98.
23. Giuseppe Garibaldi, *A Toast to Rebellion*, p. 240.
24. Ibid., pp. 248–49.
25. Ibid., p. 277.
26. Ibid., p. 277.
27. Ibid., p. 299.
28. Peterson and Knoles, *Pancho Villa*, p. 229.
29. Garfías, *Verdad y mito*, p. 71.
30. Peterson and Knoles, *Pancho Villa*, p. 229.
31. Ibid., p. 230.
32. Ibid., p. 230.
33. Ibid., p. 231.
34. Ibid., pp. 231–32.
35. O'Reilly, *Roving*, p. 102.
36. Ibid., p. 102.
37. Ibid., p. 104.
38. Ibid., p. 275.
39. Ibid., p. 288.
40. Patrick O'Hea, *Reminiscences of the Mexican Revolution*, p. 153.
41. Peterson and Knoles, *Pancho Villa*, p. 46.
42. Ibid., p. 48.
43. O'Hea, *Reminiscences*, p. 153–54.
44. Ibid., p. 154.
45. Ibid., p. 154.
46. Peterson and Knoles, *Pancho Villa*, p. 124.
47. Ibid., p. 124.
48. Ibid., p. 122.
49. Ibid., pp. 126–27.
50. Ibid., p. 127.
51. Ibid., pp. 191–92.
52. Ibid., p. 129.
53. Ibid., p. 147.
54. Ibid., p. 149.
55. Ibid., p. 131.
56. Ibid., p. 246.
57. Barbara Tuchman, *The Zimmerman Telegram*, p. 104.
58. Peterson and Knoles, *Pancho Villa*, p. 246.
59. Braddy, *Cock of the Walk*, p. 98.

60. Atkin, *Revolution*, p. 88.
61. Garibaldi, *A Toast to Rebellion*, pp. 191–93.
62. Ibid, p. 222.
63. Guzmán, *Memorias de Pancho Villa*, pp. 86–87.
64. Garibaldi, *A Toast to Rebellion*, p. 302.
65. Desmond Young, *Rommel*, p. 192.
66. AEKM, Michner to Mario González Muzquiz, 11/10/1982.
67. AEKM, Michner to Lord Freyberg, 11/22/1982.
68. Text of Manfred Rommel 7/12/83 letter to author:

> Dear Mr. Tuck:
> Many thanks for your letter
> of June 6, 1983. The version
> that my father spent some time
> fighting with Pancho Villa during
> the Mexican Revolution is not
> accurate. My father was never in
> Mexico in his life.
> I wish you success in your book project.
> Friendly greetings,
> (Manfred Rommel)

69. AEKM, Rubén Rocha to Michner, 1/24/1983.
70. AEKM, John Hardingham to Michner, 12/11/1982.
71. Lord Freyberg to author, 8/14/1983.
72. Lord Freyberg to author, 1/7/1984.
73. AEKM, Michner to John Hardingham, 11/10/1982.
74. AEKM, Norman Pelham Wright to Lord Freyberg, 3/11/1965.

6. Insurgent Mexico *and Insurgent Mexico*

1. Reed, *Insurgent Mexico*, p. 25.
2. JRP (HL), 2/2/1914 telegram from Max Eastman.
3. Reed, *Insurgent Mexico*, pp. 159–60.
4. Ibid., p. 30.
5. Ibid., p. 30.
6. Ibid., p. 30.
7. Garfías, *Verdad y mito*, p. 66.
8. Ibid., p. 63.
9. Reed, *Insurgent Mexico*, p. 39.
10. Ibid., p. 40.
11. Ibid., p. 43.
12. Ibid., p. 46.
13. Ibid., p. 49.
14. Ibid., p. 50.
15. Ibid., p. 48.
16. Ibid., p. 50.

17. Ibid., p. 65.
18. Ibid., p. 69.
19. Ibid., p. 69.
20. Ibid., p. 91.
21. Ibid., p. 75.
22. Ibid., p. 108.
23. Ibid., p. 113.
24. Ibid., p. 119.
25. Rosenstone, *Romantic Revolutionary*, pp. 153–54 and 399.
26. Reed, *Insurgent Mexico*, p. 102.
27. Ibid., p. 124.
28. Ibid., p. 124.
29. Ibid., p. 136.
30. Ibid., p. 133.
31. Ibid., pp. 134–35.
32. Johnson, *Heroic Mexico*, p. 192.
33. Reed, *Insurgent Mexico*, pp. 138–39.
34. Ibid., p. 139.
35. Ibid., pp. 250–51.
36. Ibid., p. 251.
37. Ibid., p. 252.
38. Ibid., p. 252.
39. JRP (HL), 3/25/1914 letter from Walter Lippmann.
40. Rosenstone, *Romantic Revolutionary*, p. 167.
41. Steffens, *Autobiography*, vol. 2, p. 715.
42. Ibid., p. 715.
43. Ibid., pp. 807–8 and 813–15.
44. Ibid., p. 732.

7. The Indispensables: Felipe Angeles and Louise Bryant

1. *Enciclopedia de México*, vol. 1, p. 305.
2. Ibid., p. 305.
3. Ibid., p. 305.
4. Ibid., p. 305.
5. Johnson, *Heroic Mexico*, pp. 94–95.
6. *Enciclopedia*, vol. 1, p. 306.
7. Blanco Moheno, *Crónica*, vol. 1, p. 125.
8. Ibid., p. 164.
9. Ibid., p. 165.
10. Ibid., p. 166.
11. Ibid., pp. 166–67.
12. Ibid., p. 168.
13. Ibid., p. 169.
14. Johnson, *Heroic Mexico*, p. 198.
15. Ibid., p. 199.

16. Ibid., p. 203.
17. Blanco Moheno, *Crónica*, vol. 1, p. 179.
18. Ibid., p. 243.
19. Johnson, *Heroic Mexico*, p. 251.
20. Ibid., p. 258.
21. Blanco Moheno, *Crónica*, vol. 1, p. 320.
22. Ibid., p. 320.
23. Ibid., pp. 363–64.
24. Garfías, *La revolución*, pp. 158–63.
25. Garfías, *Verdad y mito*, p. 111.
26. Johnson, *Heroic Mexico*, p. 288.
27. Howard F. Cline, *The United States and Mexico*, p. 174.
28. *Enciclopedia*, vol. 1, p. 307.
29. Katz, *Secret War*, pp. 276–77.
30. Garfías, La revolución, p. 193.
31. Johnson, *Heroic Mexico*, p. 363.
32. Gardner, *"Friend and Lover,"* p. 297.
33. Ibid., p. 297.
34. Ibid., pp. 270–74.
35. Ibid., p. 61.
36. JRP (HL), 7/5/1917 letter to Louise Bryant.
37. JRP (HL), Louise Bryant to John Reed, no date.
38. Orville Bullitt, *For the President*, p. 513.
39. Gardner, *"Friend and Lover,"* p. 290.
40. Ibid., p. 27.
41. Ibid., p. 104.
42. Ibid., p. 133.
43. LSP (BL), 6/11/1931 letter from James McNamara.
44. Louise Bryant, *Six Months in Russia*, p. 67.
45. Gardner, *"Friend and Lover,"* p. 130.
46. Arthur and Barbara Gelb, *O'Neill*, p. 330–31.
47. Bryant, *Six Red Months*, pp. 157–58.
48. Gardner, *"Friend and Lover,"* p. 113.
49. Ibid., p. 122.
50. Ibid., p. 140.
51. JRP (HL), Bryant to Reed, 3/23/1919.
52. JRP (HL), Bryant to Reed, 4/18/1919.
53. JRP (HL), Bryant to Reed, no date.
54. Gardner, *"Friend and Lover,"* pp. 149–52.
55. JRP (HL), Bryant to Reed, 4/16/1919.
56. JRP (HL), Reed to Bryant, 5/15/1920.
57. Gardner, *"Friend and Lover,"* p. 184.
58. JRP (HL), Bryant to Reed, 6/9/1916.
59. JRP (HL), Bryant to Reed, 11/29/1916.
60. JRP (HL), Bryant to Reed, 12/9/1916.

8. *The Organization Men: Carranza and Obregón*

1. Robert E. Quirk, *The Mexican Revolution: 1914–1915*, p. 18.
2. Ibid., pp. 9–10.
3. Moreno, *Los hombres*, p. 286.
4. *Enciclopedia*, vol. 2, p. 765.
5. Ibid., p. 765.
6. Katz, *Secret War*, pp. 29–30.
7. Garfías, *La revolución*, p. 105.
8. Blanco Moheno, *Crónica*, vol. 1, p. 291.
9. Francis C. Kelley, *Blood Stained Altars*, p. 246; Atkin, *Revolution*, p. 152.
10. Johnson, *Heroic Mexico*, p. 180.
11. Ibid., p. 178.
12. Frank Tannenbaum, *Mexico: The Struggle for Bread and Peace*, p. 63.
13. Johnson, *Heroic Mexico*, p. 180.
14. Hugh L. Scott, *Some Memories of a Soldier*, p. 516.
15. Blanco Moheno, *Crónica*, vol. 1, p. 189.
16. Ibid., p. 163.
17. Johnson, *Heroic Mexico*, p. 180.
18. Katz, *Secret War*, p. 146.
19. Taracena, *Historia extraoficial*, p. 146.
20. Ibid., p. 148.
21. Père Foix, *Pancho Villa*, pp. 193–94.
22. Taracena, *Historia extraoficial*, p. 152.
23. Ibid., p. 156.
24. Johnson, *Heroic Mexico*, p. 199.
25. Blanco Moheno, *Crónica*, p. 176.
26. Ibid., p. 177.
27. Ibid., pp. 177–78.
28. Jesús Silva Herzog, *Breve historia de la revolución mexicana*.
29. Lyle C. Brown, "The Politics of Armed Struggle in the Mexican Revolution, 1913–15," pp. 62–63.
30. Taracena, *Historia extraoficial*, p. 169.
31. Brown, "The Politics," p. 65.
32. Johnson, *Heroic Mexico*, p. 237.
33. Garfías, *Verdad y mito*, p. 99.
34. Taracena, *Historia extraoficial*, p. 174.
35. Johnson, *Heroic Mexico*, p. 252.
36. Atkin, *Revolution*, p. 250.
37. Silva Herzog, *Breve historia*, p. 122.
38. Johnson, *Heroic Mexico*, p. 261.
39. Ibid., p. 261.
40. Miguel and Gustavo Casasola, *Historia gráfica de la revolución mexicana*, Cuaderno 11, p. 969.
41. Katz, *Secret War*, p. 302.
42. Ibid., p. 284.

43. Garfás, *Verdad y mito*, p. 128.
44. Taracena, *Historia extraoficial*, p. 236.

9. *The Organization Men: Zinoviev and Radek*

1. Angelica Balabanov, *My Life as a Rebel*, p. 220.
2. Ibid., pp. 220–21.
3. Robert Conquest, *The Great Terror*, pp. 10–11.
4. Max Eastman, *Heroes I Have Known*, p. 231.
5. Michael Pearson, *The Sealed Train*, p. 38.
6. Ibid., p. 45.
7. Ruth Fischer, *Stalin and German Communism*, p. 12.
8. Katz, *Secret War*, p. 577.
9. Eastman, *Heroes*, p. 231.
10. Balabanov, *My Life as a Rebel*, p. 247.
11. Eastman, *Heroes*, p. 232.
12. Balabanov, *My Life as a Rebel*, p. 247.
13. Ibid., p. 247.
14. Warren Lerner, *Karl Radek: The Last Internationalist*, p. 4.
15. Ibid., p. 13.
16. Ibid., p. 5.
17. Ibid., p. 180.
18. R. Fischer, *Stalin*, p. 202.
19. Warren Lerner to author, 1/16/84.
20. Lerner, *Karl Radek*, p. 20.
21. Ibid., 29–30.
22. R. Fischer, *Stalin*, p. 203.
23. Lerner, *Karl Radek*, p. 46.
24. Pearson, *Sealed Train*, p. 85.
25. Ibid., pp. 96–97.
26. Ibid., p. 110.
27. Reed, *Ten Days*, p. 32.
28. Ibid., p. 33.
29. Isaac Deutscher, *The Prophet Armed*, p. 292.
30. Ibid., p. 292.
31. Ibid., p. 302.
32. Ibid., p. 304, n. 1.
33. Conquest, *Great Terror*, p. 11.
34. Rosenstone, *Romantic Revolutionary*, p. 349.
35. JRP (HL), 5/10/1919 letter from Ben H. Fletcher.
36. Reed, *Ten Days*, p. 57.
37. Ibid., p. 57.
38. Ibid., p. 57.
39. JRP (HL), Lenin memo to John Reed, 1/20/1920.
40. Balabanov, *My Life as a Rebel*, p. 188.
41. R. Fischer, *Stalin*, p. 204.

42. Ibid., p. 204.
43. Rosenstone, *Romantic Revolutionary*, p. 309.
44. JRP (HL), article in *The Liberator*, January 1910.
45. John W. Wheeler-Bennett, *The Forgotten Peace: Brest-Litovsk, March 1918*, p. 352.
46. R. Fischer, *Stalin*, p. 205.
47. Ibid., pp. 205–6.
48. Karl Radek, *Pamphlets and Portraits*, p. 56.
49. R. Fischer, *Stalin*, pp. 216–17.
50. Adam B. Ulam, *Stalin: The Man and his Era*, p. 348.
51. Vladimir and Evdokia Petrov, *Empire of Fear*, p. 68.
52. Ulam, *Stalin*, p. 425.
53. Ibid., p. 425.
54. Conquest, *Great Terror*, p. 183.
55. Ibid., p. 131.
56. Ibid., p. 116.
57. Ibid., p. 117.
58. Ibid., p. 163.
59. Louis Fischer, *The Life of Lenin*, p. 315.
60. Petrov, *Empire of Fear*, p. 69.

10. Fatal Ambush: Parral and Baku

1. Scott, *Some Memories*, p. 517.
2. Ibid., p. 517.
3. Braddy, *Cock of the Walk*, p. 78.
4. Silva Herzog, *Breve historia*, p. 184.
5. Katz, "Pancho Villa and the Attack on Columbus, New Mexico," pp. 101–130.
6. Atkin, *Revolution*, p. 302.
7. Johnson, *Heroic Mexico*, p. 310.
8. Scott, *Some Memories*, p. 518.
9. Garfías, *Verdad y mito*, p. 138.
10. Katz, *Secret War*, p. 310.
11. Atkin, *Revolution*, p. 317.
12. Katz, *Secret War*, pp. 308–9.
13. Johnson, *Heroic Mexico*, p. 315.
14. Taracena, *Historia extraoficial*, pp. 277–78.
15. Garfías, *Verdad y mito*, p. 142.
16. Ibid., p. 144.
17. Taracena, *Historia extraoficial*, p. 281.
18. Johnson, *Heroic Mexico*, p. 358.
19. Katz, *Secret War*, pp. 500–1.
20. Johnson, *Heroic Mexico*, pp. 318 and 320.
21. Ibid., pp. 318–19.
22. Katz, *Secret War*, pp. 292–93.

23. Steffens, *Autobiography*, vol. 2, p. 732.
24. Katz, *Secret War*, p. 254.
25. Ibid., p. 255.
26. Blanco Moheno, *Crónica*, vol 2, pp. 151–52.
27. Katz, *Secret War*, p. 533.
28. Atkin, *Revolution*, p. 339.
29. Johnson, *Heroic Mexico*, p. 355.
30. Garfías, *Verdad y mito*, p. 145.
31. Johnson, *Heroic Mexico*, p. 363.
32. Víctor Ceja Reyes, *Yo maté a Pancho Villa*, p. 221.
33. Johnson, *Heroic Mexico*, p. 376.
34. Ceja Reyes, *Yo maté*, pp. 70–71.
35. Ibid., p. 72–75.
36. Johnson, *Heroic Mexico*, p. 372.
37. Ceja Reyes, *Yo maté*, p. 205.
38. Ibid., p. 206.
39. Ibid., p. 207.
40. Ibid., p. 207.
41. Ibid., p. 221.
42. Gardner, *"Friend and Lover,"* p. 204.
43. JRP (HL), "Russian Notebooks," no date.
44. Gelb, *So Short a Time*, pp. 252–53.
45. Anthony Cave Brown and Charles B. MacDonald, *On a Field of Red*, p. 153.
46. Emma Goldman, *Living My Life*, p. 740.
47. Gelb, *So Short a Time*, pp. 255–56.
48. Ibid., p. 256.
49. Ibid., p. 267.
50. Rosenstone, *Romantic Revolutionary*, p. 369.
51. R. Fischer, *Stalin*, p. 140.
52. Ibid., p. 142.
53. JRP (HL), "The Convention of the Dead," *Liberator*, August 1919.
54. Eastman, *Heroes*, p. 236.
55. Theodore Draper, *The Roots of American Communism*, p. 285.
56. Gardner, *"Friend and Lover,"* p. 302.
57. Ibid., p. 302.
58. Rosenstone, *Romantic Revolutionary*, p. 377.
59. Brown and MacDonald, *On a Field of Red*, pp. 157–58.
60. Draper, *Roots*, pp. 288–89.
61. Goldman, *Living My Life*, pp. 850–51.
62. Gardner, *"Friend and Lover,"* p. 303.
63. Ibid., p. 304.
64. R. Fischer, *Stalin*, p. 112.
65. Gardner, *"Friend and Lover,"* p. 305.
66. Ibid., p. 366.
67. Ulam, *Stalin*, p. 95.
68. Eastman, *Heroes*, p. 304.

69. Edward Hallett Carr, *The Bolshevik Revolution*, vol. 3, p. 261.
70. L. Fischer, *Life of Lenin*, p. 526.
71. Eastman, *Heroes*, p. 230.
72. Ibid., p. 230.
73. L. Fischer, *Life of Lenin*, p. 526.
74. Eastman, *Heroes*, p. 233.
75. JRP (HL), handwritten archive document, no date.
76. Carr, *Bolshevik Revolution*, vol. 3, p. 267.
77. Draper, *Roots*, p. 288.
78. Eastman, *Heroes*, p. 233.
79. Draper, *Roots*, p. 285.
80. Ibid., pp. 292–93.

11. Villa and Reed as Revolutionaries: An Assessment

1. Albert Camus, *The Rebel*, p. 48.
2. Ibid., p. 47.
3. Arthur Koestler, *The Yogi and the Commissar*, pp. 15–16.
4. L. Fischer, *Life of Lenin*, p. 181.
5. Ibid., p. 193.
6. Reed, *Insurgent Mexico*, p. 127.
7. Ibid., p. 128.
8. Pynchon, *Viva Villa*, p. 258.
9. Reed, *Insurgent Mexico*, p. 130.
10. Ibid., pp. 130–31.
11. Katz, *Secret War*, pp. 139–40.
12. Reed, *Insurgent Mexico*, p. 145.
13. Katz, *Secret War*, p. 144.
14. JRP (HL), "Masses Manifesto," no date but either late 1912 or early 1913.
15. JRP (HL), "Almost Thirty," later published in the August 15 and 29 issues of *The New Republic*.
16. Gelb, *So Short a Time*, p. 202.
17. Rosenstone, *Romantic Revolutionary*, p. 388.
18. Ibid., p. 351.
19. JRP (HL), "Article on the Left Wing," summer 1919.
20. JRP (HL), Reed to Bryant, 9/2/19.
21. Rosenstone, *Romantic Revolutionary*, pp. 375–76.
22. Eastman, *Heroes*, p. 208.

Bibliography

Archives

AEKM: Archives of Emil K. Michner, México, D.F.
JRP (HL): John Reed Papers (Houghton Library), Cambridge, Mass.
LSP (BL): Lincoln Steffens Papers (Butler Library), New York, N.Y.

Other Sources

Almada, Francisco, ed., *Diccionario Chihuahuense*. Chihuahua: Universidad de Chihuahua, 1968.
A well-organized "Who's Who" and "What's What" of Mexico's largest state.

Atkin, Ronald, *Revolution: Mexico 1910–20*. London: Panther Books, 1972.
Intended more for the layman than the scholar. The author's adroit use of anecdotal material makes for enjoyable reading.

Baerlein, Henry. *Mexico: The Land of Unrest*. London: Herbert and Daniel, 1913.
Baerlein, Mexico correspondent of the *London Times*, covers the early days of the Revolution in the ripe, flamboyant style of Richard Harding Davis. His chronicle is useful for the light it casts on relatively little-known incidents.

Balabanov. Angelica. *My Life as a Rebel*. New York: Greenwood Press, 1968.
The Russian-born Balabanov, who became a leader of the Italian Socialist Party, was a friend and admirer of John Reed. Her memoir contains sharply etched, venomous (but not necessarily inaccurate) portraits of such figures as Zinoviev, Radek, and Mussolini.

Beezley, William H. *Insurgent Governor: Abraham González and the Mexican Revolution in Chihuahua.* Lincoln: University of Nebraska Press, 1973.
  Biography by an American scholar, viewing Abraham González as a symbol of *maderismo*, and *maderismo* as a symbol of moderate reform.

Blanco Moheno, Roberto. *Crónica de la revolución mexicana,* 3 vols. México: Editorial Diana, 1967.
  A caustic and incisive study by a journalist, politician, and sometime television commentator. Blanco Moheno is also author of a biography of President Lázaro Cárdenas.

Braddy, Haldeen. *Cock of the Walk: The Legend of Pancho Villa.* Albuquerque: University of New Mexico Press, 1955.
  Prolifically researched biography by an American admirer, flawed by a windy, overblown style.

Brandenburg, Frank. *The Making of Modern Mexico.* New York: Prentice-Hall, 1964.
  An examination of how the Mexican Revolution was institutionalized and how Mexico's "Revolutionary Family" has responded to the challenges of the modern world. Concentrates on the 53-year period between the fall of Porfirio Díaz and presidential accession of Gustavo Díaz Ordaz.

Brown, Anthony Cave, and MacDonald, Charles B. *On a Field of Red.* New York: Putnam, 1981.
  Comprehensive study of international Communism written more in the style of a spy thriller than a scholarly work. Minor errors of fact.

Brown, Lyle C., "The Politics of Armed Struggle in the Mexican Revolution, 1913–1915." In *Revolution in Mexico: Years of Upheaval, 1910–1940,* ed. James W. Wilkie and Albert L. Michaels. New York: Knopf, 1969.
  A political analysis of the military struggle in Mexico during those two crucial years. Covers both the Constitutionalist campaign against Huerta and Villa's split with the Carranza-Obregón faction.

Bryant, Louise. *Six Red Months in Russia.* London and West Nyack: Journeyman Press, 1982.
———. *Mirrors of Moscow.* New York: Thomas Seltzer, 1923.
  The first book covers the time of the Bolshevik Revolution. The second contains vivid, if somewhat simplistic, profiles of prominent contemporaries. All are Bolsheviks except for Enver Pasha, the Turkish warlord, and Tikhon, the Orthodox Patriarch.

Bullit, Orville. *For the President: Personal and Secret.* Boston: Houghton Mifflin, 1972.
  Selected correspondence between President Roosevelt and William Bullitt, edited by Orville Bullitt and James V. Compton. Though Bullitt is sympathetic

to his controversial brother, he avoids special pleading and is remarkably fair and objective in his observations.

Camus, Albert. *The Rebel.* New York: Knopf, 1956.
This definitive work examines all aspects of rebellion—literary, metaphysical, and historical as well as political. One of the most brilliant studies of its kind ever attempted.

Carr, Edward H. *The Bolshevik Revolution,* 3 vols. New York: Mac-Millan, 1951.
A comprehensive, and classic, three-part study of the Revolution by an eminent British historian.

Casasola, Miguel and Gustavo. *Historia gráfica de la revolución mexicana.* México: Ediciones Gustavo Casasola, 1965.
Massive pictorial and photographic history. This work has two editions, one in four volumes and the other in sixteen *cuadernos* (folders). Both cover the same material.

Ceja Reyes, Víctor. *Yo maté a Pancho Villa.* México: Populibros La Prensa, 1960.
Despite the title, this is not a confession but an investigative work by a well-known Mexican journalist. Ceja Reyes makes a convincing case to support views that the order for Villa's assassination originated at the highest levels.

Clendenen, Clarence C. *The United States and Pancho Villa: A Study in Unconventional Diplomacy.* Ithaca: Cornell University Press, 1961.
This work on Villa is refreshing for the manner in which it downplays romance and emphasizes *realpolitik.* Thoroughly and minutely researched.

Cline, Howard F. *The United States and Mexico.* Cambridge: Harvard University Press, 1953.
A Harvard historian's widely ranging study that focuses on economic and cultural factors as well as straight history. Begins with the Conquest and carries through to the early 1950s.

Conquest, Robert. *The Great Terror: Stalin's Purge of the Thirties.* New York: MacMillan, 1968.
The finest analysis of that frightful period by a non-Russian writer. Conquest perceptively shows how the plodding Stalin was able to triumph over the Revolution's "brightest and best."

Cumberland, Charles C. *Mexican Revolution: Genesis Under Madero.* Austin: University of Texas Press, 1952.
———. *Mexican Revolution: The Constitutionalist Years.* Austin and London: University of Texas Press, 1972.
As the titles indicate, Cumberland's second work is a continuation of the first. It was completed by the late David C. Bailey after Cumberland's death in 1970. Both volumes of this rigorous study are "must" reading for students of the Mexican Revolution.

Deutscher, Isaac. *The Prophet Armed. Trotsky: 1879–1921*, vol. 1. London: Oxford University Press, 1954.

————. *The Prophet Unarmed. Trotsky: 1921–29*, vol. 2. London: Oxford University Press, 1959.

————. *The Prophet Outcast. Trotsky: 1929–40*, vol. 3. London: Oxford University Press, 1963.

    In this massive trilogy on the Great Heretic, Deutscher brilliantly attains his self-imposed objective of emulating Carlyle's Cromwell biography. As Deutscher saw it, both he and Carlyle faced the problem of dragging their subjects out from under "a mountain of dead dogs."

Draper, Theodore. *The Roots of American Communism*. New York: Viking Press, 1957.

    An excellent analytical study of domestic Communism from its beginnings to the end of World War II. Particularly provocative are Draper's insights into Reed's feelings at the time of his death.

Eastman, Max. *Heroes I Have Known*. New York: Simon and Schuster, 1942.

    Twelve sparkling, totally subjective personality profiles by the ever eloquent radical firebrand who later turned conservative pundit.

Encíclopedia de México. México: Encíclopedia de México, S.A., 1977.

Estrada, Roque. *La revolución y Francisco Madero*. Guadalajara: Biblioteca Rivera, 1912.

    Only book on *maderista* era written while Madero was at the peak of his power. Detailed, turgid style relieved by incisive judgments.

Fernández Rojas, José, and Melgarejo, Luis. *La revolución mexicana*. México: Editores Rojas, 1913.

    Despite protestations of nonpartisanship, the authors' tone is strongly anti-Madero. Valuable mainly for meticulous coverage of little-known events.

Fischer, Louis. *The Life of Lenin*. New York: Harper and Row, 1964.

    Fischer, who knew Lenin, never lets his admiration for the Soviet leader transform him into an apologist. Lenin's ruthlessness and absolutist mentality are shown along with his greatness.

Fischer, Ruth. *Stalin and German Communism*. Cambridge: Harvard University Press, 1948.

    The author was a Marxist opponent of Stalin and inimical sister of Comintern agent Gerhart Eisler. Her recollections and her indictment of Stalin's dog-in-the-manger German policy are at times weakened by imprecision.

Foix, Père (Pedro). *Pancho Villa*. México: Ediciones Xochitl, 1950.

    Foix, a journalist and biographer, produced a work similar to Edgcumb Pynchon's—novelistic in style and full of improvised dialogue. At the same time, the historical material is informative and well-organized.

Gardner, Virginia. *"Friend and Lover": The Life of Louise Bryant*. New York: Horizon Press, 1982.
A convincing revisionist work, written from a feminist standpoint. Bryant is seen here as a victim of circumstance, destroyed by incurable illness and a vindictive second husband.

Garfías, Luis. *Verdad y mito de Pancho Villa*. México: Editorial Panorama, 1981.
————. *La revolución mexicana*. México: Editorial Panorama, 1982.
Both are works of a military historian and Mexican Army general. Not surprisingly, the emphasis is on combat actions. Though Garfías is anti-Villa, he recognizes Villa's soldierly abilities.

Garibaldi, Giuseppe. *A Toast to Rebellion*. New York and Indianapolis: Bobbs Merrill, 1935.
The opera-bouffe memoirs of Garibaldi's grandson and namesake, a dashing soldier of fortune. More *condottiere* and less idealist than his grandfather, Garibaldi's primary interest was adventure.

Gelb, Barbara. *So Short a Time: A Biography of John Reed and Louise Bryant*. New York: Norton, 1973.
————. Gelb, Arthur and Barbara. *O'Neill*. New York: Harper, 1960 and 1962.
The first work is the only tandem biography of Reed and Bryant. More scholarly and less romanticized than the title would indicate. The mammoth O'Neill biography, by Gelb and her husband, is of value for the light it casts on the Bryant-O'Neill relationship.

Goldman, Emma. *Living My Life*, 2 vols. New York: Knopf, 1931.
This two-part testament of a great American radical contains much of the material included in two previous books detailing her disenchantment with Soviet Communism.

Guzmán, Martín Luis. *Memorias de Pancho Villa*. México: Compañia General de Ediciones, n.d.
Guzmán, a journalist and revolutionary historian, constructed this "autobiography" on the basis of oral interviews with Villa. Ironically, he is the son of an officer who was killed fighting the *villistas*.

Herrera, Celia. *Francisco Villa ante la historia*. México: n.p., 1939.
The author, a fervent *maderista*, perceives a contrast between the "good" Madero and the "evil" Villa that is almost Manichean.

Hicks, Granville. *John Reed: The Making of a Revolutionary.* New York: MacMillan, 1936.
This nearly definitive biography is marred only by the author's bias. Though Hicks later turned against Communism, he was a Party member at the time of publication. Reed's difficulties with Zinoviev and Radek are disingenuously glossed over.

Johnson, William W. *Heroic Mexico.* New York: Doubleday, 1968.
This panoramic history of the revolution is directed mainly at the popular market. Excellent writing but minor errors of fact.

Kaplan, Justin. *Lincoln Steffens: A Biography.* New York: Simon and Schuster, 1974.
Biography can be particularly challenging when the subject is author of a classic autobiography. Kaplan meets the challenge admirably, especially in portions pertaining to Steffens's complex relationship with John Reed.

Katz, Friedrich. *The Secret War in Mexico.* Chicago and London: University of Chicago Press, 1981 and 1983.
————. "Pancho Villa and the Attack on Columbus, New Mexico." From the *American Historical Review*, February 1978 (vol. 83, no. 1), pp. 101–30.
The book is an able and comprehensive study that focuses both on Germany's role during the revolutionary period and how her maneuvers for dominance in Mexico interacted with those of the other great powers. This outstanding work is flawed only by a lamentably inadequate index. The article is a challenging argument that Villa's Columbus attack, far from being an act of rage, was in fact an astute and successful move to undermine Carranza's power position.

Kelley, Francis C. *Blood-Drenched Altars.* Milwaukee: Bruce Publishing Company, 1935.
The author, an American Catholic bishop, furnishes interesting genealogical information relating to Obregón's Irish ancestry.

Koestler, Arthur. *The Yogi and the Commissar.* New York: MacMillan, 1967.
A provocative collection of essays including social and literary comment as well as the core of Koestler's political thought.

Lerner, Warren. *Karl Radek: The Last Internationalist.* Stanford: Stanford University Press, 1970.
The only full-length biography, more sympathetic to Radek than were the views of his contemporaries. Erudite and ably researched.

Moreno, Daniel. *Los hombres de la revolución.* México: Editores Libro-Mex, 1960.
Profiles of thirty-three leading revolutionaries; contributors include scholars, journalists, and personal friends.

O'Connor, Richard. *Ambrose Bierce: A Biography.* Boston and Toronto: Little, Brown, 1967.
A lively, well-documented study of this sardonic iconoclast and his lifelong obsession with death.

O'Hea, Patrick. *Reminiscences of the Mexican Revolution.* London: Sphere Books, 1981.
The author, an Anglo-Irishman who settled in Mexico, performed consular

duties under the most adverse conditions. O'Hea relates these events with humor and compassion, in a courtly, erudite style.

O'Reilly, Edward S. ("Tex"). *Roving and Fighting*. New York: The Century Co., 1918.
Picaresque and highly entertaining adventures of a Texas-born soldier of fortune.

Pearson, Michael. *The Sealed Train*. New York: Putnam, 1975.
A well-researched work on Lenin's 1917 "sealed train" trip across Germany to Russia. Winston Churchill compared Lenin's arrival in Russia to the injection of a "plague bacillus."

Peterson, Jessie, and Knoles, Thelma Cox. *Pancho Villa: Intimate Recollections by People Who Knew Him*. New York: Hastings House, 1977.
A valuable collage of reminiscences. Contributors include Mexicans and Americans, friends and enemies, victims and supporters.

Petrov, Vladimir and Evkadia. *Empire of Fear*. London: Andre Deutsch, 1956.
Memoirs of a Soviet defector and his wife. Both were officers in the OGPU, as the KGB was then known. Contains purportedly authentic version of Radek's death.

Pynchon, Edgcumb. *Viva Villa! A Recovery of the Real Pancho Villa*. New York: Grosset and Dunlap, 1933.
Novelistic biography by a contemporary of John Reed. Contains version of "dishonored sister" incident at variance with that of Martín Luis Guzmán. Pynchon's documentation is insufficient to justify wealth of improvised dialogue.

Quirk, Robert E. *The Mexican Revolution: 1914–15*. Bloomington: University of Indiana Press, 1960.
A thoughtful and well-balanced analysis of the Revolution's two most crucial years.

Radek, Karl. *Portraits and Pamphlets*. London: Wishart Books, 1935.
A collection of Radekiana put out by an English Stalinist publisher. Radek, then in Stalin's favor (and ever at his mercy), had to write carefully. But the "Soviet Puck's" ebullient wit and sharp intelligence still manage to surface in these selections.

Reed, John. *Insurgent Mexico*. New York: International Publishers, 1969.
———. *Ten Days that Shook the World*. New York: New American Library (Mentor Series), 1967.
———. *The Education of John Reed*. New York: International Publishers, 1955.
The first two titles are re-issues of Reed's most successful books. The third is a compilation of his writings and contains two articles discussed in Chapter 4 of the text. These are "The Colorado War" and "Sold Out."

Rosenstone, Robert. *Romantic Revolutionary: A Biography of John Reed.* New York: Random House (Vintage Series), 1981.
A later biography, the original published by Knopf in 1975. Rosenstone, unlike Hicks, was not inhibited by strictures of ideological orthodoxy. What emerges is a well-conceived and eminently readable work.

Scott, Hugh L. *Some Memories of a Soldier.* New York and London: The Century, 1928.
Memoirs of Villa's closest contact among the American military. In a straightforward and informative account, Scott denounces American recognition of Carranza.

Seymour, Charles, ed. *Intimate Papers of Colonel House Arranged as a Narrative,* 4 vols. Boston: Houghton Mifflin, 1926–28.
Documents relating to the career of Wilson's *éminence grise.* Of particular interest is the House-Steffens dialogue after the Bolshevik government denounced the Fourteen Points.

Silva Herzog, Jesús. *Breve historia de la revolución mexicana.* México and Buenos Aires: Fondo de Cultura Económica, 1964.
The father of Mexico's present Treasury Secretary, an economist and expert on agrarian problems, brings his gift for orderly analysis to this concise history of the Revolution.

Steffens, Lincoln. *The Autobiography of Lincoln Steffens,* 2 vols. New York: Harcourt Brace, 1958.
———. *Lincoln Steffens Speaking.* New York: Harcourt Brace, 1938.
The *Autobiography* is relevant to this text for the light it casts on the Steffens-Reed split on Villa and Carranza. The second work, a compilation, contains an account of Steffens's bitter final meeting with Reed.

Tannenbaum, Frank. *The Struggle for Peace and Bread.* New York: Knopf, 1950.
A study of US-Mexican relations against a background of Mexico's social milieu.

Taracena, Alfonso. *Historia extraoficial de la revolución mexicana.* México: Editorial Jus, 1972.
Taracena, a historian and journalist, combines a reputation for objectivity with a technique, used in other works, of making history come to life through extensive use of anecdote.

Thomas, Hugh. *The Spanish Civil War.* London: Pelican Books, 1968.
This celebrated and definitive study is used here as a secondary source and to illustrate a point: how Villa's views on education contrasted with those of a particularly mindless *franquista* general.

Toussaint Aragón, Eugenio. *Quien y como fué Pancho Villa?* México: Editorial Universo, 1982.
Though the author is a medical doctor and not an analyst, he has undertaken a psycho-history of Villa. Salient aspects of Villa's personality, ranging from alcoholic abstention to sexual excess, are examined against a background of childhood trauma.

Tuchman, Barbara. *The Zimmerman Telegram.* New York: Ballantine Books, 1979.
Barring Tuchman's assertion that Huerta was an "Aztec," this study of Germany's clumsy Mexican diplomacy in World War I is up to her usual high standard.

Ulam, Adam. *Stalin: The Man and His Era.* New York: Viking Press, 1973.
It is not easy to write dispassionately about such a supremely malignant figure. Yet Ulam, in chronicling the Stalin Era, manages to avoid extremes of emotional outrage and insensitive equanimity.

Wheeler-Bennett, John W. *The Forgotten Peace: Brest-Litovsk, March 1918.* New York: Morrow, 1939.
An excellent study of the Germans' own "Versailles": the harsh, vindictive treaty they inflicted on the Russians before they themselves were defeated.

Winter, Ella, and Hicks, Granville. *The Letters of Lincoln Steffens,* 2 vols. New York: 1938.
A prodigious compilation by Steffens's widow and Reed's biographer.

Young, Desmond. *Rommel.* London: Collins, 1950.
An admirable biography by a British brigadier who was taken prisoner by Rommel during the North African campaign. Secondary source.

Index